THE PLANT-BASED DIET FOR BODYBUILDING

3 Books in 1: 350 Recipes All Vegan & Vegetarian with High-Protein!
Beginners Guide to Increase Muscle Mass with Healthy and Whole-Food Vegan
Recipes To Fuel Your Workouts!

By

Audrey Pottery

TABLE OF CONTENT

PART 1: INTRODUCTION TO THE PLANT-BASED DIET IS A LIFESTYLE

Overall, it's not easy to figure out which eating plan will be good for you! With so many eating regimens to choose from, how do you decide what to eat? Giving up animal products for myself, the animals, and Mother Earth sound good to me. How about you? I have never regretted my decision - on the contrary, I love this lifestyle. I enjoy the food more than ever! I have cured my eczema, lost weight, and resolved my health issues. I wanted to collect a great assortment of vegan recipes to help people lose weight and prevent some severe conditions; this collection will help you kick-start your vegan journey or stay on track if you've been vegan for a long time. While this depends on your socio-economic background, it's fair to say that starting a new diet might not be the easiest thing. But it is a worthy goal! There are many misconceptions about the vegan diet. They include some commonly held beliefs that the vegan diet is tedious, unhealthy, and challenging to maintain. This cookbook will hopefully open your eyes to how amazingly delicious and healthy plant-based meals can be.

I spent a significant part of my life trying to maintain a healthy weight. Eventually, I realized that there is no instant solution, no shortcut or magic wand! Finally, I gave up on diets and decided to find an eating plan that would support my overall wellness. And voila! The secret to a healthy diet is simpler than I ever thought! The vegan diet is best known for its simplicity; following this diet regime; you should focus on plant-based foods and avoid animal-based foods. If you're following a vegetarian diet or thinking about trying this lifestyle, I've created this list of plant-based, low-cost foods to make your grocery shopping easier to manage.

VEGETABLES: Try to include different types of vegetables, from surface vegetables to root vegetables that grow underground.

FRUIT: Pick affordable fruit that is on sale or in season. Add frozen fruit to your shopping list because it is just as nutritious as fresh produce. It can be used in smoothies, toppings, compotes, or preserves. On the other hand, nuts generally contain many antioxidants, especially polyphenols; it has been shown that eating nuts can prevent heart disease and some types of cancer.

NUTS AND SEEDS: Nuts and seeds offer several dietary benefits. Nuts and seeds not only provide essential nutrients but are also a variety of flavors. This "ready-to-eat" food is a perfect snack with dried fruit and trail mix, essential vegan foods to store for an emergency.

RICE AND GRAINS: Rice and grains are versatile foods that are easy to incorporate into the vegan diet. Leftovers reheat beautifully and can be served at any time of day, turning simple, inexpensive ingredients into a complete meal. I always make sure my pantry contains healthy butter like tahini or peanut butter.

BEANS AND LEGUMES: Legumes and beans are very affordable, and there is no end to the variety of tasty dishes you can cook with them. These humble yet powerful foods are packed with vitamins, minerals, protein, and dietary fiber. Besides being super healthy and versatile, legumes pair very well with other vegan proteins, vegetables, and grains.

HEALTHY FATS: Don't underestimate the importance of quality fats in vegan cooking. Coconut oil, olive oil, and avocado are always good to have on hand.

NON-CHAIN PRODUCTS: Using a plant-based cheese or milk will add flavor, texture, and nutrition to your meals. While you can find fantastic products on the market, I've included my favorite recipes for vegan feta, vegan ricotta, and plant-based milk in this collection.

HERBS, SPICES, AND CONDIMENTS: A handful of fresh herbs will add that extra something to your soups, stews, sauces, or casseroles. Vegan condiments such as mustard, ketchup, mayonnaise, and plant-based sauces can be used in salads, casseroles, and spreads. Grains and legumes will help you get the most out of your vegan dishes. Herbs and spices are naturally plant-based, but play it safe and look for a label that says "Suitable for vegans."

BAKING GOODS & CANNED GOODS: These vegan essentials include all types of flour, baking powder, baking soda, and yeast. Besides, cocoa powder, vegan chocolate, and sweeteners are good to have on hand. When it comes to healthy vegan sweeteners, opt for fresh or dried fruit, agave syrup, maple syrup, and stevia. When it comes to canned goods, stock your pantry with cooking essentials like tomatoes, sauerkraut, pickles, low-sodium chickpeas and beans, coconut milk, green chilies, pumpkin puree, tomato sauce, low-sodium corn, and artichoke hearts. To make sure you have nutritious, delicious, quality meals for you and your family, building a healthy vegan pantry is half the battle.

Eating plant-based is one of the best and healthiest diets in the world. Healthy vegan diets include lots of fresh produce, whole grains, legumes, and healthy fats like seeds and nuts. They abound in antioxidants, minerals, vitamins, and dietary fiber.

Current scientific research has pointed out that increasing plant-based foods is associated with a lower risk of mortality from cardiovascular disease, type 2 diabetes, hypertension, and obesity. Vegan food plans often rely heavily on healthy foods, avoiding animal products loaded with antibiotics, additives, and hormones. Besides, consuming a higher percentage of essential amino acids with animal protein can be detrimental to human health. Since animal products contain much more fat than plant-based foods, it's no shock that studies have shown that meat-eaters have nine times the obesity rate of vegans.

One of the most significant benefits of the vegetarian diet is weight loss. While many people choose to live a vegetarian life for ethical reasons, the diet itself can help you reach your weight loss goals. If you're struggling to shift the pounds, you might consider trying a plant-based diet. How exactly? As a vegan, you'll cut back on high-calorie foods like whole dairy, fatty fish, pork, and other cholesterol-containing foods like eggs. Try replacing these foods with fiber- and protein-rich alternatives that will keep you full longer. The key is to focus on nutrient-dense, clean and natural foods and avoid empty calories like sugar, saturated fat, and highly processed foods. Here are some tricks that help me maintain my weight on the vegan diet for years. I eat vegetables as my main dish; I consume good fats in moderation - a good fat like olive oil is not fattening; I exercise regularly, and I cook at home.

As a long-term vegan, I've learned to simplify my diet by planning meals in advance and keeping pantry supplies on hand. Remember - even if you don't strictly follow a plant-based diet, eating more natural foods is a fantastic accomplishment!

This collection contains the best plant-based recipes I've ever tried. The recipes are selected into categories based on food groups, so you can easily plan your meals. If you've always wanted to make your hummus, tahini, starter burgers, creams, and dressings, I've got you covered. This cookbook includes recipes for homemade versions of our favorite vegan substitutes like peanut butter, cashew cheese, coconut yogurt, chia eggs, flax eggs, plant-based protein sources, and so on.

Still, think vegan products are expensive or difficult to recreate at home? With this cookbook, you can turn any regular meal into a veg-friendly wonder! Making plant-based milk, cheese, or burgers at home is as simple as making any other typical recipe. On that note, I'm sharing my all-time favorite vegan recipes, the ones I always come back. I hope you'll enjoy this diet as much as I do!

1) PORRIDGE WITH STRAWBERRIES AND COCONUT

Preparation Time: 12 minutes

Servings: 2

Ingredients:

- ✓ 1 tbsp flax seed powder
- ✓ 1 oz olive oil
- ✓ 1 tbsp coconut flour

Ingredients:

- ✓ 1 pinch ground chia seeds
- ✓ 5 tbsp coconut cream
- ✓ Thawed frozen strawberries

Directions:

- ❖ In a small bowl, mix the flax seed powder with the 3 tbsp water, and allow soaking for 5 minutes.
- ❖ Place a non-stick saucepan over low heat and pour in the olive oil, vegan "flax egg," coconut flour, chia seeds, and coconut cream.
- ❖ Cook the mixture while stirring continuously until your desired consistency is achieved. Turn the heat off and spoon the porridge into serving bowls.
- ❖ Top with 4 to 6 strawberries and serve immediately.

2) BROCCOLI BROWNS

Preparation Time: 35 minutes

Servings: 4

Ingredients:

- ✓ 3 tbsp flax seed powder
- ✓ 1 head broccoli, cut into florets
- ✓ ½ white onion, grated

Ingredients:

- ✓ 1 tsp salt
- ✓ 1 tbsp freshly ground black pepper
- ✓ 5 tbsp plant butter, for frying

Directions:

- ❖ In a small bowl, mix the flax seed powder with 9 tbsp water, and allow soaking for 5 minutes. Pour the broccoli into a food processor and pulse a few times until smoothly grated.
- ❖ Transfer the broccoli into a bowl, add the vegan "flax egg," white onion, salt, and black pepper. Use a spoon to mix the ingredients evenly and set aside 5 to 10 minutes to firm up a bit. Place a large non-stick skillet over medium heat and drop 1/3 of the plant butter to melt until no longer shimmering.
- ❖ Ladle scoops of the broccoli mixture into the skillet (about 3 to 4 hash browns per batch). Flatten the pancakes to measure 3 to 4 inches in diameter, and fry until golden brown on one side, 4 minutes. Turn the pancakes with a spatula and cook the other side to brown too, another 5 minutes.
- ❖ Transfer the hash browns to a serving plate and repeat the frying process for the remaining broccoli mixture. Serve the hash browns warm with green salad.

3) AVOCADO SANDWICH WITHOUT BREAD

Preparation Time: 10 minutes

Servings: 2

Ingredients:

- ✓ 1 avocado, sliced
- ✓ 1 large red tomato, sliced
- ✓ 2 oz gem lettuce leaves

Ingredients:

- ✓ ½ oz plant butter
- ✓ 1 oz tofu, sliced
- ✓ Freshly chopped parsley to garnish

Directions:

- ❖ Put the avocado on a plate and place the tomato slices by the avocado. Arrange the lettuce (with the inner side facing you) on a flat plate to serve as the base of the sandwich.
- ❖ To assemble the sandwich, smear each leaf of the lettuce with plant butter, and arrange some tofu slices in the leaves. Then, share the avocado and tomato slices on each cheese. Garnish with parsley and serve.

4) TOFU SCRAMBLE

Preparation Time: 46 minutes

Servings: 4

Ingredients:

✓ 8 oz water-packed extra firm tofu

✓ 2 tbsp plant butter for frying

✓ 1 green bell pepper, finely chopped

✓ 1 tomato, finely chopped

Ingredients:

✓ 2 tbsp freshly chopped scallions

✓ Salt and black pepper to taste

✓ 1 tsp Mexican-style chili powder

✓ 3 oz grated plant-based Parmesan

Directions:

❖ Place the tofu in between two parchment papers to drain liquid for about 30 minutes.

❖ Melt the plant butter in a large non-stick skillet until no longer foaming. Crumble the tofu into the plant butter and fry until golden brown, stirring occasionally, making sure not to break the tofu into tiny pieces. The goal is to have the tofu like scrambled eggs, about 4 to 6 minutes.

❖ Stir in the bell pepper, tomato, scallions, and cook until the vegetables are soft, about 4 minutes. Then, season with salt, black pepper, chili powder, and stir in the cheese to incorporate and melt for about 2 minutes. Spoon the scramble into a serving platter and serve warm

5) LEMON AND ALMOND WAFFLES

Preparation Time: 20 minutes

Servings: 4

Ingredients:

✓ 2 tbsp flax seed powder

✓ 2/3 cup almond flour

✓ 2 ½ tsp baking powder

✓ A pinch salt

✓ 1 ½ cups almond milk

Ingredients:

✓ 2 tbsp plant butter

✓ 1 cup fresh almond butter

✓ 2 tbsp pure maple syrup

✓ 1 tsp fresh lemon juice

Directions:

❖ In a medium bowl, mix the flaxseed powder with 6 tbsp water and allow soaking for 5 minutes. Add the almond flour, baking powder, salt, and almond milk. Mix until well combined. Preheat a waffle iron and brush with some plant butter. Pour in a quarter cup of the batter, close the iron and cook until the waffles are golden and crisp, 2-3 minutes.

❖ Transfer the waffles to a plate and make more waffles using the same process and ingredient proportions. In a bowl, mix the almond butter with the maple syrup and lemon juice. Spread the top with the almond-lemon mixture and serve

6) ALMOND FLOUR MUFFINS

Preparation Time: 20 minutes

Preparation Time:

Servings: 4

Ingredients:

✓ 2 tbsp flax seed powder

✓ 2 tbsp almond flour

✓ ½ tsp baking powder

Ingredients:

✓ 1 pinch of salt

✓ 3 tbsp plant butter

Directions:

❖ In a small bowl, mix the flax seed with 6 tbsp water until evenly combined and leave to soak for 5 minutes. In another bowl, evenly combine the almond flour, baking powder, and salt. Then, pour in the vegan "flax egg" and whisk again. Let the batter sit for 5 minutes to set.

❖ Melt plant butter in a frying pan and add the mixture in four dollops. Fry until golden brown on one side, then flip the bread with a spatula and fry further until golden brown. Serve

7) BERRY BOWL

Preparation Time: 10 minutes

Preparation Time:

Preparation Time: 2

Ingredients:

- ✓ 1 ½ cups coconut milk
- ✓ 2 small-sized bananas
- ✓ 1 cup mixed berries, frozen

Ingredients:

- ✓ 2 tbsp almond butter
- ✓ 1 tbsp chia seeds
- ✓ 2 tbsp granola

Directions:

- ❖ Add the coconut milk, bananas, berries, almond butter and chia seeds.
- ❖ Puree until creamy, uniform and smooth.
- ❖ Divide the blended mixture between serving bowls and top with granola. Serve immediately

8) BANANA AND FIGS OATMEAL

Preparation Time: 15 minutes

Preparation Time:

Preparation Time: 2

Ingredients:

- ✓ 1 ½ cups almond milk
- ✓ 1/2 cup rolled oats
- ✓ A pinch of sea salt
- ✓ A pinch of grated nutmeg

Ingredients:

- ✓ 1/3 tsp cinnamon
- ✓ 3 dried figs, chopped
- ✓ 2 bananas, peeled and sliced
- ✓ 1 tbsp maple syrup

Directions:

- ❖ In a deep saucepan, bring the milk to a rapid boil. Add in the oats, cover the saucepan and turn the heat to medium.
- ❖ Add in the salt, nutmeg and cinnamon. Continue to cook for about 12 minutes, stirring periodically.
- ❖ Spoon the mixture into serving bowls; top with figs and bananas; add a few drizzles of the maple syrup to each serving and serve warm. Enjoy

9) GRANOLA WITH DRIED CURRANTS

Preparation Time: 25 minutes

Preparation Time:

Preparation Time: 12

Ingredients:

- ✓ 1/2 cup coconut oil
- ✓ 1/3 cup maple syrup
- ✓ 1 tsp vanilla paste
- ✓ 1/2 tsp ground cardamom
- ✓ 1 tsp ground cinnamon
- ✓ 1/3 tsp Himalayan salt

Ingredients:

- ✓ 4 cups old-fashioned oats
- ✓ 1/2 cup pecans, chopped
- ✓ 1/2 cup walnuts, chopped
- ✓ 1/4 cup pepitas
- ✓ 1 cup dried currants

Directions:

- ❖ Begin by preheating your oven to 290 degrees F; line a large baking sheet with a piece parchment paper.
- ❖ Then, thoroughly combine the coconut oil, maple syrup, vanilla paste, cardamom, cinnamon and Himalayan salt.
- ❖ Gradually add in the oats, nuts and seeds; toss to coat well.
- ❖ Spread the mixture out onto the prepared baking sheet.
- ❖ Bake in the middle of the oven, stirring halfway through the cooking time, for about 20 minutes or until golden brown.
- ❖ Stir in the dried currants and let your granola cool completely before storing. Store in an airtight container.
- ❖ Serve with your favorite plant-based milk or yogurt. Enjoy

10) BANANA PANCAKES

Preparation Time: 25 minutes

Preparation Time:

Preparation Time: 4

Ingredients:

- ✓ 2 tbsp ground flaxseeds
- ✓ 1/2 cup oat flour
- ✓ 1/2 cup coconut flour
- ✓ 1/2 cup instant oats
- ✓ 1 tsp baking powder
- ✓ 1/4 tsp kosher salt

Ingredients:

- ✓ 1/4 tsp ground cardamom
- ✓ 1/4 tsp ground cinnamon
- ✓ 1/2 tsp coconut extract
- ✓ 1 cup banana
- ✓ 2 tbsp coconut oil, at room temperature

Ingredients:

- ❖ To make the "flax" egg, in a small mixing dish, whisk 2 tbsp of the ground flaxseeds with 4 tbsp of the water. Let it sit for at least 15 minutes.
- ❖ In a mixing bowl, thoroughly combine the flour, oats, baking powder and spices. Add in the flax egg and mashed banana. Mix until everything is well incorporated.
- ❖ Heat 1/2 tbsp of the coconut oil in a frying pan over medium-low flame. Spoon about 1/4 cup of the batter into the frying pan; fry your pancake for approximately 3 minutes per side.
- ❖ Repeat until you run out of batter. Serve with your favorite fixings and enjoy

11) PESTO BREAD

Preparation Time: 35 minutes

Preparation Time:

Preparation Time: 6

Ingredients:

- ✓ 1 ½ cups grated plant-based mozzarella cheese
- ✓ 1 tbsp flax seed powder
- ✓ 4 tbsp coconut flour
- ✓ ½ cup almond flour
- ✓ ½ tsp salt

Ingredients:

- ✓ 1 tsp baking powder
- ✓ 5 tbsp plant butter
- ✓ 2 oz pesto
- ✓ Olive oil for brushing

Ingredients:

- ❖ First, mix the flax seed powder with 3 tbsp water in a bowl, and set aside to soak for 5 minutes.
- ❖ Preheat oven to 350 F and line a baking sheet with parchment paper. In a bowl, evenly combine the coconut flour, almond flour, salt, and baking powder. Melt the plant butter and cheese in a deep skillet over medium heat and stir in the vegan "flax egg." Mix in the flour mixture until a firm dough forms.
- ❖ Turn the heat off, transfer the mixture in between two parchment papers, and then use a rolling pin to flatten out the dough of about an inch's thickness.
- ❖ Remove the parchment paper on top and spread the pesto all over the dough. Now, use a knife to cut the dough into strips, twist each piece, and place it on the baking sheet.
- ❖ Brush with olive oil and bake for 15 to 20 minutes until golden brown.
- ❖ Remove the bread twist; allow cooling for a few minutes, and serve with warm almond milk

12) CREAMY BREAD WITH SESAME

Preparation Time: 40 minutes

Preparation Time:

Preparation Time: 6

Ingredients:

- ✓ 4 tbsp flax seed powder
- ✓ 2/3 cup cashew cream cheese
- ✓ 4 tbsp sesame oil + for brushing
- ✓ 1 cup coconut flour

Ingredients:

- ✓ 2 tbsp psyllium husk powder
- ✓ 1 tsp salt
- ✓ 1 tsp baking powder
- ✓ 1 tbsp sesame seeds

Ingredients:

- ❖ In a bowl, mix the flax seed powder with 1 ½ cups water until smoothly combined and set aside to soak for 5 minutes. Preheat oven to 400 F. When the vegan "flax egg" is ready, beat in the cream cheese and sesame oil until well mixed.
- ❖ Whisk in the coconut flour, psyllium husk powder, salt, and baking powder until adequately blended.
- ❖ Grease a 9 x 5 inches baking tray with cooking spray, and spread the dough in the tray. Allow the mixture to stand for 5 minutes and then brush with some sesame oil.
- ❖ Sprinkle with the sesame seeds and bake the dough for 30 minutes or until golden brown on top and set within. Take out the bread and allow cooling for a few minutes. Slice and serve

13) DIFFERENT SEEDS BREAD

Preparation Time: 55 minutes

Preparation Time:

Preparation Time: 6

Ingredients:

- ✓ 3 tbsp ground flax seeds
- ✓ ¾ cup coconut flour
- ✓ 1 cup almond flour
- ✓ 3 tsp baking powder
- ✓ 5 tbsp sesame seeds
- ✓ ½ cup chia seeds
- ✓ 1 tsp ground caraway seeds
- ✓ 1 tsp hemp seeds

Ingredients:

- ✓ ¼ cup psyllium husk powder
- ✓ 1 tsp salt
- ✓ 2/3 cup cashew cream cheese
- ✓ ½ cup melted coconut oil
- ✓ ¾ cup coconut cream
- ✓ 1 tbsp poppy seeds

Ingredients:

- ❖ Preheat oven to 350 F and line a loaf pan with parchment paper.
- ❖ For the vegan "flax egg," whisk flax seed powder with ½ cup of water and let the mixture sit to soak for 5 minutes. In a bowl, evenly combine the coconut flour, almond flour, baking powder, sesame seeds, chia seeds, ground caraway seeds, hemp seeds, psyllium husk powder, and salt.
- ❖ In another bowl, use an electric hand mixer to whisk the cream cheese, coconut oil, coconut whipping cream, and vegan "flax egg." Pour the liquid ingredients into the dry ingredients, and continue whisking with the hand mixer until a dough forms. Transfer the dough to the loaf pan, sprinkle with poppy seeds, and bake in the oven for 45 minutes or until a knife inserted into the bread comes out clean. Remove the parchment paper with the bread, and allow cooling on a rack

14) NAAN BREAD

Preparation Time: 25 minutes

Preparation Time:

Preparation Time: 6

Ingredients:

- ✓ ¾ cup almond flour
- ✓ 2 tbsp psyllium husk powder
- ✓ ½ tsp salt
- ✓ ½ tsp baking powder
- ✓ 1/3 cup olive oil

Ingredients:

- ✓ Plant butter for frying
- ✓ 4 oz plant butter
- ✓ 2 garlic cloves, minced

Ingredients:

- ❖ In a bowl, mix the almond flour, psyllium husk powder, salt, and baking powder.
- ❖ Mix in some olive oil and 2 cups of boiling water to combine the ingredients, like a thick porridge. Stir thoroughly and allow the dough to rise for 5 minutes.
- ❖ Divide the dough into 6 to 8 pieces and mold into balls. Place the balls on parchment paper and flatten with your hands.
- ❖ Melt the plant butter in a frying pan and fry the naan on both sides to have a beautiful, golden color. Transfer the naan to a plate and keep warm in the oven. For the garlic butter, add the remaining plant butter to the frying pan and sauté the garlic until fragrant, about 3 minutes. Pour the garlic butter into a bowl and serve as a dip along with the naan

15) MUSHROOM AND SPINACH CHICKPEA OMELETTE

Preparation Time: 25 minutes

Servings: 4

Ingredients:

- ✓ 1 cup chickpea flour
- ✓ ½ tsp onion powder
- ✓ ½ tsp garlic powder
- ✓ ¼ tsp white pepper
- ✓ 1/3 cup nutritional yeast
- ✓ ½ tsp baking soda
- ✓ 1 green bell pepper, chopped
- ✓ 3 scallions, chopped
- ✓ 1 cup sautéed button mushrooms
- ✓ ½ cup chopped fresh spinach
- ✓ 1 cup halved cherry tomatoes
- ✓ 1 tbsp fresh parsley leaves

Directions:

- ❖ In a medium bowl, mix the chickpea flour, onion powder, garlic powder, white pepper, nutritional yeast, and baking soda until well combined. Heat a medium skillet over medium heat and add a quarter of the batter. Swirl the pan to spread the batter across the pan. Scatter a quarter each of the bell pepper, scallions, mushrooms, and spinach on top and cook until the bottom part of the omelet sets, 1-2 minutes.
- ❖ Carefully flip the omelet and cook the other side until set and golden brown. Transfer the omelet to a plate and make the remaining omelets. Serve the omelet with the tomatoes and garnish with the parsley leaves

16) COCONUT-RASPBERRY PANCAKES

Preparation Time: 25 minutes

Servings: 4

Ingredients:

- ✓ 2 tbsp flax seed powder
- ✓ ½ cup coconut milk
- ✓ ¼ cup fresh raspberries, mashed
- ✓ ½ cup oat flour
- ✓ 1 tsp baking soda
- ✓ A pinch salt
- ✓ 1 tbsp coconut sugar
- ✓ 2 tbsp pure date syrup
- ✓ ½ tsp cinnamon powder
- ✓ 2 tbsp unsweetened coconut flakes
- ✓ 2 tsp plant butter
- ✓ Fresh raspberries for garnishing

Directions:

- ❖ In a medium bowl, mix the flax seed powder with the 6 tbsp water and thicken for 5 minutes. Mix in coconut milk and raspberries. Add the oat flour, baking soda, salt, coconut sugar, date syrup, and cinnamon powder. Fold in the coconut flakes until well combined.
- ❖ Working in batches, melt a quarter of the butter in a non-stick skillet and add ¼ cup of the batter. Cook until set beneath and golden brown, 2 minutes. Flip the pancake and cook on the other side until set and golden brown, 2 minutes. Transfer to a plate and make the remaining pancakes using the rest of the ingredients in the same proportions. Garnish the pancakes with some raspberries and serve warm

17) BLUEBERRY-CHIA PUDDING

Preparation Time: 5 minutes + chilling time

Servings: 2

Ingredients:

- ✓ ¾ cup coconut milk
- ✓ ½ tsp vanilla extract
- ✓ ½ cup blueberries
- ✓ 2 tbsp chia seeds
- ✓ Chopped walnuts to garnish

Directions:

- ❖ In a blender, pour the coconut milk, vanilla extract, and half of the blueberries. Process the ingredients at high speed until the blueberries have incorporated into the liquid.
- ❖ Open the blender and mix in the chia seeds. Share the mixture into two breakfast jars, cover, and refrigerate for 4 hours to allow the mixture to gel. Garnish the pudding with the remaining blueberries and walnuts. Serve immediately

18) POTATO AND CAULIFLOWER BROWNS

Preparation Time: 35 minutes

Servings: 4

Ingredients:

- ✓ 3 tbsp flax seed powder
- ✓ 2 large potatoes, shredded
- ✓ 1 big head cauliflower, riced
- ✓ ½ white onion, grated
- ✓ Salt and black pepper to taste
- ✓ 4 tbsp plant butter

Directions:

- ❖ In a medium bowl, mix the flaxseed powder and 9 tbsp water. Allow thickening for 5 minutes for the vegan "flax egg." Add the potatoes, cauliflower, onion, salt, and black pepper to the vegan "flax egg" and mix until well combined. Allow sitting for 5 minutes to thicken.
- ❖ Working in batches, melt 1 tbsp of plant butter in a non-stick skillet and add 4 scoops of the hash brown mixture to the skillet. Make sure to have 1 to 2-inch intervals between each scoop.
- ❖ Use the spoon to flatten the batter and cook until compacted and golden brown on the bottom part, 2 minutes. Flip the hash browns and cook further for 2 minutes or until the vegetable cook and is golden brown. Transfer to a paper-towel-lined plate to drain grease. Make the remaining hash browns using the remaining ingredients. Serve warm

19) PISTACHIOS-PUMPKIN CAKE

Preparation Time: 70 minutes

Servings: 4

Ingredients:

- ✓ 2 tbsp flaxseed powder
- ✓ 3 tbsp vegetable oil
- ✓ ¾ cup canned pumpkin puree
- ✓ ½ cup pure corn syrup
- ✓ 3 tbsp pure date sugar
- ✓ 1 ½ cups whole-wheat flour
- ✓ ½ tsp cinnamon powder
- ✓ ½ tsp baking powder
- ✓ ¼ tsp cloves powder
- ✓ ½ tsp allspice powder
- ✓ ½ tsp nutmeg powder
- ✓ 2 tbsp chopped pistachios

Directions:

- ❖ Preheat the oven to 350 F and lightly coat an 8 x 4-inch loaf pan with cooking spray. In a bowl, mix the flax seed powder with 6 tbsp water and allow thickening for 5 minutes to make the vegan "flax egg."
- ❖ In a bowl, whisk the vegetable oil, pumpkin puree, corn syrup, date sugar, and vegan "flax egg." In another bowl, mix the flour, cinnamon powder, baking powder, cloves powder, allspice powder, and nutmeg powder. Add this mixture to the wet batter and mix until well combined. Pour the batter into the loaf pan, sprinkle the pistachios on top, and gently press the nuts onto the batter to stick.
- ❖ Bake in the oven for 50-55 minutes or until a toothpick inserted into the cake comes out clean. Remove the cake onto a wire rack, allow cooling, slice, and serve

20) BELL PEPPER WITH SCRAMBLED TOFU

Preparation Time: 20 minutes

Servings: 4

Ingredients:

- ✓ 2 tbsp plant butter, for frying
- ✓ 1 (14 oz) pack firm tofu, crumbled
- ✓ 1 red bell pepper, chopped
- ✓ 1 green bell pepper, chopped
- ✓ 1 tomato, finely chopped
- ✓ 2 tbsp chopped fresh green onions
- ✓ Salt and black pepper to taste
- ✓ 1 tsp turmeric powder
- ✓ 1 tsp Creole seasoning
- ✓ ½ cup chopped baby kale
- ✓ ¼ cup grated plant-based Parmesan

Directions:

- ❖ Melt the plant butter in a skillet over medium heat and add the tofu. Cook with occasional stirring until the tofu is light golden brown while, making sure not to break the tofu into tiny bits but to have scrambled egg resemblance, 5 minutes.
- ❖ Stir in the bell peppers, tomato, green onions, salt, black pepper, turmeric powder, and Creole seasoning. Sauté until the vegetables soften, 5 minutes. Mix in the kale to wilt, 3 minutes and then half of the plant-based Parmesan cheese.
- ❖ Allow melting for 1 to 2 minutes and then turn the heat off. Top with the remaining cheese and serve warm

21) ORIGINAL FRENCH TOAST

Preparation Time: 20 minutes

Servings: 2

Ingredients:

- ✓ 1 tbsp ground flax seeds
- ✓ 1 cup coconut milk
- ✓ 1/2 tsp vanilla paste
- ✓ A pinch of sea salt
- ✓ A pinch of grated nutmeg
- ✓ 1/2 tsp ground cinnamon
- ✓ 1/4 tsp ground cloves
- ✓ 1 tbsp agave syrup
- ✓ 4 slices bread

Directions:

- ❖ In a mixing bowl, thoroughly combine the flax seeds, coconut milk, vanilla, salt, nutmeg, cinnamon, cloves and agave syrup.
- ❖ Dredge each slice of bread into the milk mixture until well coated on all sides.
- ❖ Preheat an electric griddle to medium heat and lightly oil it with a nonstick cooking spray.
- ❖ Cook each slice of bread on the preheated griddle for about 3 minutes per side until golden brown.
- ❖ Enjoy

22) FRYBREAD WITH PEANUT BUTTER AND JAM

Preparation Time: 20 minutes

Servings: 3

Ingredients:

- ✓ 1 cup all-purpose flour
- ✓ 1/2 tsp baking powder
- ✓ 1/2 tsp sea salt
- ✓ 1 tsp coconut sugar
- ✓ 1/2 cup warm water
- ✓ 3 tsp olive oil
- ✓ 3 tbsp peanut butter
- ✓ 3 tbsp raspberry jam

Directions:

- ❖ Thoroughly combine the flour, baking powder, salt and sugar. Gradually add in the water until the dough comes together.
- ❖ Divide the dough into three balls; flatten each ball to create circles.
- ❖ Heat 1 tsp of the olive oil in a frying pan over a moderate flame. Fry the first bread for about 9 minutes or until golden brown. Repeat with the remaining oil and dough.
- ❖ Serve the frybread with the peanut butter and raspberry jam. Enjoy

23) PUDDING WITH SULTANAS ON CIABATTA BREAD

Preparation Time: 2 hours 10 minutes

Servings: 4

Ingredients:

- ✓ 2 cups coconut milk, unsweetened
- ✓ 1/2 cup agave syrup
- ✓ 1 tbsp coconut oil
- ✓ 1/2 tsp vanilla essence
- ✓ 1/2 tsp ground cardamom
- ✓ 1/4 tsp ground cloves
- ✓ 1/2 tsp ground cinnamon
- ✓ 1/4 tsp Himalayan salt
- ✓ 3/4 pound stale ciabatta bread, cubed
- ✓ 1/2 cup sultana raisins

Directions:

- ❖ In a mixing bowl, combine the coconut milk, agave syrup, coconut oil, vanilla, cardamom, ground cloves, cinnamon and Himalayan salt.
- ❖ Add the bread cubes to the custard mixture and stir to combine well. Fold in the sultana raisins and allow it to rest for about 1 hour on a counter.
- ❖ Then, spoon the mixture into a lightly oiled casserole dish.
- ❖ Bake in the preheated oven at 350 degrees F for about 1 hour or until the top is golden brown.
- ❖ Place the bread pudding on a wire rack for 10 minutes before slicing and serving

24) VEGAN BANH MI

Preparation Time: 35 minutes

Servings: 4

Ingredients:

- ✓ 1/2 cup rice vinegar
- ✓ 1/4 cup water
- ✓ 1/4 cup white sugar
- ✓ 2 carrots, cut into 1/16-inch-thick matchsticks
- ✓ 1/2 cup white (daikon) radish, cut into 1/16-inch-thick matchsticks
- ✓ 1 white onion, thinly sliced
- ✓ 2 tbsp olive oil
- ✓ 12 ounces firm tofu, cut into sticks
- ✓ 1/4 cup vegan mayonnaise

- ✓ 1 ½ tbsp soy sauce
- ✓ 2 cloves garlic, minced
- ✓ 1/4 cup fresh parsley, chopped
- ✓ Kosher salt and ground black pepper, to taste
- ✓ 2 standard French baguettes, cut into four pieces
- ✓ 4 tbsp fresh cilantro, chopped
- ✓ 4 lime wedges

Directions:

- ❖ Bring the rice vinegar, water and sugar to a boil and stir until the sugar has dissolved, about 1 minute. Allow it to cool.
- ❖ Pour the cooled vinegar mixture over the carrot, daikon radish and onion; allow the vegetables to marinate for at least 30 minutes.
- ❖ While the vegetables are marinating, heat the olive oil in a frying pan over medium-high heat. Once hot, add the tofu and sauté for 8 minutes, stirring occasionally to promote even cooking.
- ❖ Then, mix the mayo, soy sauce, garlic, parsley, salt and ground black pepper in a small bowl.
- ❖ Slice each piece of the baguette in half the long way Then, toast the baguette halves under the preheated broiler for about 3 minutes.
- ❖ To assemble the banh mi sandwiches, spread each half of the toasted baguette with the mayonnaise mixture; fill the cavity of the bottom half of the bread with the fried tofu sticks, marinated vegetables and cilantro leaves.
- ❖ Lastly, squeeze the lime wedges over the filling and top with the other half of the baguette. Enjoy

25) BREAKFAST NUTTY OATMEAL MUFFINS

Preparation Time: 30 minutes

Servings: 9

Ingredients:

- ✓ 1 ½ cups rolled oats
- ✓ 1/2 cup shredded coconut, unsweetened
- ✓ 3/4 tsp baking powder
- ✓ 1/4 tsp salt
- ✓ 1/4 tsp vanilla extract
- ✓ 1/4 tsp coconut extract

- ✓ 1/4 tsp grated nutmeg
- ✓ 1/2 tsp cardamom
- ✓ 3/4 cup coconut milk
- ✓ 1/3 cup canned pumpkin
- ✓ 1/4 cup agave syrup
- ✓ 1/4 cup golden raisins
- ✓ 1/4 cup pecans, chopped

Directions:

- ❖ Begin by preheating your oven to 360 degrees F. Spritz a muffin tin with a nonstick cooking oil.
- ❖ In a mixing bowl, thoroughly combine all the ingredients, except for the raisins and pecans.
- ❖ Fold in the raisins and pecans and scrape the batter into the prepared muffin tin.
- ❖ Bake your muffins for about 25 minutes or until the top is set. Enjoy

SOUPS, STEW AND SALADS

26) SPINACH AND KALE SOUP WITH FRIED COLLARDS

Preparation Time: 16 minutes

Servings: 4

Ingredients:

- 4 tbsp plant butter
- 1 cup fresh spinach, chopped
- 1 cup fresh kale, chopped
- 1 large avocado
- 3 ½ cups coconut cream

- 4 cups vegetable broth
- 3 tbsp chopped fresh mint leaves
- Salt and black pepper to taste
- Juice from 1 lime
- 1 cup collard greens, chopped
- 2 garlic cloves, minced
- 1 pinch of green cardamom powder

Directions:

- Melt 2 tbsp of plant butter in a saucepan over medium heat and sauté spinach and kale for 5 minutes. Turn the heat off. Add the avocado, coconut cream, vegetable broth, salt, and pepper. Puree the ingredients with an immersion blender until smooth. Pour in the lime juice and set aside.
- Melt the remaining plant butter in a pan and add the collard greens, garlic, and cardamom; sauté until the garlic is fragrant and has achieved a golden brown color, about 4 minutes. Fetch the soup into serving bowls and garnish with fried collards and mint. Serve warm

27) GOULASH TOFU SOUP

Preparation Time: 25 minutes

Servings: 4

Ingredients:

- 1 ½ cups extra-firm tofu, crumbled
- 3 tbsp plant butter
- 1 white onion
- 2 garlic cloves
- 8 oz chopped butternut squash
- 1 red bell pepper
- 1 tbsp paprika powder
- ¼ tsp red chili flakes

- 1 tbsp dried basil
- ½ tbsp crushed cardamom seeds
- Salt and black pepper to taste
- 1 ½ cups crushed tomatoes
- 4 cups vegetable broth
- 1 ½ tsp red wine vinegar
- Chopped cilantro to serve

Directions:

- Melt plant butter in a pot over medium heat and sauté onion and garlic for 3 minutes. Stir in tofu and cook for 3 minutes; add the butternut squash, bell pepper, paprika, red chili flakes, basil, cardamom seeds, salt, and pepper. Cook for 2 minutes. Pour in tomatoes and vegetable broth. Bring to a boil, reduce the heat and simmer for 10 minutes. Mix in red wine vinegar. Garnish with cilantro and serve

28) MUSHROOM SOUP OF MEDLEY

Preparation Time: 40 minutes

Servings: 4

Ingredients:

- ✓ 4 oz unsalted plant butter
- ✓ 1 small onion, finely chopped
- ✓ 1 clove garlic, minced
- ✓ 5 oz button mushrooms, chopped
- ✓ 5 oz cremini mushrooms, chopped
- ✓ 5 oz shiitake mushrooms, chopped
- ✓ ½ lb celery root, chopped
- ✓ ½ tsp dried rosemary
- ✓ 1 vegetable stock cube, crushed
- ✓ 1 tbsp plain vinegar
- ✓ 1 cup coconut cream
- ✓ 4 – 6 leaves basil, chopped

Directions:

- ❖ Place a saucepan over medium-high heat, add the plant butter to melt, then sauté the onion, garlic, mushrooms, and celery root in the butter until golden brown and fragrant, about 6 minutes. Fetch out some mushrooms and reserve for garnishing. Add the rosemary, 3 cups of water, stock cube, and vinegar. Stir the mixture and bring it to a boil for 6 minutes. After, reduce the heat and simmer the soup for 15 minutes or until the celery is soft.
- ❖ Mix in the coconut cream and puree the ingredients using an immersion blender. Simmer for 2 minutes. Spoon the soup into serving bowls, garnish with the reserved mushrooms and basil. Serve

29) DILL CAULIFLOWER SOUP

Preparation Time: 26 minutes

Servings: 4

Ingredients:

- ✓ 2 tbsp coconut oil
- ✓ ½ lb celery root, trimmed
- ✓ 1 garlic clove
- ✓ 1 medium white onion
- ✓ ¼ cup fresh dill, roughly chopped
- ✓ 1 tsp cumin powder
- ✓ ¼ tsp nutmeg powder
- ✓ 1 head cauliflower, cut into florets
- ✓ 3 ½ cups seasoned vegetable stock
- ✓ 5 oz plant butter
- ✓ Juice from 1 lemon
- ✓ ¼ cup coconut whipping cream

Directions:

- ❖ Set a pot over medium heat, add the coconut oil and allow heating until no longer shimmering.
- ❖ Add the celery root, garlic clove, and onion; sauté the vegetables until fragrant and soft, about 5 minutes. Stir in the dill, cumin, and nutmeg, and fry further for 1 minute. Mix in the cauliflower florets and vegetable stock. Bring the soup to a boil for 12 to 15 minutes or until the cauliflower is soft. Turn the heat off. Add the plant butter and lemon juice. Puree the ingredients with an immersion blender until smooth. Mix in coconut whipping cream and season the soup with salt and black pepper. Serve warm

30) FENNEL BROCCOLI SOUP

Preparation Time: 25 minutes

Servings: 4

Ingredients:

- ✓ 1 fennel bulb, chopped
- ✓ 10 oz broccoli, cut into florets
- ✓ 3 cups vegetable stock
- ✓ Salt and black pepper to taste
- ✓ 1 garlic clove
- ✓ 1 cup cashew cream cheese
- ✓ 3 oz plant butter
- ✓ ½ cup chopped fresh oregano

Directions:

- ❖ Put the fennel and broccoli into a pot, and cover with the vegetable stock. Bring the ingredients to a boil over medium heat until the vegetables are soft, about 10 minutes. Season the liquid with salt and black pepper, and drop in the garlic. Simmer the soup for 5 to 7 minutes and turn the heat off.
- ❖ Pour the cream cheese, plant butter, and oregano into the soup; puree the ingredients with an immersion blender until completely smooth. Adjust the taste with salt and black pepper. Spoon the soup into serving bowls and serve

31) BEAN SOUP ASIAN-STYLE

Preparation Time: 55 minutes

Servings: 4

Ingredients:

- ✓ 1 cup canned cannellini beans
- ✓ 2 tsp curry powder
- ✓ 2 tsp olive oil
- ✓ 1 red onion, diced
- ✓ 1 tbsp minced fresh ginger
- ✓ 2 cubed sweet potatoes
- ✓ 1 cup sliced zucchini
- ✓ Salt and black pepper to taste
- ✓ 4 cups vegetable stock
- ✓ 1 bunch spinach, chopped
- ✓ Toasted sesame seeds

Directions:

- ❖ Mix the beans with 1 tsp of curry powder until well combined. Warm the oil in a pot over medium heat. Place the onion and ginger and cook for 5 minutes until soft. Add in sweet potatoes and cook for 10 minutes. Put in zucchini and cook for 5 minutes. Season with the remaining curry, pepper, and salt.
- ❖ Pour in the stock and bring to a boil. Lower the heat and simmer for 25 minutes. Stir in beans and spinach. Cook until the spinach wilts and remove from the heat. Garnish with sesame seeds to serve

32) TORTILLA MEXICAN SOUP

Preparation Time: 40 minutes

Servings: 4

Ingredients:

- ✓ 1 (14.5-oz) can diced tomatoes
- ✓ 1 (4-oz) can green chiles, chopped
- ✓ 2 tbsp olive oil
- ✓ 1 cup canned sweet corn
- ✓ 1 red onion, chopped
- ✓ 2 garlic cloves, minced
- ✓ 2 jalapeño peppers, sliced
- ✓ 4 cups vegetable broth
- ✓ 8 oz seitan, cut into ¼-inch strips
- ✓ Salt and black pepper to taste
- ✓ ¼ cup chopped fresh cilantro
- ✓ 3 tbsp fresh lime juice
- ✓ 4 corn tortillas, cut into strips
- ✓ 1 ripe avocado, chopped

Directions:

- ❖ Preheat oven to 350 F. Heat the oil in a pot over medium heat. Place sweet corn, garlic, jalapeño, and onion and cook for 5 minutes. Stir in broth, seitan, tomatoes, canned chiles, salt, and pepper. Bring to a boil, then lower the heat and simmer for 20 minutes. Put in the cilantro and lime juice, stir. Adjust the seasoning.
- ❖ Meanwhile, arrange the tortilla strips on a baking sheet and bake for 8 minutes until crisp. Serve the soup into bowls and top with tortilla strips and avocado

33) BEAN SPICY SOUP

Preparation Time: 40 minutes

Servings: 4

Ingredients:

- ✓ 2 tbsp olive oil
- ✓ 1 medium onion, chopped
- ✓ 2 large garlic cloves, minced
- ✓ 1 carrot, chopped
- ✓ 1 (15.5-oz) can cannellini beans, drained
- ✓ 5 cups vegetable broth
- ✓ ¼ tsp crushed red pepper
- ✓ Salt and black pepper to taste
- ✓ 3 cups chopped baby spinach

Directions:

- ❖ Heat oil in a pot over medium heat. Place in carrot, onion, and garlic and cook for 3 minutes. Put in beans, broth, red pepper, salt, and black pepper and stir. Bring to a boil, then lower the heat and simmer for 25 minutes. Stir in baby spinach and cook for 5 minutes until the spinach wilts. Serve warm

VEGETABLES AND SIDE DISHES

34) WINE AND LEMON BRAISED ARTICHOKES

Preparation Time: 35 minutes

Servings: 4

Ingredients:

- ✓ 1 large lemon, freshly squeezed
- ✓ 1 ½ pounds artichokes, trimmed, tough outer leaves and chokes removed
- ✓ 2 tbsp mint leaves, finely chopped
- ✓ 2 tbsp cilantro leaves, finely chopped
- ✓ 2 tbsp basil leaves, finely chopped
- ✓ 2 cloves garlic, minced
- ✓ 1/4 cup dry white wine
- ✓ 1/4 cup extra-virgin olive oil, plus more for drizzling
- ✓ Sea salt and freshly ground black pepper, to taste

Directions:

- ❖ Fill a bowl with water and add in the lemon juice. Place the cleaned artichokes in the bowl, keeping them completely submerged.
- ❖ In another small bowl, thoroughly combine the herbs and garlic. Rub your artichokes with the herb mixture.
- ❖ Pour the wine and olive oil in a saucepan; add the artichokes to the saucepan. Turn the heat to a simmer and continue to cook, covered, for about 30 minutes until the artichokes are crisp-tender.
- ❖ To serve, drizzle the artichokes with the cooking juices, season them with the salt and black pepper and enjoy

35) ROASTED CARROTS WITH HERBS

Preparation Time: 25 minute

Servings: 4

Ingredients:

- ✓ 2 pounds carrots, trimmed and halved lengthwise
- ✓ 4 tbsp olive oil
- ✓ 1 tsp granulated garlic
- ✓ 1 tsp paprika
- ✓ Sea salt and freshly ground black pepper
- ✓ 2 tbsp fresh cilantro, chopped
- ✓ 2 tbsp fresh parsley, chopped
- ✓ 2 tbsp fresh chives, chopped

Directions:

- ❖ Start by preheating your oven to 400 degrees F.
- ❖ Toss the carrots with the olive oil, granulated garlic, paprika, salt and black pepper. Arrange them in a single layer on a parchment-lined roasting sheet.
- ❖ Roast the carrots in the preheated oven for about 20 minutes, until fork-tender.
- ❖ Toss the carrots with the fresh herbs and serve immediately. Enjoy

36) BRAISED GREEN BEANS

Preparation Time: 15 minutes

Servings: 4

Ingredients:

- ✓ 4 tbsp olive oil
- ✓ 1 carrot, cut into matchsticks
- ✓ 1 ½ pounds green beans, trimmed
- ✓ 4 garlic cloves, peeled
- ✓ 1 bay laurel
- ✓ 1 ½ cups vegetable broth
- ✓ Sea salt and ground black pepper, to taste
- ✓ 1 lemon, cut into wedges

Directions:

- ❖ Heat the olive oil in a saucepan over medium flame. Once hot, fry the carrots and green beans for about 5 minutes, stirring periodically to promote even cooking.
- ❖ Add in the garlic and bay laurel and continue sautéing an additional 1 minute or until fragrant.
- ❖ Add in the broth, salt and black pepper and continue to simmer, covered, for about 9 minutes or until the green beans are tender.
- ❖ Taste, adjust the seasonings and serve with lemon wedges. Enjoy

37) SPRING ROASTED VEGETABLES

Preparation Time: 45 minutes

Servings: 4

Ingredients:

- ✓ 1/2 pound carrots, slice into 1-inch chunks
- ✓ 1/2 pound parsnips, slice into 1-inch chunks
- ✓ 1/2 pound celery, slice into 1-inch chunks
- ✓ 1/2 pound sweet potatoes, slice into 1-inch chunks
- ✓ 1 large onion, slice into wedges
- ✓ 1/4 cup olive oil
- ✓ 1 tsp red pepper flakes
- ✓ 1 tsp dried basil
- ✓ 1 tsp dried oregano
- ✓ 1 tsp dried thyme
- ✓ Sea salt and freshly ground black pepper

Directions:

- ❖ Start by preheating your oven to 420 degrees F.
- ❖ Toss the vegetables with the olive oil and spices. Arrange them on a parchment-lined roasting pan.
- ❖ Roast for about 25 minutes. Stir the vegetables and continue to cook for 20 minutes more.
- ❖ Enjoy!

38) TRADITIONAL MOROCCAN TAGINE

Preparation Time: 30 minutes

Servings: 4

Ingredients:

- ✓ 3 tbsp olive oil
- ✓ 1 large shallot, chopped
- ✓ 1 tsp ginger, peeled and minced
- ✓ 4 garlic cloves, chopped
- ✓ 2 medium carrots, trimmed and chopped
- ✓ 2 medium parsnips, trimmed and chopped
- ✓ 2 medium sweet potatoes, peeled and cubed
- ✓ Sea salt and ground black pepper, to taste
- ✓ 1 tsp hot sauce
- ✓ 1 tsp fenugreek
- ✓ 1/2 tsp saffron
- ✓ 1/2 tsp caraway
- ✓ 2 large tomatoes, pureed
- ✓ 4 cups vegetable broth
- ✓ 1 lemon, cut into wedges

Directions:

- ❖ In a Dutch Oven, heat the olive oil over medium heat. Once hot, sauté the shallots for 4 to 5 minutes, until tender.
- ❖ Then, sauté the ginger and garlic for about 40 seconds or until aromatic.
- ❖ Add in the remaining ingredients, except for the lemon and bring to a boil. Immediately turn the heat to a simmer.
- ❖ Let it simmer for about 25 minutes or until the vegetables have softened. Serve with fresh lemon wedges and enjoy

39) CHINESE CABBAGE STIR-FRY

Preparation Time: 10 minutes

Servings: 3

Ingredients:

- ✓ 3 tbsp sesame oil
- ✓ 1 pound Chinese cabbage, sliced
- ✓ 1/2 tsp Chinese five-spice powder
- ✓ Kosher salt, to taste
- ✓ 1/2 tsp Szechuan pepper
- ✓ 2 tbsp soy sauce
- ✓ 3 tbsp sesame seeds, lightly toasted

Directions:

- ❖ In a wok, heat the sesame oil until sizzling. Stir fry the cabbage for about 5 minutes.
- ❖ Stir in the spices and soy sauce and continue to cook, stirring frequently, for about 5 minutes more, until the cabbage is crisp-tender and aromatic.
- ❖ Sprinkle sesame seeds over the top and serve immediately

40) SWEET MASHED CARROTS

Preparation Time: 25 minutes

Servings: 4

Ingredients:

- ✓ 1 ½ pounds carrots, trimmed
- ✓ 3 tbsp vegan butter
- ✓ 1 cup scallions, sliced
- ✓ 1 tbsp maple syrup
- ✓ 1/2 tsp garlic powder
- ✓ 1/2 tsp ground allspice
- ✓ Sea salt, to taste
- ✓ 1/2 cup soy sauce
- ✓ 2 tbsp fresh cilantro, chopped

Directions:

- ❖ Steam the carrots for about 15 minutes until they are very tender; drain well.
- ❖ In a sauté pan, melt the butter until sizzling. Now, turn the heat down to maintain an insistent sizzle.
- ❖ Now, cook the scallions until they've softened. Add in the maple syrup, garlic powder, ground allspice, salt and soy sauce for about 10 minutes or until they are caramelized.
- ❖ Add the caramelized scallions to your food processor; add in the carrots and puree the ingredients until everything is well blended.
- ❖ Serve garnished with the fresh cilantro. Enjoy

41) SAUTÉED TURNIP GREENS

Preparation Time: 15 minutes

Servings: 4

Ingredients:

- ✓ 2 tbsp olive oil
- ✓ 1 onion, sliced
- ✓ 2 garlic cloves, sliced
- ✓ 1 ½ pounds turnip greens cleaned and chopped
- ✓ 1/4 cup vegetable broth
- ✓ 1/4 cup dry white wine
- ✓ 1/2 tsp dried oregano
- ✓ 1 tsp dried parsley flakes
- ✓ Kosher salt and ground black pepper, to taste

Directions:

- ❖ In a sauté pan, heat the olive oil over a moderately high heat.
- ❖ Now, sauté the onion for 3 to 4 minutes or until tender and translucent. Add in the garlic and continue to cook for 30 seconds more or until aromatic.
- ❖ Stir in the turnip greens, broth, wine, oregano and parsley; continue sautéing an additional 6 minutes or until they have wilted completely.
- ❖ Season with salt and black pepper to taste and serve warm. Enjoy

42) YUKON GOLD MASHED POTATOES

Preparation Time: 25 minutes

Servings: 5

Ingredients:

- ✓ 2 pounds Yukon Gold potatoes, peeled and diced
- ✓ 1 clove garlic, pressed
- ✓ Sea salt and red pepper flakes, to taste
- ✓ 3 tbsp vegan butter
- ✓ 1/2 cup soy milk
- ✓ 2 tbsp scallions, sliced

Directions:

- ❖ Cover the potatoes with an inch or two of cold water. Cook the potatoes in gently boiling water for about 20 minutes.
- ❖ Then, puree the potatoes, along with the garlic, salt, red pepper, butter and milk, to your desired consistency.
- ❖ Serve garnished with fresh scallions. Enjoy

LUNCH

43) TOFU CABBAGE STIR-FRY

Preparation Time: 45 minutes

Servings: 4

Ingredients:

- ✓ 2 ½ cups baby bok choy, quartered
- ✓ 5 oz plant butter
- ✓ 2 cups tofu, cubed
- ✓ 1 tsp garlic powder
- ✓ 1 tsp onion powder
- ✓ 1 tbsp plain vinegar
- ✓ 2 garlic cloves, minced
- ✓ 1 tsp chili flakes
- ✓ 1 tbsp fresh ginger, grated
- ✓ 3 green onions, sliced
- ✓ 1 tbsp sesame oil
- ✓ 1 cup tofu mayonnaise

Directions:

❖ Melt half of the butter in a wok over medium heat, add the bok choy, and stir-fry until softened. Season with salt, black pepper, garlic powder, onion powder, and plain vinegar. Sauté for 2 minutes; set aside. Melt the remaining butter in the wok, add and sauté garlic, chili flakes, and ginger until fragrant. Put the tofu in the wok and cook until browned on all sides. Add the green onions and bok choy, heat for 2 minutes, and add the sesame oil. Stir in tofu mayonnaise, cook for 1 minute, and serve

44) SMOKED TEMPEH WITH BROCCOLI FRITTERS

Preparation Time: 40 minutes

Servings: 4

Ingredients:

- ✓ 4 tbsp flax seed powder
- ✓ 1 tbsp soy sauce
- ✓ 3 tbsp olive oil
- ✓ 1 tbsp grated ginger
- ✓ 3 tbsp fresh lime juice
- ✓ Cayenne pepper to taste
- ✓ 10 oz tempeh slices
- ✓ 1 head broccoli, grated
- ✓ 8 oz tofu, grated
- ✓ 3 tbsp almond flour
- ✓ ½ tsp onion powder
- ✓ 4 ¼ oz plant butter
- ✓ ½ cup mixed salad greens
- ✓ 1 cup tofu mayonnaise
- ✓ Juice of ½ a lemon

Directions:

❖ In a bowl, mix the flax seed powder with 12 tbsp water and set aside to soak for 5 minutes. In another bowl, combine soy sauce, olive oil, grated ginger, lime juice, salt, and cayenne pepper. Brush the tempeh slices with the mixture. Heat a grill pan over medium and grill the tempeh on both sides until golden brown and nicely smoked. Remove the slices to a plate.

❖ In another bowl, mix the tofu with broccoli. Add in vegan "flax egg," almond flour, onion powder, salt, and black pepper. Mix and form 12 patties out of the mixture. Melt the plant butter in a skillet and fry the patties on both sides until golden brown. Remove to a plate. Add the grilled tempeh with the broccoli fritters and salad greens. Mix the tofu mayonnaise with the lemon juice and drizzle over the salad

45) CHEESY CAULIFLOWER CASSEROLE

Preparation Time: 35 minutes

Servings: 4

Ingredients:

- ✓ 2 oz plant butter
- ✓ 1 white onion, finely chopped
- ✓ ½ cup celery stalks, finely chopped
- ✓ 1 green bell pepper, chopped
- ✓ Salt and black pepper to taste
- ✓ 1 small head cauliflower, chopped
- ✓ 1 cup tofu mayonnaise
- ✓ 4 oz grated plant-based Parmesan
- ✓ 1 tsp red chili flakes

Directions:

❖ Preheat oven to 400 F. Season onion, celery, and bell pepper with salt and black pepper. In a bowl, mix cauliflower, tofu mayonnaise, Parmesan cheese, and red chili flakes. Pour the mixture into a greased baking dish and add the vegetables; mix to distribute. Bake for 20 minutes. Remove and serve warm

46) MUSHROOM CURRY PIE

Preparation Time: 70 minutes

Servings: 6

Ingredients:

- ✓ Piecrust:
- ✓ 1 tbsp flax seed powder + 3 tbsp water
- ✓ ¾ cup coconut flour
- ✓ 4 tbsp chia seeds
- ✓ 4 tbsp almond flour
- ✓ 1 tbsp psyllium husk powder
- ✓ 1 tsp baking powder
- ✓ 1 pinch of salt
- ✓ 3 tbsp olive oil
- ✓ 4 tbsp water

- ✓ Filling:
- ✓ 1 cup chopped shiitake mushrooms
- ✓ 1 cup tofu mayonnaise
- ✓ 3 tbsp flax seed powder + 9 tbsp water
- ✓ ½ red bell pepper, finely chopped
- ✓ 1 tsp turmeric
- ✓ ½ tsp paprika
- ✓ ½ tsp garlic powder
- ✓ ½ cup cashew cream cheese
- ✓ 1 ¼ cups grated plant-based Parmesan

Directions:

- ❖ In two separate bowls, mix the different portions of flax seed powder with the respective quantity of water and set aside to absorb for 5 minutes.
- ❖ Preheat oven to 350 F. When the vegan "flax egg" is ready, pour the smaller quantity into a food processor, add in the pie crust ingredients and blend until a ball forms out of the dough. Line a springform pan with parchment paper and grease with cooking spray. Spread the dough on the bottom of the pan and bake for 15 minutes. In a bowl, add the remaining flax egg and all the filling ingredients, combine the mixture, and fill the piecrust. Bake for 40 minutes. Serve sliced

47) TOFU AND SPINACH LASAGNA WITH RED SAUCE

Preparation Time: 65 minutes

Servings: 4

Ingredients:

- ✓ 2 tbsp plant butter
- ✓ 1 white onion, chopped
- ✓ 1 garlic clove, minced
- ✓ 2 ½ cups crumbled tofu
- ✓ 3 tbsp tomato paste
- ✓ ½ tbsp dried oregano
- ✓ Salt and black pepper to taste
- ✓ 1 cup baby spinach

- ✓ 8 tbsp flax seed powder
- ✓ 1 ½ cup cashew cream cheese
- ✓ 5 tbsp psyllium husk powder
- ✓ 2 cups coconut cream
- ✓ 5 oz grated plant-based mozzarella
- ✓ 2 oz grated plant-based Parmesan
- ✓ ½ cup fresh parsley, finely chopped

Directions:

- ❖ Melt plant butter in a medium pot and sauté onion and garlic until fragrant and soft, about 3 minutes. Stir in tofu and cook until brown. Mix in tomato paste, oregano, salt, and black pepper. Pour ½ cup of water into the pot, stir, and simmer the ingredients until most of the liquid has evaporated.
- ❖ Preheat oven to 300 F. Mix flax seed powder with 1 ½ cups water in a bowl to make vegan "flax egg." Allow sitting to thicken for 5 minutes. Combine vegan "flax egg" with cashew cream cheese and salt. Add psyllium husk powder a bit at a time while whisking and allow the mixture to sit for a few minutes. Line a baking sheet with parchment paper and spread the mixture in. Cover with another parchment paper and flatten the dough into the sheet. Bake for 10-12 minutes. Slice the pasta into sheets.
- ❖ In a bowl, combine coconut cream and two-thirds of the plant-based mozzarella cheese. Fetch out 2 tbsp of the mixture and reserve. Mix in plant-based Parmesan cheese, salt, pepper, and parsley. Set aside. Grease a baking dish with cooking spray, layer a single line of pasta, spread with some tomato sauce, 1/3 of the spinach, and ¼ of the coconut cream mixture. Repeat layering the ingredients twice in the same manner, making sure to top the final layer with the coconut cream mixture and the reserved cream cheese. Bake for 30 minutes at 400 F. Slice and serve with salad

48) AVOCADO COCONUT PIE

Preparation Time: 80 minutes

Servings: 4

Ingredients:

- Piecrust:
- 1 tbsp flax seed powder + 3 tbsp water
- 1 cup coconut flour
- 4 tbsp chia seeds
- 1 tbsp psyllium husk powder
- 1 tsp baking soda
- 1 pinch salt
- 3 tbsp coconut oil
- 4 tbsp water

- ✓ Filling:
- ✓ 2 ripe avocados, chopped
- ✓ 1 cup tofu mayonnaise
- ✓ 3 tbsp flax seed powder + 9 tbsp water
- ✓ 2 tbsp fresh parsley, chopped
- ✓ 1 jalapeno, finely chopped
- ✓ ½ tsp onion powder
- ✓ ¼ tsp salt
- ✓ ½ cup cream cheese
- ✓ 1 ¼ cups grated plant-based Parmesan

Directions:

- ❖ In 2 separate bowls, mix the different portions of flax seed powder with the respective quantity of water. Allow absorbing for 5 minutes.
- ❖ Preheat oven to 350 F. In a food processor, add the piecrust ingredients and the smaller portion of the vegan "flax egg." Blend until the resulting dough forms into a ball. Line a springform pan with parchment paper and spread the dough in the pan. Bake for 10-15 minutes.
- ❖ Put the avocado in a bowl and add the tofu mayonnaise, remaining vegan "flax egg," parsley, jalapeno, onion powder, salt, cream cheese, and plant-based Parmesan. Combine well. Remove the piecrust when ready and fill with the creamy mixture. Bake for 35 minutes. Cool before slicing and serving

49) GREEN AVOCADO CARBONARA

Preparation Time: 30 minutes

Servings: 4

Ingredients:

- 8 tbsp flax seed powder
- 1 ½ cups cashew cream cheese
- 5 ½ tbsp psyllium husk powder
- 1 avocado, chopped
- 1 ¾ cups coconut cream
- Juice of ½ lemon

- ✓ 1 tsp onion powder
- ✓ ½ tsp garlic powder
- ✓ ¼ cup olive oil
- ✓ Salt and black pepper to taste
- ✓ ½ cup grated plant-based Parmesan
- ✓ 4 tbsp toasted pecans

Directions:

- ❖ Preheat oven to 300 F.
- ❖ In a medium bowl, mix the flax seed powder with 1 ½ cups water and allow sitting to thicken for 5 minutes. Add the cashew cream cheese, salt, and psyllium husk powder. Whisk until smooth batter forms. Line a baking sheet with parchment paper, pour in the batter, and cover with another parchment paper. Use a rolling pin to flatten the dough into the sheet. Bake for 10-12 minutes. Remove, take off the parchment papers and use a sharp knife to slice the pasta into thin strips lengthwise. Cut each piece into halves, pour into a bowl, and set aside.
- ❖ In a blender, combine avocado, coconut cream, lemon juice, onion powder, and garlic powder; puree until smooth. Pour the olive oil over the pasta and stir to coat properly. Pour the avocado sauce on top and mix. Season with salt and black pepper. Divide the pasta into serving plates, garnish with Parmesan cheese and pecans, and serve immediately

50) MUSHROOM AND GREEN BEAN BIRYANI

Preparation Time: 50 minutes

Servings: 4

Ingredients:

- 1 cup brown rice
- 3 tbsp plant butter
- 3 medium white onions, chopped
- 6 garlic cloves, minced
- 1 tsp ginger puree
- 1 tbsp turmeric powder + for dusting
- ¼ tsp cinnamon powder
- 2 tsp garam masala

- ✓ ½ tsp cardamom powder
- ✓ ½ tsp cayenne powder
- ✓ ½ tsp cumin powder
- ✓ 1 tsp smoked paprika
- ✓ 3 large tomatoes, diced
- ✓ 2 green chilies, minced
- ✓ 1 tbsp tomato puree
- ✓ 1 cup chopped cremini mushrooms
- ✓ 1 cup chopped mustard greens
- ✓ 1 cup plant-based yogurt

Directions:

- ❖ Melt the butter in a large pot and sauté the onions until softened, 3 minutes. Mix in the garlic, ginger, turmeric, cardamom powder, garam masala, cardamom powder, cayenne pepper, cumin powder, paprika, and salt. Stir-fry for 1-2 minutes.
- ❖ Stir in the tomatoes, green chili, tomato puree, and mushrooms. Once boiling, mix in the rice and cover with water. Cover the pot and cook over medium heat until the liquid absorbs and the rice is tender, 15-20 minutes. Open the lid and fluff in the mustard greens and half of the parsley. Dish the food, top with the coconut yogurt, garnish with the remaining parsley, and serve warm

51) BAKED CHEESY SPAGHETTI SQUASH

Preparation Time: 40 minutes

Servings: 4

Ingredients:

- ✓ 2 lb spaghetti squash
- ✓ 1 tbsp coconut oil
- ✓ Salt and black pepper to taste
- ✓ 2 tbsp melted plant butter
- ✓ ½ tbsp garlic powder
- ✓ 1/5 tsp chili powder
- ✓ 1 cup coconut cream
- ✓ 2 oz cashew cream cheese
- ✓ 1 cup plant-based mozzarella
- ✓ 2 oz grated plant-based Parmesan
- ✓ 2 tbsp fresh cilantro, chopped
- ✓ Olive oil for drizzling

Directions:

- ❖ Preheat oven to 350 F.
- ❖ Cut the squash in halves lengthwise and spoon out the seeds and fiber. Place on a baking dish, brush with coconut oil, and season with salt and pepper. Bake for 30 minutes. Remove and use two forks to shred the flesh into strands.
- ❖ Empty the spaghetti strands into a bowl and mix with plant butter, garlic and chili powders, coconut cream, cream cheese, half of the plant-based mozzarella and plant-based Parmesan cheeses. Spoon the mixture into the squash cups and sprinkle with the remaining mozzarella cheese. Bake further for 5 minutes. Sprinkle with cilantro and drizzle with some oil. Serve

52) KALE AND MUSHROOM PIEROGIS

Preparation Time: 45 minutes

Servings: 4

Ingredients:

- ✓ Stuffing:
- ✓ 2 tbsp plant butter
- ✓ 2 garlic cloves, finely chopped
- ✓ 1 small red onion, finely chopped
- ✓ 3 oz baby Bella mushrooms, sliced
- ✓ 2 oz fresh kale
- ✓ ½ tsp salt
- ✓ ¼ tsp freshly ground black pepper
- ✓ ½ cup dairy-free cream cheese
- ✓ 2 oz plant-based Parmesan, grated
- ✓ Pierogi:
- ✓ 1 tbsp flax seed powder
- ✓ ½ cup almond flour
- ✓ 4 tbsp coconut flour
- ✓ ½ tsp salt
- ✓ 1 tsp baking powder
- ✓ 1 ½ cups grated plant-based Parmesan
- ✓ 5 tbsp plant butter
- ✓ Olive oil for brushing

Directions:

- ❖ Put the plant butter in a skillet and melt over medium heat, then add and sauté the garlic, red onion, mushrooms, and kale until the mushrooms brown. Season the mixture with salt and black pepper and reduce the heat to low. Stir in the cream cheese and plant-based Parmesan cheese and simmer for 1 minute. Turn the heat off and set the filling aside to cool.
- ❖ Make the pierogis: In a small bowl, mix the flax seed powder with 3 tbsp water and allow sitting for 5 minutes. In a bowl, combine almond flour, coconut flour, salt, and baking powder. Put a small pan over low heat, add, and melt the plant-based Parmesan cheese and plant butter while stirring continuously until smooth batter forms. Turn the heat off.
- ❖ Pour the vegan "flax egg" into the cream mixture, continue stirring while adding the flour mixture until a firm dough forms. Mold the dough into four balls, place on a chopping board, and use a rolling pin to flatten each into ½ inch thin round pieces. Spread a generous amount of stuffing on one-half of each dough, then fold over the filling, and seal the dough with your fingers. Brush with olive oil, place on a baking sheet, and bake for 20 minutes at 380 F. Serve with salad

53) VEGAN MUSHROOM PIZZA

Preparation Time: 35 minutes

Servings: 4

Ingredients:

- ✓ 2 tsp plant butter
- ✓ 1 cup chopped button mushrooms
- ✓ ½ cup sliced mixed bell peppers
- ✓ Salt and black pepper to taste
- ✓ 1 pizza crust
- ✓ 1 cup tomato sauce
- ✓ 1 cup plant-based Parmesan cheese
- ✓ 5-6 basil leaves

Directions:

- ❖ Melt plant butter in a skillet and sauté mushrooms and bell peppers for 10 minutes until softened. Season with salt and black pepper. Put the pizza crust on a pizza pan, spread the tomato sauce all over, and scatter vegetables evenly on top. Sprinkle with plant-based Parmesan cheese. Bake for 20 minutes until the cheese has melted. Garnish with basil and serve

54) GRILLED ZUCCHINI WITH SPINACH AVOCADO PESTO

Preparation Time: 20 minutes

Servings: 4

Ingredients:

- ✓ 3 oz spinach, chopped
- ✓ 1 ripe avocado, chopped
- ✓ Juice of 1 lemon
- ✓ 1 garlic clove, minced
- ✓ 2 oz pecans
- ✓ Salt and black pepper to taste
- ✓ ¾ cup olive oil
- ✓ 2 zucchini, sliced
- ✓ 1 tbsp fresh lemon juice
- ✓ 2 tbsp melted plant butter
- ✓ 1 ½ lb tempeh slices

Directions:

- ❖ Place the spinach in a food processor along with the avocado, lemon juice, garlic, and pecans. Blend until smooth and then season with salt and black pepper. Add the olive oil and process a little more. Pour the pesto into a bowl and set aside.
- ❖ Place zucchini in a bowl. Season with the remaining lemon juice, salt, black pepper, and the plant butter. Also, season the tempeh with salt and black pepper, and brush with olive oil. Preheat a grill pan and cook both the tempeh and zucchini slices until browned on both sides. Plate the tempeh and zucchini, spoon some pesto to the side, and serve immediately

55) EGGPLANT FRIES WITH CHILI AIOLI AND BEET SALAD

Preparation Time: 35 minutes

Servings: 4

Ingredients:

- ✓ Eggplant Fries:
- ✓ 2 tbsp flax seed powder
- ✓ 2 eggplants, sliced
- ✓ 2 cups almond flour
- ✓ Salt and black pepper to taste
- ✓ 2 tbsp olive oil
- ✓ Beet salad:
- ✓ 3½ oz beets, peeled and thinly cut
- ✓ 3½ oz red cabbage, grated
- ✓ 2 tbsp fresh cilantro
- ✓ 2 tbsp olive oil
- ✓ 1 tbsp freshly squeezed lime juice
- ✓ Salt and black pepper to taste
- ✓ Spicy Aioli:
- ✓ 1 tbsp flax seed powder
- ✓ 2 garlic cloves, minced
- ✓ ¾ cup light olive oil
- ✓ ½ tsp red chili flakes
- ✓ 1 tbsp freshly squeezed lemon juice
- ✓ 3 tbsp dairy-free yogurt

Directions:

- ❖ Preheat oven to 400 F. In a bowl, combine the flax seed powder with 6 tbsp water and allow sitting to thicken for 5 minutes. In a deep plate, mix almond flour, salt, and black pepper. Dip the eggplant slices into the vegan "flax egg," then in the almond flour, and then in the vegan "flax egg," and finally in the flour mixture. Place the eggplants on a greased baking sheet and drizzle with olive oil. Bake until the fries are crispy and brown, about 15 minutes.
- ❖ For the aioli, mix the flax seed powder with 3 tbsp water in a bowl and set aside to thicken for 5 minutes. Whisk in garlic while pouring in the olive oil gradually. Stir in red chili flakes, salt, black pepper, lemon juice, and dairy-free yogurt. Adjust the taste with salt, garlic, or yogurt as desired.
- ❖ For the beet salad, in a salad bowl, combine the beets, red cabbage, cilantro, olive oil, lime juice, salt, and black pepper. Use two spoons to toss the ingredients until properly combined. Serve the eggplant fries with the chili aioli and beet salad

56) TOFU SKEWERS WITH SALSA VERDE AND SQUASH MASH

Preparation Time: 20 minutes

Servings: 4

Ingredients:

- ✓ 7 tbsp fresh cilantro, finely chopped
- ✓ 4 tbsp fresh basil, finely chopped
- ✓ 2 garlic cloves
- ✓ Juice of ½ lemon
- ✓ 4 tbsp capers
- ✓ 2⁄3 cup olive oil
- ✓ 1 lb extra firm tofu, cubed
- ✓ ½ tbsp sugar-free BBQ sauce
- ✓ 1 tbsp melted plant butter
- ✓ 3 cups butternut squash, cubed
- ✓ ½ cup cold plant butter
- ✓ 2 oz grated plant-based Parmesan

Directions:

- ❖ In a blender, add cilantro, basil, garlic, lemon juice, capers, olive oil, salt, and pepper. Process until smooth; set aside. Thread the tofu cubes on wooden skewers. Season with salt and brush with BBQ sauce. Melt plant butter in a grill pan and fry the tofu until browned. Remove to a plate. Pour the squash into a pot, add some lightly salted water, and bring the vegetable to a boil until soft, about 6 minutes. Drain and pour into a bowl. Add the cold plant butter, plant-based Parmesan cheese, salt, and black pepper. Mash the vegetable with an immersion blender until the consistency of mashed potatoes is achieved. Serve the tofu skewers with the mashed cauliflower and salsa verde

57) MUSHROOM LETTUCE WRAPS

Preparation Time: 25 minutes

Servings: 4

Ingredients:

- ✓ 2 tbsp plant butter
- ✓ 4 oz baby Bella mushrooms, sliced
- ✓ 1 ½ lb tofu, crumbled
- ✓ 1 iceberg lettuce, leaves extracted
- ✓ 1 cup grated plant-based cheddar
- ✓ 1 large tomato, sliced

Directions:

- ❖ Melt the plant butter in a skillet, add in mushrooms and sauté until browned and tender, about 6 minutes. Transfer to a plate. Add the tofu to the skillet and cook until brown, about 10 minutes. Spoon the tofu and mushrooms into the lettuce leaves, sprinkle with the plant-based cheddar cheese, and share the tomato slices on top. Serve the burger immediately

58) CLASSIC GARLICKY RICE

Preparation Time: 20 minutes

Servings: 4

Ingredients:

- ✓ 4 tbsp olive oil
- ✓ 4 cloves garlic, chopped
- ✓ 1 ½ cups white rice
- ✓ 2 ½ cups vegetable broth

Directions:

- ❖ In a saucepan, heat the olive oil over a moderately high flame. Add in the garlic and sauté for about 1 minute or until aromatic.
- ❖ Add in the rice and broth. Bring to a boil; immediately turn the heat to a gentle simmer.
- ❖ Cook for about 15 minutes or until all the liquid has absorbed. Fluff the rice with a fork, season with salt and pepper and serve hot

59) BROWN RICE WITH VEGETABLES AND TOFU

Preparation Time: 45 minutes

Servings: 4

Ingredients:

- ✓ 4 tsp sesame seeds
- ✓ 2 spring garlic stalks, minced
- ✓ 1 cup spring onions, chopped
- ✓ 1 carrot, trimmed and sliced
- ✓ 1 celery rib, sliced
- ✓ 1/4 cup dry white wine
- ✓ 10 ounces tofu, cubed
- ✓ 1 ½ cups long-grain brown rice, rinsed thoroughly
- ✓ 2 tbsp soy sauce
- ✓ 2 tbsp tahini
- ✓ 1 tbsp lemon juice

Directions:

- ❖ In a wok or large saucepan, heat 2 tsp of the sesame oil over medium-high heat. Now, cook the garlic, onion, carrot and celery for about 3 minutes, stirring periodically to ensure even cooking.
- ❖ Add the wine to deglaze the pan and push the vegetables to one side of the wok. Add in the remaining sesame oil and fry the tofu for 8 minutes, stirring occasionally.
- ❖ Bring 2 ½ cups of water to a boil over medium-high heat. Bring to a simmer and cook the rice for about 30 minutes or until it is tender; fluff the rice and stir it with the soy sauce and tahini.
- ❖ Stir the vegetables and tofu into the hot rice; add a few drizzles of the fresh lemon juice and serve warm. Enjoy

60) AMARANTH PORRIDGE

Preparation Time: 35 minutes

Servings: 4

Ingredients:

- ✓ 3 cups water
- ✓ 1 cup amaranth
- ✓ 1/2 cup coconut milk
- ✓ 4 tbsp agave syrup
- ✓ A pinch of kosher salt
- ✓ A pinch of grated nutmeg

Directions:

- ❖ Bring the water to a boil over medium-high heat; add in the amaranth and turn the heat to a simmer.
- ❖ Let it cook for about 30 minutes, stirring periodically to prevent the amaranth from sticking to the bottom of the pan.
- ❖ Stir in the remaining ingredients and continue to cook for 1 to 2 minutes more until cooked through. Enjoy

DINNER

61) BLACK-EYED PEA OAT BAKE

Preparation Time: 25 minutes

Servings: 4

Ingredients:

- ✓ 1 carrot, shredded
- ✓ 1 onion, chopped
- ✓ 2 garlic cloves, minced
- ✓ 1 (15.5-oz) can black-eyed peas
- ✓ ¾ cup whole-wheat flour
- ✓ ¾ cup quick-cooking oats
- ✓ ½ cup breadcrumbs
- ✓ ¼ cup minced fresh parsley
- ✓ 1 tbsp soy sauce
- ✓ ½ tsp dried sage
- ✓ Salt and black pepper to taste

Directions:

- ❖ Preheat oven to 360 F.
- ❖ Combine the carrot, onion, garlic, and peas and pulse until creamy and smooth in a blender. Add in flour, oats, breadcrumbs, parsley, soy sauce, sage, salt, and pepper. Blend until ingredients are evenly mixed. Spoon the mixture into a greased loaf pan. Bake for 40 minutes until golden. Allow it to cool down for a few minutes before slicing. Serve immediately

62) PAPRIKA FAVA BEAN PATTIES

Preparation Time: 15 minutes

Servings: 4

Ingredients:

- ✓ 4 tbsp olive oil
- ✓ 1 minced onion
- ✓ 1 garlic clove, minced
- ✓ 1 (15.5-oz) can fava beans
- ✓ 1 tbsp minced fresh parsley
- ✓ ½ cup breadcrumbs
- ✓ ¼ cup almond flour
- ✓ 1 tsp smoked paprika
- ✓ ½ tsp dried thyme
- ✓ 4 burger buns, toasted
- ✓ 4 lettuce leaves
- ✓ 1 ripe tomato, sliced

Directions:

- ❖ In a blender, add onion, garlic, beans, parsley, breadcrumbs, flour, paprika, thyme, salt, and pepper. Pulse until uniform but not smooth. Shape 4 patties out of the mixture. Refrigerate for 15 minutes.
- ❖ Heat olive oil in a skillet over medium heat. Fry the patties for 10 minutes on both sides until golden brown. Serve in toasted buns with lettuce and tomato slices

63) WALNUT LENTIL BURGERS

Preparation Time: 70 minutes

Servings: 4

Ingredients:

- ✓ 2 tbsp olive oil
- ✓ 1 cup dry lentils, rinsed
- ✓ 2 carrots, grated
- ✓ 1 onion, diced
- ✓ ½ cup walnuts
- ✓ 1 tbsp tomato puree
- ✓ ¾ cup almond flour
- ✓ 2 tsp curry powder
- ✓ 4 whole-grain buns

Directions:

- ❖ Place lentils in a pot and cover with water. Bring to a boil and simmer for 15-20 minutes.
- ❖ Meanwhile, combine the carrots, walnuts, onion, tomato puree, flour, curry powder, salt, and pepper in a bowl. Toss to coat. Once the lentils are ready, drain and transfer into the veggie bowl. Mash the mixture until sticky. Shape the mixture into balls; flatten to make patties.
- ❖ Heat the oil in a skillet over medium heat. Brown the patties for 8 minutes on both sides. To assemble, put the cakes on the buns and top with your desired toppings

64) COUSCOUS ANDQUINOA BURGERS

Preparation Time: 20 minutes

Servings: 4

Ingredients:

- ✓ 2 tbsp olive oil
- ✓ ¼ cup couscous
- ✓ ¼ cup boiling water
- ✓ 2 cups cooked quinoa
- ✓ 2 tbsp balsamic vinegar
- ✓ 3 tbsp chopped olives
- ✓ ½ tsp garlic powder
- ✓ Salt to taste
- ✓ 4 burger buns
- ✓ Lettuce leaves, for serving
- ✓ Tomato slices, for serving

Directions:

- ❖ Preheat oven to 350 F.
- ❖ In a bowl, place the couscous with boiling water. Let sit covered for 5 minutes. Once the liquid is absorbed, fluff with a fork. Add in quinoa and mash them to form a chunky texture. Stir in vinegar, olive oil, olives, garlic powder, and salt.
- ❖ Shape the mixture into 4 patties. Arrange them on a greased tray and bake for 25-30 minutes. To assemble, place the patties on the buns and top with lettuce and tomato slices. Serve

65) BEAN AND PECAN SANDWICHES

Preparation Time: 20 minutes

Servings: 4

Ingredients:

- ✓ 1 onion, chopped
- ✓ 1 garlic clove, crushed
- ✓ ¾ cup pecans, chopped
- ✓ ¾ cup canned black beans
- ✓ ¾ cup almond flour
- ✓ 2 tbsp minced fresh parsley
- ✓ 1 tbsp soy sauce
- ✓ 1 tsp Dijon mustard + to serve
- ✓ Salt and black pepper to taste
- ✓ ½ tsp ground sage
- ✓ ½ tsp sweet paprika
- ✓ 2 tbsp olive oil
- ✓ Bread slices
- ✓ Lettuce leaves and sliced tomatoes

Directions:

- ❖ Put the onion, garlic, and pecans in a blender and pulse until roughly ground. Add in the beans and pulse until everything is well combined. Transfer to a large mixing bowl and stir in the flour, parsley, soy sauce, mustard, salt, sage, paprika, and pepper. Mold patties out of the mixture.
- ❖ Heat the oil in a skillet over medium heat. Brown the patties for 10 minutes on both sides. To assemble, lay patties on the bread slices and top with mustard, lettuce, and tomato slices

66) HOMEMADE KITCHARI

Preparation Time: 40 minutes

Servings: 5

Ingredients:

- ✓ 4 cups chopped cauliflower and broccoli florets
- ✓ ½ cup split peas
- ✓ ½ cup brown rice
- ✓ 1 red onion, chopped
- ✓ 1 (14.5-oz) can diced tomatoes
- ✓ 3 garlic cloves, minced
- ✓ 1 jalapeño pepper, seeded
- ✓ ½ tsp ground ginger
- ✓ 1 tsp ground turmeric
- ✓ 1 tsp olive oil
- ✓ 1 tsp fennel seeds
- ✓ Juice of 1 large lemon
- ✓ Salt and black pepper to taste

Directions:

- ❖ In a food processor, place the onion, tomatoes with juices, garlic, jalapeño pepper, ginger, turmeric, and 2 tbsp of water. Pulse until ingredients are evenly mixed.
- ❖ Heat the oil in a pot over medium heat. Cook the cumin and fennel seeds for 2-3 minutes, stirring often. Pour in the puréed mixture, split peas, rice, and 3 cups of water. Bring to a boil, then lower the heat and simmer for 10 minutes. Stir in cauliflower, broccoli, and cook for another 10 minutes. Mix in lemon juice and adjust seasoning

67) PICANTE GREEN RICE

Preparation Time: 35 minutes

Servings: 4

Ingredients:

- ✓ 1 roasted bell pepper, chopped
- ✓ 3 small hot green chilies, chopped
- ✓ 2 ½ cups vegetable broth
- ✓ ½ cup chopped fresh parsley
- ✓ 1 onion, chopped
- ✓ 2 garlic cloves, chopped
- ✓ Salt and black pepper to taste
- ✓ ½ tsp dried oregano
- ✓ 3 tbsp canola oil
- ✓ 1 cup long-grain brown rice
- ✓ 1 ½ cups cooked black beans
- ✓ 2 tbsp minced fresh cilantro

Directions:

- ❖ In a food processor, place bell pepper, chilies, 1 cup of broth, parsley, onion, garlic, pepper, oregano, salt, and pepper and blend until smooth. Heat oil in a skillet over medium heat. Add in rice and veggie mixture. Cook for 5 minutes, stirring often. Add in the remaining broth and bring to a boil, lower the heat, and simmer for 15 minutes. Mix in beans and cook for another 5 minutes. Serve with cilantro

68) ASIAN QUINOA SAUTÉ

Preparation Time: 30 minutes

Servings: 4

Ingredients:

- ✓ 1 cup quinoa
- ✓ Salt to taste
- ✓ 1 head cauliflower, break into florets
- ✓ 2 tsp untoasted sesame oil
- ✓ 1 cup snow peas, cut in half
- ✓ 1 cup frozen peas
- ✓ 2 cups chopped Swiss chard
- ✓ 2 scallions, chopped
- ✓ 2 tbsp water
- ✓ 1 tsp toasted sesame oil
- ✓ 1 tbsp soy sauce
- ✓ 2 tbsp sesame seeds

Directions:

- ❖ Place quinoa with 2 cups of water and salt in a bowl. Bring to a boil, lower the heat and simmer for 15 minutes. Do not stir.
- ❖ Heat the oil in a skillet over medium heat and sauté the cauliflower for 4-5 minutes. Add in snow peas and stir well. Stir in Swiss chard, scallions, and 2 tbsp of water; cook until wilted, about 5 minutes. Season with salt.
- ❖ Drizzle with sesame oil and soy sauce and cook for 1 minute. Divide the quinoa in bowls and top with the cauliflower mixture. Garnish with sesame seeds and soy sauce to serve

69) FARRO AND BLACK BEAN LOAF

Preparation Time: 50 minutes

Servings: 6

Ingredients:

- ✓ 3 tbsp olive oil
- ✓ 1 onion, minced
- ✓ 1 cup faro
- ✓ 2 (15.5-oz) cans black beans, mashed

- ✓ ½ cup quick-cooking oats
- ✓ 1/3 cup whole-wheat flour
- ✓ 2 tbsp nutritional yeast
- ✓ 1 ½ tsp dried thyme
- ✓ ½ tsp dried oregano

Directions:

- ❖ Heat the oil in a pot over medium heat. Place in onion and sauté for 3 minutes. Add in faro, 2 cups of water, salt, and pepper. Bring to a boil, lower the heat and simmer for 20 minutes. Remove to a bowl.
- ❖ Preheat oven to 350 F.
- ❖ Add the mashed beans, oats, flour, yeast, thyme, and oregano to the faro bowl. Toss to combine. Taste and adjust the seasoning. Shape the mixture into a greased loaf. Bake for 20 minutes. Let cool for a few minutes. Slice and serve

70) CUBAN-STYLE MILLET

Preparation Time: 40 minutes

Servings: 4

Ingredients:

- ✓ 2 tbsp olive oil
- ✓ 1 onion, chopped
- ✓ 2 zucchinis, chopped
- ✓ 2 garlic cloves, minced

- ✓ 1 tsp dried thyme
- ✓ ½ tsp ground cumin
- ✓ 1 (15.5-oz) can black-eyed peas
- ✓ 1 cup millet
- ✓ 2 tbsp chopped fresh cilantro

Directions:

- ❖ Heat the oil in a pot over medium heat. Place in onion and sauté for 3 minutes until translucent. Add in zucchinis, garlic, thyme, and cumin and cook for 10 minutes. Put in peas, millet, and 2 ½ cups of hot water. Bring to a boil, then lower the heat and simmer for 20 minutes. Fluff the millet using a fork. Serve garnished with cilantro

71) TRADITIONAL CILANTRO PILAF

Preparation Time: 30 minutes

Servings: 6

Ingredients:

- ✓ 3 tbsp olive oil
- ✓ 1 onion, minced
- ✓ 1 carrot, chopped
- ✓ 2 garlic cloves, minced
- ✓ 1 cup wild rice

- ✓ 1 ½ tsp ground fennel seeds
- ✓ ½ tsp ground cumin
- ✓ Salt and black pepper to taste
- ✓ 3 tbsp minced fresh cilantro

Directions:

- ❖ Heat the oil in a pot over medium heat. Place in onion, carrot, and garlic and sauté for 5 minutes. Stir in rice, fennel seeds, cumin, and 2 cups water. Bring to a boil, then lower the heat and simmer for 20 minutes. Remove to a bowl and fluff using a fork. Serve topped with cilantro and black pepper

72) ORIENTAL BULGUR AND WHITE BEANS

Preparation Time: 55 minutes

Servings: 4

Ingredients:

- ✓ 2 tbsp olive oil
- ✓ 3 green onions, chopped
- ✓ 1 cup bulgur
- ✓ 1 cups water
- ✓ 1 tbsp soy sauce

- ✓ Salt to taste
- ✓ 1 ½ cups cooked white beans
- ✓ 1 tbsp nutritional yeast
- ✓ 1 tbsp dried parsley

Directions:

- ❖ Heat the oil in a pot over medium heat. Place in green onions and sauté for 3 minutes. Stir in bulgur, water, soy sauce, and salt. Bring to a boil, then lower the heat and simmer for 20-22 minutes. Mix in beans and yeast. Cook for 5 minutes. Serve topped with parsley

73) ONE-POT RED LENTILS WITH MUSHROOMS

Preparation Time: 25 minutes

Servings: 4

Ingredients:

- ✓ 2 tsp olive oil
- ✓ 2 cloves garlic, minced
- ✓ 2 tsp grated fresh ginger
- ✓ ½ tsp ground cumin
- ✓ ½ tsp fennel seeds
- ✓ 1 cup mushrooms, chopped
- ✓ 1 large tomato, chopped
- ✓ 1 cup dried red lentils
- ✓ 2 tbsp lemon juice

Directions:

- ❖ Heat the oil in a pot over medium heat. Place in the garlic and ginger and cook for 3 minutes. Stir in cumin, fennel, mushrooms, tomato, lentils, and 2 ¼ cups of water. Bring to a boil, then lower the heat and simmer for 15 minutes. Mix in lemon juice and serve

74) COLORFUL RISOTTO WITH VEGETABLES

Preparation Time: 35 minutes

Servings: 5

Ingredients:

- ✓ 2 tbsp sesame oil
- ✓ 1 onion, chopped
- ✓ 2 bell peppers, chopped
- ✓ 1 parsnip, trimmed and chopped
- ✓ 1 carrot, trimmed and chopped
- ✓ 1 cup broccoli florets
- ✓ 2 garlic cloves, finely chopped
- ✓ 1/2 tsp ground cumin
- ✓ 2 cups brown rice
- ✓ Sea salt and black pepper, to taste
- ✓ 1/2 tsp ground turmeric
- ✓ 2 tbsp fresh cilantro, finely chopped

Directions:

- ❖ Heat the sesame oil in a saucepan over medium-high heat.
- ❖ Once hot, cook the onion, peppers, parsnip, carrot and broccoli for about 3 minutes until aromatic.
- ❖ Add in the garlic and ground cumin; continue to cook for 30 seconds more until aromatic.
- ❖ Place the brown rice in a saucepan and cover with cold water by 2 inches. Bring to a boil. Turn the heat to a simmer and continue to cook for about 30 minutes or until tender.
- ❖ Stir the rice into the vegetable mixture; season with salt, black pepper and ground turmeric; garnish with fresh cilantro and serve immediately. Enjoy

75) AMARANT GRITS WITH WALNUTS

Preparation Time: 35 minutes

Servings: 4

Ingredients:

- ✓ 2 cups water
- ✓ 2 cups coconut milk
- ✓ 1 cup amaranth
- ✓ 1 cinnamon stick
- ✓ 1 vanilla bean
- ✓ 4 tbsp maple syrup
- ✓ 4 tbsp walnuts, chopped

Directions:

- ❖ Bring the water and coconut milk to a boil over medium-high heat; add in the amaranth, cinnamon and vanilla and turn the heat to a simmer.
- ❖ Let it cook for about 30 minutes, stirring periodically to prevent the amaranth from sticking to the bottom of the pan.
- ❖ Top with maple syrup and walnuts. Enjoy

76) BARLEY PILAF WITH WILD MUSHROOMS

Preparation Time: 45 minutes

Servings: 4

Ingredients:

- ✓ 2 tbsp vegan butter
- ✓ 1 small onion, chopped
- ✓ 1 tsp garlic, minced
- ✓ 1 jalapeno pepper, seeded and minced
- ✓ 1 pound wild mushrooms, sliced
- ✓ 1 cup medium pearl barley, rinsed
- ✓ 2 ¾ cups vegetable broth

Directions:

- ❖ Melt the vegan butter in a saucepan over medium-high heat.
- ❖ Once hot, cook the onion for about 3 minutes until just tender.
- ❖ Add in the garlic, jalapeno pepper, mushrooms; continue to sauté for 2 minutes or until aromatic.
- ❖ Add in the barley and broth, cover and continue to simmer for about 30 minutes. Once all the liquid has absorbed, allow the barley to rest for about 10 minutes fluff with a fork.
- ❖ Taste and adjust the seasonings. Enjoy

77) SWEET CORNBREAD MUFFINS

Preparation Time: 30 minutes

Servings: 8

Ingredients:

- ✓ 1 cup all-purpose flour
- ✓ 1 cup yellow cornmeal
- ✓ 1 tsp baking powder
- ✓ 1 tsp baking soda
- ✓ 1 tsp kosher salt

- ✓ 1/2 cup sugar
- ✓ 1/2 tsp ground cinnamon
- ✓ 1 1/2 cups almond milk
- ✓ 1/2 cup vegan butter, melted
- ✓ 2 tbsp applesauce

Directions:

- ❖ Start by preheating your oven to 420 degrees F. Now, spritz a muffin tin with a nonstick cooking spray.
- ❖ In a mixing bowl, thoroughly combine the flour, cornmeal, baking soda, baking powder, salt, sugar and cinnamon.
- ❖ Gradually add in the milk, butter and applesauce, whisking constantly to avoid lumps.
- ❖ Scrape the batter into the prepared muffin tin. Bake your muffins for about 25 minutes or until a tester inserted in the middle comes out dry and clean.
- ❖ Transfer them to a wire rack to rest for 5 minutes before unmolding and serving. Enjoy

78) ACRYLIC RICE PUDDING WITH DRIED FIGS

Preparation Time: 45 minutes

Servings: 4

Ingredients:

- ✓ 2 cups water
- ✓ 1 cup medium-grain white rice
- ✓ 3 ½ cups coconut milk
- ✓ 1/2 cup coconut sugar

- ✓ 1 cinnamon stick
- ✓ 1 vanilla bean
- ✓ 1/2 cup dried figs, chopped
- ✓ 4 tbsp coconut, shredded

Directions:

- ❖ In a saucepan, bring the water to a boil over medium-high heat. Immediately turn the heat to a simmer, add in the rice and let it cook for about 20 minutes.
- ❖ Add in the milk, sugar and spices and continue to cook for 20 minutes more, stirring constantly to prevent the rice from sticking to the pan.
- ❖ Top with dried figs and coconut; serve your pudding warm or at room temperature. Enjoy

79) POTAGE AU QUINOA

Preparation Time: 25 minutes

Servings: 4

Ingredients:

- ✓ 2 tbsp olive oil
- ✓ 1 onion, chopped
- ✓ 4 medium potatoes, peeled and diced
- ✓ 1 carrot, trimmed and diced
- ✓ 1 parsnip, trimmed and diced

- ✓ 1 jalapeno pepper, seeded and chopped
- ✓ 4 cups vegetable broth
- ✓ 1 cup quinoa
- ✓ Sea salt and ground white pepper, to taste

Directions:

- ❖ In a heavy-bottomed pot, heat the olive oil over medium-high heat. Sauté the onion, potatoes, carrots, parsnip and pepper for about 5 minutes or until they've softened.
- ❖ Add in the vegetable broth and quinoa; bring to a boil.
- ❖ Immediately turn the heat to a simmer for about 15 minutes or until the quinoa is tender.
- ❖ Season with salt and pepper to taste. Puree your potage with an immersion blender. Reheat the potage just before serving and enjoy

80) SORGHUM BOWL WITH ALMONDS

Preparation Time: :15 minutes

Servings: 4

Ingredients:

- ✓ 1 cup sorghum
- ✓ 3 cups almond milk
- ✓ A pinch of sea salt
- ✓ A pinch of grated nutmeg

- ✓ 1/2 tsp ground cinnamon
- ✓ 1/4 tsp ground cardamom
- ✓ 1 tsp crystallized ginger
- ✓ 4 tbsp brown sugar
- ✓ 4 tbsp almonds, slivered

Directions:

- ❖ Place the sorghum, almond milk, salt, nutmeg, cinnamon, cardamom and crystallized ginger in a saucepan; simmer gently for about 15 minutes.
- ❖ Add in the brown sugar, stir and spoon the porridge into serving bowls.
- ❖ Top with almonds and serve immediately. Enjoy

81) BULGUR MUFFINS WITH RAISINS

Preparation Time: 20 minutes

Servings: 6

Ingredients:

- ✓ 1 cup bulgur, cooked
- ✓ 4 tbsp coconut oil, melted
- ✓ 1 tsp baking powder
- ✓ 1 tsp baking soda
- ✓ 2 tbsp flax egg
- ✓ 1 ¼ cups all-purpose flour
- ✓ 1/2 cup coconut flour
- ✓ 1 cup coconut milk
- ✓ 4 tbsp brown sugar
- ✓ 1/2 cup raisins, packed

Directions:

- ❖ Start by preheating your oven to 420 degrees F. Spritz a muffin tin with a nonstick cooking oil.
- ❖ Thoroughly combine all the dry ingredients. Add in the cooked bulgur.
- ❖ In another bowl, whisk all the wet ingredients; add the wet mixture to the bulgur mixture; fold in the raisins.
- ❖ Mix until everything is well combined, but not overmixed; spoon the batter into the prepared muffin.
- ❖ Now, bake your muffins for about 16 minutes or until a tester comes out dry and clean. Enjoy

82) OLD-FASHIONED PILAF

Preparation Time: 45 minutes

Servings: 4

Ingredients:

- ✓ 2 tbsp sesame oil
- ✓ 1 shallot, sliced
- ✓ 2 bell peppers, seeded and sliced
- ✓ 3 cloves garlic, minced
- ✓ 10 ounces oyster mushrooms, cleaned and sliced
- ✓ 2 cups brown rice
- ✓ 2 tomatoes, pureed
- ✓ 2 cups vegetable broth
- ✓ Salt and black pepper, to taste
- ✓ 1 cup sweet corn kernels
- ✓ 1 cup green peas

Directions:

- ❖ Heat the sesame oil in a saucepan over medium-high heat.
- ❖ Once hot, cook the shallot and peppers for about 3 minutes until just tender.
- ❖ Add in the garlic and oyster mushrooms; continue to sauté for 1 minute or so until aromatic.
- ❖ In a lightly oiled casserole dish, place the rice, flowed by the mushroom mixture, tomatoes, broth, salt, black pepper, corn and green peas.
- ❖ Bake, covered, at 375 degrees F for about 40 minutes, stirring after 20 minutes. Enjoy

83) FREEKEH SALAD WITH ZA'ATAR

Preparation Time: 35 minutes

Servings: 4

Ingredients:

- ✓ 1 cup freekeh
- ✓ 2 ½ cups water
- ✓ 1 cup grape tomatoes, halved
- ✓ 2 bell peppers, seeded and sliced
- ✓ 1 habanero pepper, seeded and sliced
- ✓ 1 onion, thinly sliced
- ✓ 2 tbsp fresh cilantro, chopped
- ✓ 2 tbsp fresh parsley, chopped
- ✓ 2 ounces green olives, pitted and sliced
- ✓ 1/4 cup extra-virgin olive oil
- ✓ 2 tbsp lemon juice
- ✓ 1 tsp deli mustard
- ✓ 1 tsp za'atar
- ✓ Sea salt and ground black pepper, to taste

Directions:

- ❖ Place the freekeh and water in a saucepan. Bring to a boil over medium-high heat.
- ❖ Immediately turn the heat to a simmer for 30 to 35 minutes, stirring occasionally to promote even cooking. Let it cool completely.
- ❖ Toss the cooked freekeh with the remaining ingredients. Toss to combine well.
- ❖ Enjoy

84) VEGETABLE AMARANTH SOUP

Preparation Time: 30 minutes

Servings: 4

Ingredients:

- ✓ 2 tbsp olive oil
- ✓ 1 small shallot, chopped
- ✓ 1 carrot, trimmed and chopped
- ✓ 1 parsnip, trimmed and chopped
- ✓ 1 cup yellow squash, peeled and chopped
- ✓ 1 tsp fennel seeds
- ✓ 1 tsp celery seeds
- ✓ 1 tsp turmeric powder
- ✓ 1 bay laurel
- ✓ 1/2 cup amaranth
- ✓ 2 cups cream of celery soup
- ✓ 2 cups water
- ✓ 2 cups collard greens, torn into pieces
- ✓ Sea salt and ground black pepper, to taste

Directions:

- ❖ In a heavy-bottomed pot, heat the olive oil until sizzling. Once hot, sauté the shallot, carrot, parsnip and squash for 5 minutes or until just tender.
- ❖ Then, sauté the fennel seeds, celery seeds, turmeric powder and bay laurel for about 30 seconds, until aromatic.
- ❖ Add in the amaranth, soup and water. Turn the heat to a simmer. Cover and let it simmer for 15 to 18 minutes.
- ❖ Afterwards, add in the collard greens, season with salt and black pepper and continue to simmer for 5 minutes longer. Enjoy

85) POLENTA WITH MUSHROOMS AND CHICKPEAS

Preparation Time: 25 minutes

Servings: 4

Ingredients:

- ✓ 3 cups vegetable broth
- ✓ 1 cup yellow cornmeal
- ✓ 2 tbsp olive oil
- ✓ 1 onion, chopped
- ✓ 1 bell pepper, seeded and sliced
- ✓ 1 pound Cremini mushrooms, sliced
- ✓ 2 garlic cloves, minced
- ✓ 1/2 cup dry white wine
- ✓ 1/2 cup vegetable broth
- ✓ Kosher salt and freshly ground black pepper, to taste
- ✓ 1 tsp paprika
- ✓ 1 cup canned chickpeas, drained

Directions:

- ❖ In a medium saucepan, bring the vegetable broth to a boil over medium-high heat. Now, add in the cornmeal, whisking continuously to prevent lumps.
- ❖ Reduce the heat to a simmer. Continue to simmer, whisking periodically, for about 18 minutes, until the mixture has thickened.
- ❖ Meanwhile, heat the olive oil in a saucepan over a moderately high heat. Cook the onion and pepper for about 3 minutes or until just tender and fragrant.
- ❖ Add in the mushrooms and garlic; continue to sauté, gradually adding the wine and broth, for 4 more minutes or until cooked through. Season with salt, black pepper and paprika. Stir in the chickpeas.
- ❖ Spoon the mushroom mixture over your polenta and serve warm. Enjoy

86) TEFF SALAD WITH AVOCADO AND BEANS

Preparation Time: 20 minutes + chilling time

Servings: 2

Ingredients:

- ✓ 2 cups water
- ✓ 1/2 cup teff grain
- ✓ 1 tsp fresh lemon juice
- ✓ 3 tbsp vegan mayonnaise
- ✓ 1 tsp deli mustard
- ✓ 1 small avocado, pitted, peeled and sliced
- ✓ 1 small red onion, thinly sliced
- ✓ 1 small Persian cucumber, sliced
- ✓ 1/2 cup canned kidney beans, drained
- ✓ 2 cups baby spinach

Directions:

- ❖ In a deep saucepan, bring the water to a boil over high heat. Add in the teff grain and turn the heat to a simmer.
- ❖ Continue to cook, covered, for about 20 minutes or until tender. Let it cool completely.
- ❖ Add in the remaining ingredients and toss to combine. Serve at room temperature. Enjoy

87) OVERNIGHT OATMEAL WITH WALNUTS

Preparation Time: 5 minutes + chilling time

Servings: 3

Ingredients:

- ✓ 1 cup old-fashioned oats
- ✓ 3 tbsp chia seeds
- ✓ 1 ½ cups coconut milk
- ✓ 3 tsp agave syrup
- ✓ 1 tsp vanilla extract
- ✓ 1/2 tsp ground cinnamon
- ✓ 3 tbsp walnuts, chopped
- ✓ A pinch of salt
- ✓ A pinch of grated nutmeg

Directions:

- ❖ Divide the ingredients between three mason jars.
- ❖ Cover and shake to combine well. Let them sit overnight in your refrigerator.
- ❖ You can add some extra milk before serving. Enjoy

88) COLORFUL SPELT SALAD

Preparation Time: 50 minutes + chilling time

Servings: 4

Ingredients:

- ✓ 3 ½ cups water
- ✓ 1 cup dry spelt
- ✓ 1 cup canned kidney beans, drained
- ✓ 1 bell pepper, seeded and diced
- ✓ 2 medium tomatoes, diced
- ✓ 2 tbsp basil, chopped
- ✓ 2 tbsp parsley, chopped
- ✓ 2 tbsp mint, chopped
- ✓ 1/4 cup extra-virgin olive oil
- ✓ 1 tsp deli mustard
- ✓ 1 tbsp fresh lime juice
- ✓ 1 tbsp white vinegar
- ✓ Sea salt and cayenne pepper, to taste

Directions:

- ❖ Bring the water to a boil over medium-high heat. Now, add in the spelt, turn the heat to a simmer and continue to cook for approximately 50 minutes, until the spelt is tender. Drain and allow it to cool completely.
- ❖ Toss the spelt with the remaining ingredients; toss to combine well and place the salad in your refrigerator until ready to serve.
- ❖ Enjoy

SNACKS

89) KENTUCKY CAULIFLOWER WITH MASHED PARSNIPS

Preparation Time: 35 minutes

Servings: 6

Ingredients:

- ½ cup unsweetened almond milk
- ¼ cup coconut flour
- ¼ tsp cayenne pepper
- ½ cup whole-grain breadcrumbs
- ½ cup grated plant-based mozzarella
- 30 oz cauliflower florets
- 1 lb parsnips, peeled and quartered
- 3 tbsp melted plant butter
- A pinch of nutmeg
- 1 tsp cumin powder
- 1 cup coconut cream
- 2 tbsp sesame oil

Directions:

- ❖ Preheat oven to 425 F and line a baking sheet with parchment paper.
- ❖ In a small bowl, combine almond milk, coconut flour, and cayenne pepper. In another bowl, mix salt, breadcrumbs, and plant-based mozzarella cheese. Dip each cauliflower floret into the milk mixture, coating properly, and then into the cheese mixture. Place the breaded cauliflower on the baking sheet and bake in the oven for 30 minutes, turning once after 15 minutes.
- ❖ Make slightly salted water in a saucepan and add the parsnips. Bring to boil over medium heat for 15 minutes or until the parsnips are fork-tender. Drain and transfer to a bowl. Add in melted plant butter, cumin powder, nutmeg, and coconut cream. Puree the ingredients using an immersion blender until smooth. Spoon the parsnip mash into serving plates and drizzle with some sesame oil. Serve with the baked cauliflower when ready

90) SPINACH CHIPS WITH GUACAMOLE HUMMUS

Preparation Time: 30 minutes

Servings: 4

Ingredients:

- ½ cup baby spinach
- 1 tbsp olive oil
- ½ tsp plain vinegar
- 3 large avocados, chopped
- ½ cup chopped parsley + for garnish
- ½ cup melted plant butter
- ¼ cup pumpkin seeds
- ¼ cup sesame paste
- Juice from ½ lemon
- 1 garlic clove, minced
- ½ tsp coriander powder
- Salt and black pepper to taste

Directions:

- ❖ Preheat oven to 300 F. Put spinach in a bowl and toss with olive oil, vinegar, and salt. Place in a parchment paper-lined baking sheet and bake until the leaves are crispy but not burned, about 15 minutes.
- ❖ Place avocado into the bowl of a food processor. Add in parsley, plant butter, pumpkin seeds, sesame paste, lemon juice, garlic, coriander powder, salt, and black pepper. Puree until smooth. Spoon the hummus into a bowl and garnish with parsley. Serve with spinach chips

91) BUTTERED CARROT NOODLES WITH KALE

Preparation Time: 15 minutes

Servings: 4

Ingredients:

- 2 large carrots
- ¼ cup vegetable broth
- 4 tbsp plant butter
- 1 garlic clove, minced
- 1 cup chopped kale
- Salt and black pepper to taste

Directions:

- ❖ Peel the carrots with a slicer and run both through a spiralizer to form noodles.
- ❖ Pour the vegetable broth into a saucepan and add the carrot noodles. Simmer (over low heat) the carrots for 3 minutes. Strain through a colander and set the vegetables aside.
- ❖ Place a large skillet over medium heat and melt the plant butter. Add the garlic and sauté until softened and put in the kale; cook until wilted. Pour the carrots into the pan, season with salt and black pepper, and stir-fry for 3 to 4 minutes. Spoon the vegetables into a bowl and serve with pan-grilled tofu

92) PARSLEY PUMPKIN NOODLES

Preparation Time: 15 minutes

Servings: 4

Ingredients:

- ¼ cup plant butter
- ½ cup chopped onion
- 1 lb pumpkin, spiralized
- 1 bunch kale, sliced
- ¼ cup chopped fresh parsley
- Salt and black pepper to taste

Directions:

- Mel butter in a skillet over medium heat. Place the onion and cook for 3 minutes. Add in pumpkin and cook for another 7-8 minutes. Stir in kale and cook for another 2 minutes, until the kale wilts. Sprinkle with parsley, salt, and pepper and serve

93) CURRY CAULI RICE WITH MUSHROOMS

Preparation Time: 15 minutes

Servings: 4

Ingredients:

- 8 oz baby Bella mushrooms, stemmed and sliced
- 2 large heads cauliflower
- 2 tbsp toasted sesame oil, divided
- 1 onion, chopped
- 3 garlic cloves, minced
- Salt and black pepper to taste
- ½ tsp curry powder
- 1 tsp freshly chopped parsley
- 2 scallions, thinly sliced

Directions:

- Use a knife to cut the entire cauliflower head into 6 pieces and transfer to a food processor. With the grater attachment, shred the cauliflower into a rice-like consistency.
- Heat half of the sesame oil in a large skillet over medium heat and then add the onion and mushrooms. Sauté for 5 minutes or until the mushrooms are soft.
- Add the garlic and sauté for 2 minutes or until fragrant. Pour in the cauliflower and cook until the rice has slightly softened, about 10 minutes.
- Season with salt, black pepper, and curry powder; then, mix the ingredients to be well combined. After, turn the heat off and stir in the parsley and scallions. Dish the cauli rice into serving plates and serve warm

94) MIXED SEED CRACKERS

Preparation Time: 57 minutes

Servings: 6

Ingredients:

- 1/3 cup sesame seed flour
- 1/3 cup pumpkin seeds
- 1/3 cup sunflower seeds
- 1/3 cup sesame seeds
- 1/3 cup chia seeds
- 1 tbsp psyllium husk powder
- 1 tsp salt
- ¼ cup plant butter, melted
- 1 cup boiling water

Directions:

- Preheat oven to 300 F.
- Combine the sesame seed flour with the pumpkin seeds, sunflower seeds, sesame seeds, chia seeds, psyllium husk powder, and salt. Pour in the plant butter and hot water and mix the ingredients until a dough forms with a gel-like consistency.
- Line a baking sheet with parchment paper and place the dough on the sheet. Cover the dough with another parchment paper and, with a rolling pin, flatten the dough into the baking sheet. Remove the parchment paper on top.
- Tuck the baking sheet in the oven and bake for 45 minutes. Allow the crackers to cool and dry in the oven, about 10 minutes. After, remove the sheet and break the crackers into small pieces. Serve

DESSERTS

95) VANILLA BROWNIES

Preparation Time: 30 minutes + chilling time

Servings: 4

Ingredients:

- ✓ 2 tbsp flaxseed powder
- ✓ ¼ cup cocoa powder
- ✓ ½ cup almond flour
- ✓ ½ tsp baking powder
- ✓ ½ cup erythritol
- ✓ 10 tbsp plant butter
- ✓ 2 oz dairy-free dark chocolate
- ✓ ½ tsp vanilla extract

Directions:

- ❖ Preheat oven to 375 F and line a baking sheet with parchment paper. Mix the flaxseed powder with 6 tbsp water in a bowl and allow thickening for 5 minutes. In a separate bowl, mix cocoa powder, almond flour, baking powder, and erythritol until no lumps. In another bowl, add the plant butter and dark chocolate and melt both in the microwave for 30 seconds to 1 minute.

- ❖ Whisk the vegan "flax egg" and vanilla into the chocolate mixture, then pour the mixture into the dry ingredients. Combine evenly. Pour the batter onto the paper-lined baking sheet and bake for 20 minutes. Cool completely and refrigerate for 2 hours. When ready, slice into squares and serve

96) VEGAN CHEESECAKE WITH BLUEBERRIES

Preparation Time: 1 hour 30 minutes + chilling

time

Servings: 6

Ingredients:

- ✓ 2 oz plant butter
- ✓ 1 ¼ cups almond flour
- ✓ 3 tbsp Swerve sugar
- ✓ 1 tsp vanilla extract
- ✓ 3 tbsp flaxseed powder
- ✓ 2 cups cashew cream cheese
- ✓ ½ cup coconut cream
- ✓ 1 tsp lemon zest
- ✓ 2 oz fresh blueberries

Directions:

- ❖ Preheat oven to 350 F and grease a springform pan with cooking spray. Line with parchment paper.

- ❖ To make the crust, melt the plant butter in a skillet over low heat until nutty in flavor. Turn the heat off and stir in almond flour, 2 tbsp of Swerve sugar, and half of the vanilla until a dough forms. Press the mixture into the springform pan and bake for 8 minutes.

- ❖ Mix flaxseed powder with 9 tbsp water and allow sitting for 5 minutes to thicken. In a bowl, combine cashew cream cheese, coconut cream, remaining Swerve sugar, lemon zest, remaining vanilla extract, and vegan "flax egg." Remove the crust from the oven and pour the mixture on top. Use a spatula to layer evenly. Bake the cake for 15 minutes at 400 F. Then, reduce the heat to 230 F and bake for 45-60 minutes. Remove to cool completely. Refrigerate overnight and scatter the blueberries on top. Serve

97) LIME AVOCADO ICE CREAM

Preparation Time: 10 minutes

Servings: 4

Ingredients:

- ✓ 2 large avocados, pitted
- ✓ Juice and zest of 3 limes
- ✓ 1/3 cup erythritol
- ✓ 1 ¾ cups coconut cream
- ✓ ¼ tsp vanilla extract

Directions:

- ❖ In a blender, combine the avocado pulp, lime juice and zest, erythritol, coconut cream, and vanilla extract. Process until the mixture is smooth. Pour the mixture into your ice cream maker and freeze based on the manufacturer's instructions. When ready, remove and scoop the ice cream into bowls. Serve immediately

98) VANILLA WHITE CHOCOLATE PUDDING

Preparation Time: 20 minutes+ cooling time   **Servings: 4**

Ingredients:

- ✓ 3 tbsp flaxseed + 9 tbsp water
- ✓ 3 tbsp corn-starch
- ✓ 1 cup cashew cream
- ✓ 2 ½ cups almond milk
- ✓ ½ pure date sugar
- ✓ 1 tbsp vanilla caviar
- ✓ 6 oz white chocolate chips
- ✓ Whipped coconut cream
- ✓ Sliced bananas and raspberries

Directions:

- ❖ In a small bowl, mix the flaxseed powder with water and allow thickening for 5 minutes to make the vegan "flax egg." In a large bowl, whisk the corn-starch and cashew cream until smooth. Beat in the vegan "flax egg" until well combined.
- ❖ Pour the almond milk into a pot and whisk in the date sugar. Cook over medium heat while frequently stirring until the sugar dissolves. Reduce the heat to low and simmer until steamy and bubbly around the edges.
- ❖ Pour half of the almond milk mixture into the vegan "flax egg" mix, whisk well and pour this mixture into the remaining milk content in the pot. Whisk continuously until well combined. Bring the new mixture to a boil over medium heat while still frequently stirring and scraping all the pot's corners, 2 minutes.
- ❖ Turn the heat off, stir in the vanilla caviar, then the white chocolate chips until melted. Spoon the mixture into a bowl, allow cooling for 2 minutes, cover with plastic wraps, making sure to press the plastic onto the surface of the pudding, and refrigerate for 4 hours. Remove the pudding from the fridge, take off the plastic wrap, and whip for about a minute. Spoon the dessert into serving cups, swirl some coconut whipping cream on top, and top with the bananas and raspberries. Enjoy

99) GRANDMA´S APRICOT TARTE TATIN

Preparation Time: 30 minutes+ cooling time   **Servings: 4**

Ingredients:

- ✓ 4 tbsp flaxseed powder
- ✓ ¼ cup almond flour
- ✓ 3 tbsp whole-wheat flour
- ✓ ½ tsp salt
- ✓ ¼ cup cold plant butter, crumbled
- ✓ 3 tbsp pure maple syrup
- ✓ 4 tbsp melted plant butter
- ✓ 3 tsp pure maple syrup
- ✓ 1 tsp vanilla extract
- ✓ 1 lemon, juiced
- ✓ 12 apricots, halved and pitted
- ✓ ½ cup coconut cream
- ✓ 4 fresh basil leaves

Directions:

- ❖ Preheat the oven to 350 F and grease a large pie pan with cooking spray.
- ❖ In a medium bowl, mix the flaxseed powder with 12 tbsp water and allow thickening for 5 minutes.
- ❖ In a large bowl, combine the flours and salt. Add the plant butter and using an electric hand mixer, whisk until crumbly. Pour in the vegan "flax egg" and maple syrup and mix until smooth dough forms. Flatten the dough on a flat surface, cover with plastic wrap, and refrigerate for 1 hour.
- ❖ Dust a working surface with almond flour, remove the dough onto the surface, and using a rolling pin, flatten the dough into a 1-inch diameter circle. Set aside. In a large bowl, mix the plant butter, maple syrup, vanilla, and lemon juice. Add the apricots to the mixture and coat well.
- ❖ Arrange the apricots (open side down) in the pie pan and lay the dough on top. Press to fit and cut off the dough hanging on the edges. Brush the top with more plant butter and bake in the oven for 35 to 40 minutes or until golden brown and puffed up.
- ❖ Remove the pie pan from the oven, allow cooling for 5 minutes, and run a butter knife around the edges of the pastry. Invert the dessert onto a large plate, spread the coconut cream on top, and garnish with the basil leaves. Slice and serve

100) SOUTHERN APPLE COBBLER WITH RASPBERRIES

Preparation Time: 50 minutes

Servings: 4

Ingredients:

- ✓ 3 apples, chopped
- ✓ 2 tbsp pure date sugar
- ✓ 1 cup fresh raspberries
- ✓ 2 tbsp unsalted plant butter
- ✓ ½ cup whole-wheat flour
- ✓ 1 cup toasted rolled oats
- ✓ 2 tbsp pure date sugar
- ✓ 1 tsp cinnamon powder

Directions:

- ❖ Preheat the oven to 350 F and grease a baking dish with some plant butter.
- ❖ Add apples, date sugar, and 3 tbsp of water to a pot. Cook over low heat until the date sugar melts and then mix in the raspberries. Cook until the fruits soften, 10 minutes. Pour and spread the fruit mixture into the baking dish and set aside.
- ❖ In a blender, add the plant butter, flour, oats, date sugar, and cinnamon powder. Pulse a few times until crumbly. Spoon and spread the mixture on the fruit mix until evenly layered. Bake in the oven for 25 to 30 minutes or until golden brown on top. Remove the dessert, allow cooling for 2 minutes, and serve

101) CHOCOLATE PEPPERMINT MOUSSE

Preparation Time: 10 minutes + chilling time

Servings: 4

Ingredients:

- ✓ ¼ cup Swerve sugar, divided
- ✓ 4 oz cashew cream cheese, softened
- ✓ 3 tbsp cocoa powder
- ✓ ¾ tsp peppermint extract
- ✓ ½ tsp vanilla extract
- ✓ 1/3 cup coconut cream

Directions:

- ❖ Put 2 tbsp of Swerve sugar, cashew cream cheese, and cocoa powder in a blender. Add the peppermint extract, ¼ cup warm water, and process until smooth. In a bowl, whip vanilla extract, coconut cream, and the remaining Swerve sugar using a whisk. Fetch out 5-6 tbsp for garnishing. Fold in the cocoa mixture until thoroughly combined. Spoon the mousse into serving cups and chill in the fridge for 30 minutes. Garnish with the reserved whipped cream and serve

102) RASPBERRIES TURMERIC PANNA COTTA

Preparation Time: 10 minutes + chilling time

Servings: 6

Ingredients:

- ✓ ½ tbsp powdered vegetarian gelatin
- ✓ 2 cups coconut cream
- ✓ ¼ tsp vanilla extract
- ✓ 1 pinch turmeric powder
- ✓ 1 tbsp erythritol
- ✓ 1 tbsp chopped toasted pecans
- ✓ 12 fresh raspberries

Directions:

- ❖ Mix gelatin and ½ tsp water and allow sitting to dissolve. Pour coconut cream, vanilla extract, turmeric, and erythritol into a saucepan and bring to a boil over medium heat, then simmer for 2 minutes. Turn the heat off. Stir in the gelatin until dissolved. Pour the mixture into 6 glasses, cover with plastic wrap, and refrigerate for 2 hours or more. Top with the pecans and raspberries and serve

103) BAKED APPLES FILLED WITH NUTS

Preparation Time: 35 minutes + cooling time

Servings: 4

Ingredients:

- ✓ 4 gala apples
- ✓ 3 tbsp pure maple syrup
- ✓ 4 tbsp almond flour
- ✓ 6 tbsp pure date sugar
- ✓ 6 tbsp plant butter, cold and cubed
- ✓ 1 cup chopped mixed nuts

Directions:

- ❖ Preheat the oven the 400 F.
- ❖ Slice off the top of the apples and use a melon baller or spoon to scoop out the cores of the apples. In a bowl, mix the maple syrup, almond flour, date sugar, butter, and nuts. Spoon the mixture into the apples and then bake in the oven for 25 minutes or until the nuts are golden brown on top and the apples soft. Remove the apples from the oven, allow cooling, and serve

104) MINT ICE CREAM

Preparation Time: 10 minutes + chilling time

Servings: 4

Ingredients:

- ✓ 2 avocados, pitted
- ✓ 1 ¼ cups coconut cream
- ✓ ½ tsp vanilla extract
- ✓ 2 tbsp erythritol
- ✓ 2 tsp chopped mint leaves

Directions:

- ❖ Into a blender, spoon the avocado pulps, pour in the coconut cream, vanilla extract, erythritol, and mint leaves. Process until smooth. Pour the mixture into your ice cream maker and freeze according to the manufacturer's instructions. When ready, remove and scoop the ice cream into bowls. Serve

105) CARDAMOM COCONUT FAT BOMBS

Preparation Time: 10 minutes

Servings: 6

Ingredients:

- ✓ ½ cup grated coconut
- ✓ 3 oz plant butter, softened
- ✓ ¼ tsp green cardamom powder
- ✓ ½ tsp vanilla extract
- ✓ ¼ tsp cinnamon powder

Directions:

- ❖ Pour the grated coconut into a skillet and roast until lightly brown. Set aside to cool. In a bowl, combine butter, half of the coconut, cardamom, vanilla, and cinnamon. Form balls from the mixture and roll each one in the remaining coconut. Refrigerate until ready to serve

106) CINNAMON FAUX RICE PUDDING

Preparation Time: 25 minutes

Servings: 6

Ingredients:

- ✓ 1 ¼ cups coconut cream
- ✓ 1 tsp vanilla extract
- ✓ 1 tsp cinnamon powder
- ✓ 1 cup mashed tofu
- ✓ 2 oz fresh strawberries

Directions:

- ❖ Pour the coconut cream into a bowl and whisk until a soft peak forms. Mix in the vanilla and cinnamon. Lightly fold in the vegan cottage cheese and refrigerate for 10 to 15 minutes to set. Spoon into serving glasses, top with the strawberries and serve immediately

PART 2: INTRODUCTION - WHAT DOES IT MEAN PLANT-BASED DIET?

A human diet is categorized into two parts, plant-derived foods and animal-derived foods. When comparing nutritional values, plant-based foods offer more than animal-based foods. From macronutrients including carbohydrates, proteins, and fats to vitamins and minerals essential to the human body, everything can come from plants, making animal proteins less critical in a healthy, balanced diet. Although this has not been widely accepted for some time, scientific discoveries and years of research into the human diet have led to people's confidence in plant-based diets. These foods provide many health benefits. Consuming an entirely plant-based diet can prevent a person from eating unhealthy saturated fats and other harmful elements that could lead to toxicity in the body or increase certain diseases' risk. As we discuss the merits of this diet and the dos and don'ts, you will also learn the basics of the diet and find practical recipes that fit this specific eating plan. All of the recipes are divided into broad categories suited to meet your daily needs, from breakfast to appetizers, snacks, desserts, dressings, and more.

Vegan, vegetarian, or plant-based? With so much dietary jargon everywhere, it's hard to distinguish between them. Simplifying, a plant-based diet is anything that comes from plants, whether it's vegetables, fruits, grains, oils, milk, seeds, nuts, flours, or legumes. This diet limits animal consumption, whether it is meat, milk, or fat. Because of these characteristics, we can say that a plant-based diet is another term for a vegan diet as both diets are highly restrictive on animal consumption, even if it is eggs or processed dairy products. Every ingredient must come from plants. In this sense, a plant-based diet is a slightly different approach as it does not restrict the use of eggs, yogurt, cheese, etc. In a plant-based diet, these should be replaced with vegan substitutes.

PLANT-BASED DIET AND ITS BENEFITS

Now that you know what the plant-based diet is, it's essential to look at the myriad of benefits it has to offer. It's hard to stick to a diet that makes you drastically change your current way of eating if you don't have a good reason. That's the goal of this chapter. This book wants to give you a good reason to achieve your health and weight loss goals using a plant-based diet.

MORE ENERGY

Within a few days of eating this type of diet, you'll feel energized because you'll have the nutrients you need. The foods you eat will also have a higher water content, which can hydrate your skin and make you feel better in general. Plant-based foods are easier to digest and lighter, so you'll feel better than ever in just a few days. Plus, when you eat right, you'll sleep better. When you rich your body with the vitamins and minerals it needs, you'll help your body relax and sleep peacefully. Calcium and magnesium can help relax your body for peaceful rest, which this diet is complete.

LOWERS CHOLESTEROL

Plants do not contain cholesterol, which includes saturated forms like coffee or chocolate. When you live a plant-based diet, you reduce the amount of cholesterol you take to almost zero. A plant-based diet lowers your heart disease risk, as cholesterol is a major cause of strokes and heart attacks.

AVOID CHRONIC DISEASES

Chronic diseases, including diabetes, cancer, and obesity, are low in societies that follow a plant-based lifestyle. This diet has been shown to help fight chronic disease by reducing chronic inflammation, high blood sugar, stress and provides your body with the nutrients it needs.

LOWERS BLOOD PRESSURE

A plant-based diet reduces blood pressure as well as stress and anxiety. Foods rich in potassium include seeds, whole grains, almonds, beans, berries, and grains. However, meat contains almost no potassium, which is why a plant-based diet offers a better way to control blood pressure.

MAINTAINS BLOOD SUGAR LEVELS

A plant-based diet has a lot of protein. Protein can lower blood sugar production and, in turn, make you feel full longer. Besides, a plant-based diet can help reduce stress levels by lowering cortisone levels in the body. Cortisol is a stress hormone.

WEIGHT LOSS

In societies that follow a predominantly plant-based lifestyle, there is also less obesity, which we've already covered as a chronic disease. Since you're taking in more vitamins and nutrients as well as fiber, which your body needs to break down while you're eating a plant-based lifestyle, you're also likely to stay full longer, which means you'll eat less overall. Burning more calories than you take in, you will lose weight, so eating less is an essential part of that.

THE PLANT-BASED DIET SHOPPING LIST

While this shopping list doesn't include everything for the original recipes, this shopping list will help you keep your pantry stocked with the basics.

NUTS

Any type of dried fruit is recommended in a plant-based diet, but it's helpful to have peanuts and walnuts on hand. You can also store cashews and almonds, as they are regularly used in a variety of dishes.

FRUIT

Any whole fruit is available in the plant-based diet. However, it is recommended to avoid dried fruits and fruit juices because of the amount of sugar they will introduce into your diet.

VEGETABLES: STARCHY

This includes all types of potatoes, whole corn, legumes of all kinds. This consists of all beans and lentils, root vegetables, and even quinoa. These are filling parts of your meals that are high in fiber.

OMEGA 3 SOURCES

With an entirely plant-based diet, you will need sources of omega 3. These include ground flaxseeds and chia seeds.

WHOLE GRAINS

You need some type of grain in your plant-based diet. Whole grains are always recommended, including entire wheat, brown rice, and oats. Overly processed oats will not give you the nutrients you need.

VEGETABLES: NON-STARCHY

These vegetables are excellent for your body because they are full of nutrients and help you get the vitamins you need. This includes leafy greens like kale, spinach, lettuce, etc. You can also use eggplant, zucchini, tomatoes, and broccoli as non-starchy bases.

SPICES

As far as spices go, any spice is allowed. This includes dried spices and fresh herbs.

CONSUME SPARINGLY

These are plant-based foods, but they are not as healthy for you as other vegetables. So, even though you can have them, it is recommended to use them sparingly. This includes added sweeteners. Examples of added sweeteners are fruit juice concentrate, natural sugars, honey, and maple syrup. Pumpkin seeds, sesame seeds, sunflower seeds, and nuts should also be consumed on a limited basis. So should coconuts and avocados. You should also limit refined proteins from wheat or soybeans

DRINKS

You can have almost any beverage in your plant-based diet. However, it is recommended to drink unsweetened plant-based milk, caffeine-free tea, caffeine-free coffee, and green tea.

107) PUDDING WITH SULTANAS ON CIABATTA BREAD

Preparation Time: 2 hours 10 minutes   **Servings: 4**

Ingredients:

- ✓ 2 cups coconut milk, unsweetened
- ✓ 1/2 cup agave syrup
- ✓ 1 tbsp coconut oil
- ✓ 1/2 tsp vanilla essence
- ✓ 1/2 tsp ground cardamom
- ✓ 1/4 tsp ground cloves
- ✓ 1/2 tsp ground cinnamon
- ✓ 1/4 tsp Himalayan salt
- ✓ 3/4 pound stale ciabatta bread, cubed
- ✓ 1/2 cup sultana raisins

Directions:

- ❖ In a mixing bowl, combine the coconut milk, agave syrup, coconut oil, vanilla, cardamom, ground cloves, cinnamon and Himalayan salt.
- ❖ Add the bread cubes to the custard mixture and stir to combine well. Fold in the sultana raisins and allow it to rest for about 1 hour on a counter.
- ❖ Then, spoon the mixture into a lightly oiled casserole dish.
- ❖ Bake in the preheated oven at 350 degrees F for about 1 hour or until the top is golden brown.
- ❖ Place the bread pudding on a wire rack for 10 minutes before slicing and serving

108)   VEGAN BANH MI

Preparation Time: 35 minutes   **Servings: 4**

Ingredients:

- ✓ 1/2 cup rice vinegar
- ✓ 1/4 cup water
- ✓ 1/4 cup white sugar
- ✓ 2 carrots, cut into 1/16-inch-thick matchsticks
- ✓ 1/2 cup white (daikon) radish, cut into 1/16-inch-thick matchsticks
- ✓ 1 white onion, thinly sliced
- ✓ 2 tbsp olive oil
- ✓ 12 ounces firm tofu, cut into sticks
- ✓ 1/4 cup vegan mayonnaise
- ✓ 1 ½ tbsp soy sauce
- ✓ 2 cloves garlic, minced
- ✓ 1/4 cup fresh parsley, chopped
- ✓ Kosher salt and ground black pepper, to taste
- ✓ 2 standard French baguettes, cut into four pieces
- ✓ 4 tbsp fresh cilantro, chopped
- ✓ 4 lime wedges

Directions:

- ❖ Bring the rice vinegar, water and sugar to a boil and stir until the sugar has dissolved, about 1 minute. Allow it to cool.
- ❖ Pour the cooled vinegar mixture over the carrot, daikon radish and onion; allow the vegetables to marinate for at least 30 minutes.
- ❖ While the vegetables are marinating, heat the olive oil in a frying pan over medium-high heat. Once hot, add the tofu and sauté for 8 minutes, stirring occasionally to promote even cooking.
- ❖ Then, mix the mayo, soy sauce, garlic, parsley, salt and ground black pepper in a small bowl.
- ❖ Slice each piece of the baguette in half the long way Then, toast the baguette halves under the preheated broiler for about 3 minutes.
- ❖ To assemble the banh mi sandwiches, spread each half of the toasted baguette with the mayonnaise mixture; fill the cavity of the bottom half of the bread with the fried tofu sticks, marinated vegetables and cilantro leaves.
- ❖ Lastly, squeeze the lime wedges over the filling and top with the other half of the baguette. Enjoy

109)   BREAKFAST NUTTY OATMEAL MUFFINS

Preparation Time: 30 minutes   **Servings: 9**

Ingredients:

- ✓ 1 ½ cups rolled oats
- ✓ 1/2 cup shredded coconut, unsweetened
- ✓ 3/4 tsp baking powder
- ✓ 1/4 tsp salt
- ✓ 1/4 tsp vanilla extract
- ✓ 1/4 tsp coconut extract
- ✓ 1/4 tsp grated nutmeg
- ✓ 1/2 tsp cardamom
- ✓ 3/4 cup coconut milk
- ✓ 1/3 cup canned pumpkin
- ✓ 1/4 cup agave syrup
- ✓ 1/4 cup golden raisins
- ✓ 1/4 cup pecans, chopped

Directions:

- ❖ Begin by preheating your oven to 360 degrees F. Spritz a muffin tin with a nonstick cooking oil.
- ❖ In a mixing bowl, thoroughly combine all the ingredients, except for the raisins and pecans.
- ❖ Fold in the raisins and pecans and scrape the batter into the prepared muffin tin.
- ❖ Bake your muffins for about 25 minutes or until the top is set. Enjoy

110) SMOOTHIE BOWL OF RASPBERRY AND CHIA

Preparation Time: 10 minutes

Servings: 2

Ingredients:

- ✓ 1 cup coconut milk
- ✓ 2 small-sized bananas, peeled
- ✓ 1 ½ cups raspberries, fresh or frozen
- ✓ 2 dates, pitted
- ✓ 1 tbsp coconut flakes
- ✓ 1 tbsp pepitas
- ✓ 2 tbsp chia seeds

Directions:

- ❖ In your blender or food processor, mix the coconut milk with the bananas, raspberries and dates.
- ❖ Process until creamy and smooth. Divide the smoothie between two bowls.
- ❖ Top each smoothie bowl with the coconut flakes, pepitas and chia seeds. Enjoy

111) BREAKFAST OATS WITH WALNUTS AND CURRANTS

Preparation Time: 10 minutes

Servings: 2

Ingredients:

- ✓ 1 cup water
- ✓ 1 ½ cups oat milk
- ✓ 1 ½ cups rolled oats
- ✓ A pinch of salt
- ✓ A pinch of grated nutmeg
- ✓ 1/4 tsp cardamom
- ✓ 1 handful walnuts, roughly chopped
- ✓ 4 tbsp dried currants

Directions:

- ❖ In a deep saucepan, bring the water and milk to a rolling boil. Add in the oats, cover the saucepan and turn the heat to medium.
- ❖ Add in the salt, nutmeg and cardamom. Continue to cook for about 12 to 13 minutes more, stirring occasionally.
- ❖ Spoon the mixture into serving bowls; top with walnuts and currants. Enjoy

112) APPLESAUCE PANCAKES WITH COCONUT

Preparation Time: 50 minutes

Servings: 8

Ingredients:

- ✓ 1 ¼ cups whole-wheat flour
- ✓ 1 tsp baking powder
- ✓ 1/4 tsp sea salt
- ✓ 1/2 tsp coconut sugar
- ✓ 1/4 tsp ground cloves
- ✓ 1/4 tsp ground cardamom
- ✓ 1/2 tsp ground cinnamon
- ✓ 3/4 cup oat milk
- ✓ 1/2 cup applesauce, unsweetened
- ✓ 2 tbsp coconut oil
- ✓ 8 tbsp coconut, shredded
- ✓ 8 tbsp pure maple syrup

Directions:

- ❖ In a mixing bowl, thoroughly combine the flour, baking powder, salt, sugar and spices. Gradually add in the milk and applesauce.
- ❖ Heat a frying pan over a moderately high flame and add a small amount of the coconut oil.
- ❖ Once hot, pour the batter into the frying pan. Cook for approximately 3 minutes until the bubbles form; flip it and cook on the other side for 3 minutes longer until browned on the underside. Repeat with the remaining oil and batter.
- ❖ Serve with shredded coconut and maple syrup. Enjoy

113) VEGGIE PANINI

Preparation Time: 30 minutes

Servings: 4

Ingredients:

- ✓ 1 tbsp olive oil
- ✓ 1 cup sliced button mushrooms
- ✓ Salt and black pepper to taste
- ✓ 1 ripe avocado, sliced
- ✓ 2 tbsp freshly squeezed lemon juice
- ✓ 1 tbsp chopped parsley
- ✓ ½ tsp pure maple syrup
- ✓ 8 slices whole-wheat ciabatta
- ✓ 4 oz sliced plant-based Parmesan

Directions:

- ❖ Heat the olive oil in a medium skillet over medium heat and sauté the mushrooms until softened, 5 minutes. Season with salt and black pepper. Turn the heat off.
- ❖ Preheat a panini press to medium heat, 3 to 5 minutes. Mash the avocado in a medium bowl and mix in the lemon juice, parsley, and maple syrup. Spread the mixture on 4 bread slices, divide the mushrooms and plant-based Parmesan cheese on top.
- ❖ Cover with the other bread slices and brush the top with olive oil. Grill the sandwiches one after another in the heated press until golden brown, and the cheese is melted.
- ❖ Serve

114) CHEDDAR GRITS AND SOY CHORIZO

Preparation Time: 25 minutes

Servings: 6

Ingredients:

- ✓ 1 cup quick-cooking grits
- ✓ ½ cup grated plant-based cheddar
- ✓ 2 tbsp peanut butter
- ✓ 1 cup soy chorizo, chopped
- ✓ 1 cup corn kernels
- ✓ 2 cups vegetable broth

Directions:

- ❖ Preheat oven to 380 F.
- ❖ Pour the broth in a pot and bring to a boil over medium heat. Stir in salt and grits. Lower the heat and cook until the grits are thickened, stirring often. Turn the heat off, put in the plant-based cheddar cheese, peanut butter, soy chorizo, and corn and mix well.
- ❖ Spread the mixture into a greased baking dish and bake for 45 minutes until slightly puffed and golden brown. Serve right away

115) VANILLA CREPES AND BERRY CREAM COMPOTE TOPPING

Preparation Time: 35 minutes

Servings: 4

Ingredients:

- ✓ For the berry cream:
- ✓ 2 tbsp plant butter
- ✓ 2 tbsp pure date sugar
- ✓ 1 tsp vanilla extract
- ✓ ½ cup fresh blueberries
- ✓ ½ cup fresh raspberries
- ✓ ½ cup whipped coconut cream
- ✓ For the crepes:
- ✓ 2 tbsp flax seed powder
- ✓ 1 tsp vanilla extract
- ✓ 1 tsp pure date sugar
- ✓ ¼ tsp salt
- ✓ 2 cups almond flour
- ✓ 1 ½ cups almond milk
- ✓ 1 ½ cups water
- ✓ 3 tbsp plant butter for frying

Directions:

- ❖ Melt butter in a pot over low heat and mix in the date sugar, and vanilla. Cook until the sugar melts and then toss in berries. Allow softening for 2-3 minutes. Set aside to cool.
- ❖ In a medium bowl, mix the flax seed powder with 6 tbsp water and allow to thicken for 5 minutes to make the vegan "flax egg." Whisk in vanilla, date sugar, and salt. Pour in a quarter cup of almond flour and whisk, then a quarter cup of almond milk, and mix until no lumps remain. Repeat the mixing process with the remaining almond flour and almond milk in the same quantities until exhausted.
- ❖ Mix in 1 cup of water until the mixture is runny like that of pancakes and add the remaining water until it is lighter. Brush a large non-stick skillet with some butter and place over medium heat to melt. Pour 1 tbsp of the batter into the pan and swirl the skillet quickly and all around to coat the pan with the batter. Cook until the batter is dry and golden brown beneath, about 30 seconds.
- ❖ Use a spatula to carefully flip the crepe and cook the other side until golden brown too. Fold the crepe onto a plate and set aside. Repeat making more crepes with the remaining batter until exhausted. Plate the crepes, top with the whipped coconut cream and the berry compote. Serve immediately

116) BREAKFAST NAAN BREAD WITH MANGO JAM

Preparation Time: 40 minutes

Servings: 4

Ingredients:

- ✓ ¾ cup almond flour
- ✓ 1 tsp salt + extra for sprinkling
- ✓ 1 tsp baking powder
- ✓ 1/3 cup olive oil
- ✓ 2 cups boiling water
- ✓ 2 tbsp plant butter for frying
- ✓ 4 cups heaped chopped mangoes
- ✓ 1 cup pure maple syrup
- ✓ 1 lemon, juiced
- ✓ A pinch of saffron powder
- ✓ 1 tsp cardamom powder

Directions:

- ❖ In a large bowl, mix the almond flour, salt, and baking powder. Mix in the olive oil and boiling water until smooth, thick batter forms. Allow the dough to rise for 5 minutes. Form balls out of the dough, place each on a baking paper, and use your hands to flatten the dough.
- ❖ Working in batches, melt the plant butter in a large skillet and fry the dough on both sides until set and golden brown on each side, 4 minutes per bread. Transfer to a plate and set aside for serving.
- ❖ Add mangoes, maple syrup, lemon juice, and 3 tbsp water in a pot and cook until boiling, 5 minutes. Mix in saffron and cardamom powders and cook further over low heat until the mangoes soften. Mash the mangoes with the back of the spoon until relatively smooth with little chunks of mangoes in a jam.
- ❖ Cool completely. Spoon the jam into sterilized jars and serve with the naan bread

117) CRISPY CORN CAKES

Preparation Time: 35 minutes

Servings: 4

Ingredients:

- ✓ 1 tbsp flaxseed powder
- ✓ 2 cups yellow cornmeal
- ✓ 1 tsp salt
- ✓ 2 tsp baking powder
- ✓ 4 tbsp olive oil
- ✓ 1 cup tofu mayonnaise for serving

Directions:

- ❖ In a bowl, mix the flax seed powder with 3 tbsp water and allow thickening for 5 minutes to form the vegan "flax egg." Mix in 1 cup of water and then whisk in the cornmeal, salt, and baking powder until soup texture forms but not watery.
- ❖ Heat a quarter of the olive oil in a griddle pan and pour in a quarter of the batter. Cook until set and golden brown beneath, 3 minutes. Flip the cake and cook the other side until set and golden brown too. Plate the cake and make three more with the remaining oil and batter.
- ❖ Top the cakes with some tofu mayonnaise before serving

118) CHIA COCONUT PUDDING

Preparation Time: 5 minutes+ cooling time

Servings: 4

Ingredients:

- ✓ 1 cup coconut milk
- ✓ ½ tsp vanilla extract
- ✓ 3 tbsp chia seeds
- ✓ ½ cup granola
- ✓ 2/3 cup chopped sweet nectarine

Directions:

- ❖ In a medium bowl, mix the coconut milk, vanilla, and chia seeds until well combined. Divide the mixture between 4 breakfast cups and refrigerate for at least 4 hours to allow the mixture to gel.
- ❖ Top with the granola and nectarine. Serve

119) CHOCOLATE AND CARROT BREAD WITH RAISINS

Preparation Time: 75 minutes

Servings: 4

Ingredients:

- ✓ 1 ½ cup whole-wheat flour
- ✓ ¼ cup almond flour
- ✓ ¼ tsp salt
- ✓ ¼ tsp cloves powder
- ✓ ¼ tsp cayenne pepper
- ✓ 1 tbsp cinnamon powder
- ✓ ½ tsp nutmeg powder
- ✓ 1 ½ tsp baking powder
- ✓ 2 tbsp flax seed powder
- ✓ ½ cup pure date sugar
- ✓ ¼ cup pure maple syrup
- ✓ ¾ tsp almond extract
- ✓ 1 tbsp grated lemon zest
- ✓ ½ cup unsweetened applesauce
- ✓ ¼ cup olive oil
- ✓ 4 carrots, shredded
- ✓ 3 tbsp unsweetened chocolate chips
- ✓ 2/3 cup black raisins

Directions:

- ❖ Preheat oven to 375 F and line a loaf tin with baking paper. In a bowl, mix all the flours, salt, cloves powder, cayenne pepper, cinnamon powder, nutmeg powder, and baking powder.
- ❖ In another bowl, mix the flax seed powder, 6 tbsp water, and allow thickening for 5 minutes. Mix in the date sugar, maple syrup, almond extract, lemon zest, applesauce, and olive oil. Combine both mixtures until smooth and fold in the carrots, chocolate chips, and raisins.
- ❖ Pour the mixture into a loaf pan and bake in the oven until golden brown on top or a toothpick inserted into the bread comes out clean, 45-50 minutes. Remove from the oven, transfer the bread onto a wire rack to cool, slice, and serve

120) FRENCH TOASTS TROPICAL STYLE

Preparation Time: 55 minutes

Servings: 4

Ingredients:

- ✓ 2 tbsp flax seed powder
- ✓ 1 ½ cups unsweetened almond milk
- ✓ ½ cup almond flour
- ✓ 2 tbsp maple syrup + extra for drizzling
- ✓ 2 pinches of salt
- ✓ ½ tbsp cinnamon powder
- ✓ ½ tsp fresh lemon zest
- ✓ 1 tbsp fresh pineapple juice
- ✓ 8 whole-grain bread slices

Directions:

- ❖ Preheat the oven to 400 F and lightly grease a roasting rack with olive oil. Set aside.
- ❖ In a medium bowl, mix the flax seed powder with 6 tbsp water and allow thickening for 5 to 10 minutes. Whisk in the almond milk, almond flour, maple syrup, salt, cinnamon powder, lemon zest, and pineapple juice. Soak the bread on both sides in the almond milk mixture and allow sitting on a plate for 2 to 3 minutes.
- ❖ Heat a large skillet over medium heat and place the bread in the pan. Cook until golden brown on the bottom side. Flip the bread and cook further until golden brown on the other side, 4 minutes in total. Transfer to a plate, drizzle some maple syrup on top and serve immediately

121) CREPES WITH MUSHROOM

Preparation Time: 25 minutes   Servings: 4

Ingredients:

- ✓ 1 cup whole-wheat flour
- ✓ 1 tsp onion powder
- ✓ ½ tsp baking soda
- ✓ ¼ tsp salt
- ✓ 1 cup pressed, crumbled tofu
- ✓ ⅓ cup plant-based milk
- ✓ ¼ cup lemon juice
- ✓ 2 tbsp extra-virgin olive oil
- ✓ ½ cup finely chopped mushrooms
- ✓ ½ cup finely chopped onion
- ✓ 2 cups collard greens

Directions:

- ❖ Combine the flour, onion powder, baking soda, and salt in a bowl. Blitz the tofu, milk, lemon juice, and oil in a food processor over high speed for 30 seconds. Pour over the flour mixture and mix to combine well. Add in the mushrooms, onion, and collard greens.
- ❖ Heat a skillet and grease with cooking spray. Lower the heat and spread a ladleful of the batter across the surface of the skillet. Cook for 4 minutes on both sides or until set. Remove to a plate. Repeat the process until no batter is left, greasing with a little more oil, if needed. Serve

122) FRENCH TOAST WITH CINNAMON-BANANA

Preparation Time: 25 minutes   Servings: 3

Ingredients:

- ✓ 1/3 cup coconut milk
- ✓ 1/2 cup banana, mashed
- ✓ 2 tbsp besan (chickpea flour)
- ✓ 1/2 tsp baking powder
- ✓ 1/2 tsp vanilla paste
- ✓ A pinch of sea salt
- ✓ 1 tbsp agave syrup
- ✓ 1/2 tsp ground allspice
- ✓ A pinch of grated nutmeg
- ✓ 6 slices day-old sourdough bread
- ✓ 2 bananas, sliced
- ✓ 2 tbsp brown sugar
- ✓ 1 tsp ground cinnamon

Directions:

- ❖ To make the batter, thoroughly combine the coconut milk, mashed banana, besan, baking powder, vanilla, salt, agave syrup, allspice and nutmeg.
- ❖ Dredge each slice of bread into the batter until well coated on all sides.
- ❖ Preheat an electric griddle to medium heat and lightly oil it with a nonstick cooking spray.
- ❖ Cook each slice of bread on the preheated griddle for about 3 minutes per side until golden brown.
- ❖ Garnish the French toast with the bananas, brown sugar and cinnamon. Enjoy

123) INDIAN TRADITIONAL ROTI

Preparation Time: 30 minutes   Servings: 5

Ingredients:

- ✓ 2 cups bread flour
- ✓ 1 tsp baking powder
- ✓ 1/2 tsp salt
- ✓ 3/4 warm water
- ✓ 1 cup vegetable oil, for frying

Directions:

- ❖ Thoroughly combine the flour, baking powder and salt in a mixing bowl. Gradually add in the water until the dough comes together.
- ❖ Divide the dough into five balls; flatten each ball to create circles.
- ❖ Heat the olive oil in a frying pan over a moderately high flame. Fry the first bread, turning it over to promote even cooking; fry it for about 10 minutes or until golden brown.
- ❖ Repeat with the remaining dough. Transfer each roti to a paper towel-lined plate to drain the excess oil.
- ❖ Enjoy

124) CHIA CHOCOLATE PUDDING

Preparation Time: 10 minutes + chilling time   Servings: 4

Ingredients:

- ✓ 4 tbsp unsweetened cocoa powder
- ✓ 4 tbsp maple syrup
- ✓ 1 2/3 cups coconut milk
- ✓ A pinch of grated nutmeg
- ✓ A pinch of ground cloves
- ✓ 1/2 tsp ground cinnamon
- ✓ 1/2 cup chia seeds

Directions:

- ❖ Add the cocoa powder, maple syrup, milk and spices to a bowl and stir until everything is well incorporated.
- ❖ Add in the chia seeds and stir again to combine well. Spoon the mixture into four jars, cover and place in your refrigerator overnight.
- ❖ On the actual day, stir with a spoon and serve. Enjoy

125) EASY BREAKFAST POLENTA

Preparation Time: 20 minutes   **Servings: 2**

Ingredients:

- ✓ 2 cups vegetable broth
- ✓ 1/2 cup cornmeal
- ✓ 1/2 tsp sea salt
- ✓ 1/4 tsp ground black pepper, to taste
- ✓ 1/4 tsp red pepper flakes, crushed
- ✓ 2 tbsp olive oil

Directions:

- ❖ In a medium saucepan, bring the vegetable broth to boil over medium-high heat. Now, add in the cornmeal, whisking continuously to prevent lumps.
- ❖ Season with salt, black pepper and red pepper.
- ❖ Reduce the heat to a simmer. Continue to simmer, whisking periodically, for about 18 minutes, until the mixture has thickened.
- ❖ Now, pour the olive oil into a saucepan and stir to combine well. Enjoy

126) PEPPER AND SCALLION OMELETTE

Preparation Time: 15 minutes   **Servings: 2**

Ingredients:

- ✓ 2 tbsp olive oil
- ✓ 3 scallions, chopped
- ✓ 2 bell peppers, chopped
- ✓ 6 tbsp besan (chickpea flour)
- ✓ 10 tbsp rice milk, unsweetened
- ✓ Kala namak salt and ground black pepper, to season
- ✓ 1/3 tsp red pepper flakes
- ✓ 2 tbsp fresh Italian parsley, chopped

Directions:

- ❖ Heat the olive oil in a frying pan over medium-high heat. Once hot, sauté the scallions and peppers for about 3 minutes until tender and aromatic.
- ❖ Meanwhile, whisk the chickpea flour with the milk, salt, black pepper and red pepper flakes.
- ❖ Then, pour the mixture into the frying pan.
- ❖ Cook for about 4 minutes. Turn it over and cook for an additional 3 to 4 minutes until set. Serve with fresh parsley. Enjoy

127) TRADITIONAL TOFU SCRAMBLE

Preparation Time: 15 minutes   **Servings: 2**

Ingredients:

- ✓ 1 tbsp olive oil
- ✓ 6 ounces extra-firm tofu, pressed and crumbled
- ✓ 1 cup baby spinach
- ✓ Sea salt and ground black pepper to taste
- ✓ 1/2 tsp turmeric powder
- ✓ 1/4 tsp cumin powder
- ✓ 1/2 tsp garlic powder
- ✓ 1 handful fresh chives, chopped

Directions:

- ❖ Heat the olive oil in a frying skillet over medium heat. When it's hot, add the tofu and sauté for 8 minutes, stirring occasionally to promote even cooking.
- ❖ Add in the baby spinach and aromatics and continue sautéing an additional 1 to 2 minutes.
- ❖ Garnish with fresh chives and serve warm. Enjoy

128) FRENCH TOAST WITH BANANA AND STRAWBERRY SYRUP

Preparation Time: 40 minutes   **Servings: 8**

Ingredients:

- ✓ 1 banana, mashed
- ✓ 1 cup coconut milk
- ✓ 1 tsp pure vanilla extract
- ✓ ¼ tsp ground nutmeg
- ✓ ½ tsp ground cinnamon
- ✓ 1 ½ tsp arrowroot powder
- ✓ A pinch of salt
- ✓ 8 slices whole-grain bread
- ✓ 1 cup strawberries
- ✓ 2 tbsp water
- ✓ 2 tbsp maple syrup

Directions:

- ❖ Preheat oven to 350 F.
- ❖ In a bowl, stir banana, coconut milk, vanilla, nutmeg, cinnamon, arrowroot, and salt. Dip each bread slice in the banana mixture and arrange on a baking tray. Spread the remaining banana mixture over the top. Bake for 30 minutes until the tops are lightly browned. In a pot over medium heat, put the strawberries, water, and maple syrup. Simmer for 15-10 minutes, until the berries breaking up and the liquid has reduced. Serve

129) PIMIENTO BISCUITS WITH CASHEW CHEESE

Preparation Time: 30 minutes

Servings: 4

Ingredients:

- ✓ 2 cups whole-wheat flour
- ✓ 2 tsp baking powder
- ✓ 1 tsp salt
- ✓ ½ tsp baking soda
- ✓ ½ tsp garlic powder
- ✓ ¼ tsp black pepper
- ✓ ¼ cup plant butter, cold and cubed
- ✓ ¾ cup coconut milk
- ✓ 1 cup shredded cashew cheese
- ✓ 1 (4 oz) jar chopped pimientos,
- ✓ 1 tbsp melted unsalted plant butter

Directions:

- ❖ Preheat the oven to 450 F and line a baking sheet with parchment paper. Set aside. In a medium bowl, mix the flour, baking powder, salt, baking soda, garlic powder, and black pepper. Add the cold butter using a hand mixer until the mixture is the size of small peas. Pour in ¾ of the coconut milk and continue whisking. Continue adding the remaining coconut milk, a tbspful at a time, until dough forms.
- ❖ Mix in the cashew cheese and pimientos. (If the dough is too wet to handle, mix in a little bit more flour until it is manageable). Place the dough on a lightly floured surface and flatten the dough into ½-inch thickness.
- ❖ Use a 2 ½-inch round cutter to cut out biscuits' pieces from the dough. Gather, re-roll the dough once and continue cutting out biscuits. Arrange the biscuits on the prepared pan and brush the tops with the melted butter.
- ❖ Bake for 12-14 minutes, or until the biscuits are golden brown. Cool and serve

130) RASPBERRY, ORANGE-GLAZED MUFFINS

Preparation Time: 40 minutes

Servings: 4

Ingredients:

- ✓ 2 tbsp flax seed powder
- ✓ 2 cups whole-wheat flour
- ✓ 1 ½ tsp baking powder
- ✓ A pinch salt
- ✓ ½ cup plant butter, softened
- ✓ 2 cups pure date sugar
- ✓ ½ cup oat milk
- ✓ 2 tsp vanilla extract
- ✓ 1 lemon, zested
- ✓ 1 cup dried raspberries
- ✓ 2 tbsp orange juice

Directions:

- ❖ Preheat oven to 400 F and grease 6 muffin cups with cooking spray. In a small bowl, mix the flax seed powder with 6 tbsp water and allow thickening for 5 minutes to make the vegan "flax egg." In a medium bowl, mix the flour, baking powder, and salt. In another bowl, cream the plant butter, half of the date sugar, and vegan "flax egg." Mix in the oat milk, vanilla, and lemon zest.
- ❖ Combine both mixtures, fold in raspberries, and fill muffin cups two-thirds way up with the batter. Bake for 20-25 minutes. In a medium bowl, whisk orange juice and remaining date sugar until smooth. Remove the muffins when ready and transfer to a wire rack to cool. Drizzle the glaze on top to serve

131) STRAWBERRY AND PECAN BREAKFAST

Preparation Time: 15 minutes

Servings: 2

Ingredients:

- ✓ 1 (14-oz) can coconut milk, refrigerated overnight
- ✓ 1 cup granola
- ✓ ½ cup pecans, chopped
- ✓ 1 cup sliced strawberries

Directions:

- ❖ Drain the coconut milk liquid. Layer the coconut milk solids, granola, and strawberries in small glasses. Top with chopped pecans and serve right away

132) GRANOLA WITH HAZELNUTS AND ORANGE

Preparation Time: 50 minutes

Servings: 5

Ingredients:

- ✓ 2 cups rolled oats
- ✓ ¾ cup whole-wheat flour
- ✓ 1 tbsp ground cinnamon
- ✓ 1 tsp ground ginger
- ✓ ½ cup sunflower seeds
- ✓ ½ cup hazelnuts, chopped
- ✓ ½ cup pumpkin seeds
- ✓ ½ cup shredded coconut
- ✓ 1 ¼ cups orange juice
- ✓ ½ cup dried cherries
- ✓ ½ cup goji berries

Directions:

- ❖ Preheat oven to 350 F.
- ❖ In a bowl, combine the oats, flour, cinnamon, ginger, sunflower seeds, hazelnuts, pumpkin seeds, and coconut. Pour in the orange juice, toss to mix well.
- ❖ Transfer to a baking sheet and bake for 15 minutes. Turn the granola and continue baking until it is crunchy, about 30 minutes. Stir in the cherries and goji berries and store in the fridge for up to 14 days

133) ORANGE CREPES

Preparation Time: 30 minutes

Servings: 4

Ingredients:

- ✓ 2 tbsp flax seed powder
- ✓ 1 tsp vanilla extract
- ✓ 1 tsp pure date sugar
- ✓ ¼ tsp salt

- ✓ 2 cups almond flour
- ✓ 1 ½ cups oat milk
- ✓ ½ cup melted plant butter
- ✓ 3 tbsp fresh orange juice
- ✓ 3 tbsp plant butter for frying

Directions:

- ❖ In a medium bowl, mix the flax seed powder with 6 tbsp water and allow thickening for 5 minutes to make the vegan "flax egg." Whisk in the vanilla, date sugar, and salt.
- ❖ Pour in a quarter cup of almond flour and whisk, then a quarter cup of oat milk, and mix until no lumps remain. Repeat the mixing process with the remaining almond flour and almond milk in the same quantities until exhausted.
- ❖ Mix in the plant butter, orange juice, and half of the water until the mixture is runny like pancakes. Add the remaining water until the mixture is lighter. Brush a non-stick skillet with some butter and place over medium heat to melt.
- ❖ Pour 1 tbsp of the batter into the pan and swirl the skillet quickly and all around to coat the pan with the batter. Cook until the batter is dry and golden brown beneath, about 30 seconds.
- ❖ Use a spatula to flip the crepe and cook the other side until golden brown too. Fold the crepe onto a plate and set aside. Repeat making more crepes with the remaining batter until exhausted. Drizzle some maple syrup on the crepes and serve

134) OAT BREAD WITH COCONUT

Preparation Time: 50 minutes

Servings: 4

Ingredients:

- ✓ 4 cups whole-wheat flour
- ✓ ¼ tsp salt
- ✓ ½ cup rolled oats

- ✓ 1 tsp baking soda
- ✓ 1 ¾ cups coconut milk, thick
- ✓ 2 tbsp pure maple syrup

Directions:

- ❖ Preheat the oven to 400 F.
- ❖ In a bowl, mix flour, salt, oats, and baking soda. Add in coconut milk and maple syrup and whisk until dough forms. Dust your hands with some flour and knead the dough into a ball. Shape the dough into a circle and place on a baking sheet.
- ❖ Cut a deep cross on the dough and bake in the oven for 15 minutes at 450 F. Reduce the temperature to 400 F and bake further for 20 to 25 minutes or until a hollow sound is made when the bottom of the bread is tapped. Slice and serve

135) BOWL WITH BLACK BEANS AND SPICY QUINOA

Preparation Time: 25 minutes

Servings: 4

Ingredients:

- ✓ 1 cup brown quinoa, rinsed
- ✓ 3 tbsp plant-based yogurt
- ✓ ½ lime, juiced
- ✓ 2 tbsp chopped fresh cilantro
- ✓ 1 (5 oz) can black beans, drained

- ✓ 3 tbsp tomato salsa
- ✓ ¼ avocado, sliced
- ✓ 2 radishes, shredded
- ✓ 1 tbsp pepitas (pumpkin seeds)

Directions:

- ❖ Cook the quinoa with 2 cups of slightly salted water in a medium pot over medium heat or until the liquid absorbs, 15 minutes. Spoon the quinoa into serving bowls and fluff with a fork.
- ❖ In a small bowl, mix the yogurt, lime juice, cilantro, and salt. Divide this mixture on the quinoa and top with the beans, salsa, avocado, radishes, and pepitas. Serve immediately

SOUPS, STEW AND SALADS

136) TORTILLA MEXICAN SOUP

Preparation Time: 40 minutes

Servings: 4

Ingredients:

- ✓ 1 (14.5-oz) can diced tomatoes
- ✓ 1 (4-oz) can green chiles, chopped
- ✓ 2 tbsp olive oil
- ✓ 1 cup canned sweet corn
- ✓ 1 red onion, chopped
- ✓ 2 garlic cloves, minced
- ✓ 2 jalapeño peppers, sliced
- ✓ 4 cups vegetable broth
- ✓ 8 oz seitan, cut into ¼-inch strips
- ✓ Salt and black pepper to taste
- ✓ ¼ cup chopped fresh cilantro
- ✓ 3 tbsp fresh lime juice
- ✓ 4 corn tortillas, cut into strips
- ✓ 1 ripe avocado, chopped

Directions:

- ❖ Preheat oven to 350 F. Heat the oil in a pot over medium heat. Place sweet corn, garlic, jalapeño, and onion and cook for 5 minutes. Stir in broth, seitan, tomatoes, canned chiles, salt, and pepper. Bring to a boil, then lower the heat and simmer for 20 minutes. Put in the cilantro and lime juice, stir. Adjust the seasoning.
- ❖ Meanwhile, arrange the tortilla strips on a baking sheet and bake for 8 minutes until crisp. Serve the soup into bowls and top with tortilla strips and avocado

137) MUSHROOM RICE WINE SOUP

Preparation Time: 25 minutes

Servings: 4

Ingredients:

- ✓ 2 tbsp olive oil
- ✓ 4 green onions, chopped
- ✓ 1 carrot, chopped
- ✓ 8 oz shiitake mushrooms, sliced
- ✓ 3 tbsp rice wine
- ✓ 2 tbsp soy sauce
- ✓ 4 cups vegetable broth
- ✓ Salt and black pepper to taste
- ✓ 2 tbsp parsley, chopped

Directions:

- ❖ Heat the oil in a pot over medium heat. Place the green onions and carrot and cook for 5 minutes.
- ❖ Stir in mushrooms, rice wine, soy sauce, broth, salt, and pepper. Bring to a boil, then lower the heat and simmer for 15 minutes. Top with parsley and serve warm

138) BEAN TANGY TOMATO SOUP

Preparation Time: 30 minutes

Servings: 5

Ingredients:

- ✓ 2 tsp olive oil
- ✓ 1 onion, chopped
- ✓ 2 garlic cloves, minced
- ✓ 1 cup mushrooms, chopped
- ✓ Sea salt to taste
- ✓ 1 tbsp dried basil
- ✓ ½ tbsp dried oregano
- ✓ 1 (19-oz) can diced tomatoes
- ✓ 1 (14-oz) can kidney beans, drained
- ✓ 5 cups water
- ✓ 2 cups chopped mustard greens

Directions:

- ❖ Heat the oil in a pot over medium heat. Place in the onion, garlic, mushrooms, and salt and cook for 5 minutes. Stir in basil and oregano, tomatoes, and beans. Pour in water and stir. Simmer for 20 minutes and add in mustard greens; cook for 5 minutes until greens soften. Serve immediately

139)   SPINACH AND POTATO SOUP

Preparation Time: 55 minutes   Servings: 4

Ingredients:

- ✓ ¼ tsp crushed red pepper
- ✓ 1 bay leaf
- ✓ Salt to taste
- ✓ 4 cups chopped spinach
- ✓ 1 cup green lentils, rinsed

- ✓ 2 tbsp olive oil
- ✓ 1 onion, chopped
- ✓ 2 garlic cloves, minced
- ✓ 4 cups vegetable broth
- ✓ 2 russet potatoes, cubed
- ✓ ½ tsp dried oregano

Directions:

- ❖ Warm the oil in a pot over medium heat. Place the onion and garlic and cook covered for 5 minutes. Stir in broth, potatoes, oregano, red pepper, bay leaf, lentils, and salt. Bring to a boil, then lower the heat and simmer uncovered for 30 minutes. Add in spinach and cook for another 5 minutes. Discard the bay leaf and serve immediately

140)   BEAN TURMERIC SOUP

Preparation Time: 50 minutes   Servings: 6

Ingredients:

- ✓ 1 bay leaf
- ✓ Salt to taste
- ✓ 1 tsp ground cayenne pepper
- ✓ 1 (15.5-oz) can white beans, drained
- ✓ ⅓ cup whole-wheat pasta
- ✓ ¼ tsp turmeric

- ✓ 3 tbsp olive oil
- ✓ 1 onion, chopped
- ✓ 2 carrots, chopped
- ✓ 1 sweet potato, chopped
- ✓ 1 yellow bell pepper, chopped
- ✓ 2 garlic cloves, minced
- ✓ 4 tomatoes, chopped
- ✓ 6 cups vegetable broth

Directions:

- ❖ Heat the oil in a pot over medium heat. Place onion, carrots, sweet potato, bell pepper, and garlic. Cook for 5 minutes. Add in tomatoes, broth, bay leaf, salt, and cayenne pepper. Stir and bring to a boil. Lower the heat and simmer for 10 minutes. Put in white beans and simmer for 15 more minutes.
- ❖ Cook the pasta in a pot with boiling salted water and turmeric for 8-10 minutes, until pasta is al dente. Strain and transfer to the soup. Discard the bay leaf. Spoon into a bowl and serve

141)   COCONUT ARUGULA SOUP

Preparation Time: 30 minutes   Servings: 4

Ingredients:

- ✓ 1 tbsp fresh mint, chopped
- ✓ Sea salt and black pepper to taste
- ✓ ¾ cup coconut milk

- ✓ 1 tsp coconut oil
- ✓ 1 onion, diced
- ✓ 2 cups green beans
- ✓ 4 cups water
- ✓ 1 cup arugula, chopped

Directions:

- ❖ Place a pot over medium heat and heat the coconut oil. Add in the onion and sauté for 5 minutes. Pour in green beans and water. Bring to a boil, lower the heat and stir in arugula, mint, salt, and pepper. Simmer for 10 minutes. Stir in coconut milk. Transfer to a food processor and blitz the soup until smooth. Serve

142)   ORIGINAL LENTIL SOUP WITH SWISS CHARD

Preparation Time: 25 minutes   Servings: 5

Ingredients:

- ✓ 1/2 tsp dried thyme
- ✓ 1/4 tsp ground cumin
- ✓ 5 cups roasted vegetable broth
- ✓ 1 ¼ cups brown lentils, soaked overnight and rinsed
- ✓ 2 cups Swiss chard, torn into pieces

- ✓ 2 tbsp olive oil
- ✓ 1 white onion, chopped
- ✓ 1 tsp garlic, minced
- ✓ 2 large carrots, chopped
- ✓ 1 parsnip, chopped
- ✓ 2 stalks celery, chopped
- ✓ 2 bay leaves

Directions:

- ❖ In a heavy-bottomed pot, heat the olive oil over a moderate heat. Now, sauté the vegetables along with the spices for about 3 minutes until they are just tender.
- ❖ Add in the vegetable broth and lentils, bringing it to a boil. Immediately turn the heat to a simmer and add in the bay leaves. Let it cook for about 15 minutes or until lentils are tender.
- ❖ Add in the Swiss chard, cover and let it simmer for 5 minutes more or until the chard wilts.
- ❖ Serve in individual bowls and enjoy

143) WINTER SPICY FARRO SOUP

Preparation Time: 30 minutes

Servings: 4

Ingredients:

- ✓ 2 tbsp olive oil
- ✓ 1 medium-sized leek, chopped
- ✓ 1 medium-sized turnip, sliced
- ✓ 2 Italian peppers, seeded and chopped
- ✓ 1 jalapeno pepper, minced
- ✓ 2 potatoes, peeled and diced
- ✓ 4 cups vegetable broth
- ✓ 1 cup farro, rinsed
- ✓ 1/2 tsp granulated garlic
- ✓ 1/2 tsp turmeric powder
- ✓ 1 bay laurel
- ✓ 2 cups spinach, turn into pieces

Directions:

- ❖ In a heavy-bottomed pot, heat the olive oil over a moderate heat. Now, sauté the leek, turnip, peppers and potatoes for about 5 minutes until they are crisp-tender.
- ❖ Add in the vegetable broth, farro, granulated garlic, turmeric and bay laurel; bring it to a boil.
- ❖ Immediately turn the heat to a simmer. Let it cook for about 25 minutes or until farro and potatoes have softened.
- ❖ Add in the spinach and remove the pot from the heat; let the spinach sit in the residual heat until it wilts. Enjoy

144) COLORED CHICKPEA SALAD

Preparation Time: 30 minutes

Servings: 4

Ingredients:

- ✓ 16 ounces canned chickpeas, drained
- ✓ 1 medium avocado, sliced
- ✓ 1 bell pepper, seeded and sliced
- ✓ 1 large tomato, sliced
- ✓ 2 cucumber, diced
- ✓ 1 red onion, sliced
- ✓ 1/2 tsp garlic, minced
- ✓ 1/4 cup fresh parsley, chopped
- ✓ 1/4 cup olive oil
- ✓ 2 tbsp apple cider vinegar
- ✓ 1/2 lime, freshly squeezed
- ✓ Sea salt and ground black pepper, to taste

Directions:

- ❖ Toss all the ingredients in a salad bowl.
- ❖ Place the salad in your refrigerator for about 1 hour before serving.
- ❖ Enjoy

145) MEDITERRANEAN LENTIL SALAD

Preparation Time: 20 minutes + chilling time

Servings: 5

Ingredients:

- ✓ 1 ½ cups red lentil, rinsed
- ✓ 1 tsp deli mustard
- ✓ 1/2 lemon, freshly squeezed
- ✓ 2 tbsp tamari sauce
- ✓ 2 scallion stalks, chopped
- ✓ 1/4 cup extra-virgin olive oil
- ✓ 2 garlic cloves, minced
- ✓ 1 cup butterhead lettuce, torn into pieces
- ✓ 2 tbsp fresh parsley, chopped
- ✓ 2 tbsp fresh cilantro, chopped
- ✓ 1 tsp fresh basil
- ✓ 1 tsp fresh oregano
- ✓ 1 ½ cups cherry tomatoes, halved
- ✓ 3 ounces Kalamata olives, pitted and halved

Directions:

- ❖ In a large-sized saucepan, bring 4 ½ cups of the water and the red lentils to a boil.
- ❖ Immediately turn the heat to a simmer and continue to cook your lentils for about 15 minutes or until tender. Drain and let it cool completely.
- ❖ Transfer the lentils to a salad bowl; toss the lentils with the remaining ingredients until well combined.
- ❖ Serve chilled or at room temperature. Enjoy

146) ROASTED AVOCADO AND ASPARAGUS SALAD

Preparation Time: 20 minutes + chilling time

Servings: 4

Ingredients:

- ✓ 1 pound asparagus, trimmed, cut into bite-sized pieces
- ✓ 1 white onion, chopped
- ✓ 2 garlic cloves, minced
- ✓ 1 Roma tomato, sliced
- ✓ 1/4 cup olive oil
- ✓ 1/4 cup balsamic vinegar
- ✓ 1 tbsp stone-ground mustard
- ✓ 2 tbsp fresh parsley, chopped
- ✓ 1 tbsp fresh cilantro, chopped
- ✓ 1 tbsp fresh basil, chopped
- ✓ Sea salt and ground black pepper, to taste
- ✓ 1 small avocado, pitted and diced
- ✓ 1/2 cup pine nuts, roughly chopped

Directions:

- ❖ Begin by preheating your oven to 420 degrees F.
- ❖ Toss the asparagus with 1 tbsp of the olive oil and arrange them on a parchment-lined roasting pan.
- ❖ Bake for about 15 minutes, rotating the pan once or twice to promote even cooking. Let it cool completely and place in your salad bowl.
- ❖ Toss the asparagus with the vegetables, olive oil, vinegar, mustard and herbs. Salt and pepper to taste.
- ❖ Toss to combine and top with avocado and pine nuts. Enjoy

147) GREEN BEAN CREAM SALAD WITH PINE NUTS

Preparation Time: 10 minutes + chilling time

Servings: 5

Ingredients:

- ✓ 1 ½ pounds green beans, trimmed
- ✓ 2 medium tomatoes, diced
- ✓ 2 bell peppers, seeded and diced
- ✓ 4 tbsp shallots, chopped
- ✓ 1/2 cup pine nuts, roughly chopped
- ✓ 1/2 cup vegan mayonnaise
- ✓ 1 tbsp deli mustard
- ✓ 2 tbsp fresh basil, chopped
- ✓ 2 tbsp fresh parsley, chopped
- ✓ 1/2 tsp red pepper flakes, crushed
- ✓ Sea salt and freshly ground black pepper, to taste

Directions:

- ❖ Boil the green beans in a large saucepan of salted water until they are just tender or about 2 minutes.
- ❖ Drain and let the beans cool completely; then, transfer them to a salad bowl. Toss the beans with the remaining ingredients.
- ❖ Taste and adjust the seasonings. Enjoy

148) KALE CANNELLINI BEAN SOUP

Preparation Time: 25 minutes

Servings: 5

Ingredients:

- ✓ 1 tbsp olive oil
- ✓ 1/2 tsp ginger, minced
- ✓ 1/2 tsp cumin seeds
- ✓ 1 red onion, chopped
- ✓ 1 carrot, trimmed and chopped
- ✓ 1 parsnip, trimmed and chopped
- ✓ 2 garlic cloves, minced
- ✓ 5 cups vegetable broth
- ✓ 12 ounces Cannellini beans, drained
- ✓ 2 cups kale, torn into pieces
- ✓ Sea salt and ground black pepper, to taste

Directions:

- ❖ In a heavy-bottomed pot, heat the olive over medium-high heat. Now, sauté the ginger and cumin for 1 minute or so.
- ❖ Now, add in the onion, carrot and parsnip; continue sautéing an additional 3 minutes or until the vegetables are just tender.
- ❖ Add in the garlic and continue to sauté for 1 minute or until aromatic.
- ❖ Then, pour in the vegetable broth and bring to a boil. Immediately reduce the heat to a simmer and let it cook for 10 minutes.
- ❖ Fold in the Cannellini beans and kale; continue to simmer until the kale wilts and everything is thoroughly heated. Season with salt and pepper to taste.
- ❖ Ladle into individual bowls and serve hot. Enjoy

149) MUSHROOM SOUP WITH HEARTY CREAM

Preparation Time: 15 minutes

Servings: 5

Ingredients:

- ✓ 2 tbsp soy butter
- ✓ 1 large shallot, chopped
- ✓ 20 ounces Cremini mushrooms, sliced
- ✓ 2 cloves garlic, minced
- ✓ 4 tbsp flaxseed meal
- ✓ 5 cups vegetable broth
- ✓ 1 1/3 cups full-fat coconut milk
- ✓ 1 bay leaf
- ✓ Sea salt and ground black pepper, to taste

Directions:

- ❖ In a stockpot, melt the vegan butter over medium-high heat. Once hot, cook the shallot for about 3 minutes until tender and fragrant.
- ❖ Add in the mushrooms and garlic and continue cooking until the mushrooms have softened. Add in the flaxseed meal and continue to cook for 1 minute or so.
- ❖ Add in the remaining ingredients. Let it simmer, covered and continue to cook for 5 to 6 minutes more until your soup has thickened slightly.
- ❖ Enjoy

150) ITALIAN AUTHENTIC PANZANELLA SALAD

Preparation Time: 35 minutes

Servings: 3

Ingredients:

- ✓ 3 cups artisan bread, broken into 1-inch cubes
- ✓ 3/4-pound asparagus, trimmed and cut into bite-sized pieces
- ✓ 4 tbsp extra-virgin olive oil
- ✓ 1 red onion, chopped
- ✓ 1 tsp deli mustard
- ✓ 2 medium heirloom tomatoes, diced
- ✓ 2 cups arugula
- ✓ 2 cups baby spinach
- ✓ 2 Italian peppers, seeded and sliced
- ✓ Sea salt and ground black pepper, to taste
- ✓ 2 tbsp fresh lime juice

Directions:

- ❖ Arrange the bread cubes on a parchment-lined baking sheet. Bake in the preheated oven at 310 degrees F for about 20 minutes, rotating the baking sheet twice during the baking time; reserve.
- ❖ Turn the oven to 420 degrees F and toss the asparagus with 1 tbsp of olive oil. Roast the asparagus for about 15 minutes or until crisp-tender.
- ❖ Toss the remaining ingredients in a salad bowl; top with the roasted asparagus and toasted bread.
- ❖ Enjoy

VEGETABLES AND SIDE DISHES

151)   SWEET MASHED CARROTS

Preparation Time: 25 minutes

Servings: 4

Ingredients:

- ✓ 1 ½ pounds carrots, trimmed
- ✓ 3 tbsp vegan butter
- ✓ 1 cup scallions, sliced
- ✓ 1 tbsp maple syrup
- ✓ 1/2 tsp garlic powder
- ✓ 1/2 tsp ground allspice
- ✓ Sea salt, to taste
- ✓ 1/2 cup soy sauce
- ✓ 2 tbsp fresh cilantro, chopped

Directions:

- ❖ Steam the carrots for about 15 minutes until they are very tender; drain well.
- ❖ In a sauté pan, melt the butter until sizzling. Now, turn the heat down to maintain an insistent sizzle.
- ❖ Now, cook the scallions until they've softened. Add in the maple syrup, garlic powder, ground allspice, salt and soy sauce for about 10 minutes or until they are caramelized.
- ❖ Add the caramelized scallions to your food processor; add in the carrots and puree the ingredients until everything is well blended.
- ❖ Serve garnished with the fresh cilantro. Enjoy

152)   SAUTÉED TURNIP GREENS

Preparation Time: 15 minutes

Servings: 4

Ingredients:

- ✓ 2 tbsp olive oil
- ✓ 1 onion, sliced
- ✓ 2 garlic cloves, sliced
- ✓ 1 ½ pounds turnip greens cleaned and chopped
- ✓ 1/4 cup vegetable broth
- ✓ 1/4 cup dry white wine
- ✓ 1/2 tsp dried oregano
- ✓ 1 tsp dried parsley flakes
- ✓ Kosher salt and ground black pepper, to taste

Directions:

- ❖ In a sauté pan, heat the olive oil over a moderately high heat.
- ❖ Now, sauté the onion for 3 to 4 minutes or until tender and translucent. Add in the garlic and continue to cook for 30 seconds more or until aromatic.
- ❖ Stir in the turnip greens, broth, wine, oregano and parsley; continue sautéing an additional 6 minutes or until they have wilted completely.
- ❖ Season with salt and black pepper to taste and serve warm. Enjoy

153)   YUKON GOLD MASHED POTATOES

Preparation Time: 25 minutes

Servings: 5

Ingredients:

- ✓ 2 pounds Yukon Gold potatoes, peeled and diced
- ✓ 1 clove garlic, pressed
- ✓ Sea salt and red pepper flakes, to taste
- ✓ 3 tbsp vegan butter
- ✓ 1/2 cup soy milk
- ✓ 2 tbsp scallions, sliced

Directions:

- ❖ Cover the potatoes with an inch or two of cold water. Cook the potatoes in gently boiling water for about 20 minutes.
- ❖ Then, puree the potatoes, along with the garlic, salt, red pepper, butter and milk, to your desired consistency.
- ❖ Serve garnished with fresh scallions. Enjoy

154)   AROMATIC SAUTÉED SWISS CHARD

Preparation Time: 15 minutes

Servings: 4

Ingredients:

- ✓ 2 tbsp vegan butter
- ✓ 1 onion, chopped
- ✓ 2 cloves garlic, sliced
- ✓ Sea salt and ground black pepper, to season
- ✓ 1 ½ pounds Swiss chard, torn into pieces, tough stalks removed
- ✓ 1 cup vegetable broth
- ✓ 1 bay leaf
- ✓ 1 thyme sprig
- ✓ 2 rosemary sprigs
- ✓ 1/2 tsp mustard seeds
- ✓ 1 tsp celery seeds

Directions:

- ❖ In a saucepan, melt the vegan butter over medium-high heat.
- ❖ Then, sauté the onion for about 3 minutes or until tender and translucent; sauté the garlic for about 1 minute until aromatic.
- ❖ Add in the remaining ingredients and turn the heat to a simmer; let it simmer, covered, for about 10 minutes or until everything is cooked through. Enjoy

155) CLASSIC SAUTÉED BELL PEPPERS

Preparation Time: 15 minutes

Servings: 2

Ingredients:

- ✓ 3 tbsp olive oil
- ✓ 4 bell peppers, seeded and slice into strips
- ✓ 2 cloves garlic, minced
- ✓ Salt and freshly ground black pepper, to taste
- ✓ 1 tsp cayenne pepper
- ✓ 4 tbsp dry white wine
- ✓ 2 tbsp fresh cilantro, roughly chopped

Directions:

- ❖ In a saucepan, heat the oil over medium-high heat.
- ❖ Once hot, sauté the peppers for about 4 minutes or until tender and fragrant. Then, sauté the garlic for about 1 minute until aromatic.
- ❖ Add in the salt, black pepper and cayenne pepper; continue to sauté, adding the wine, for about 6 minutes more until tender and cooked through.
- ❖ Taste and adjust the seasonings. Top with fresh cilantro and serve. Enjoy

156) MASHED ROOT VEGETABLES

Preparation Time: 25 minutes

Servings: 5

Ingredients:

- ✓ 1 pound russet potatoes, peeled and cut into chunks
- ✓ 1/2 pound parsnips, trimmed and diced
- ✓ 1/2 pound carrots, trimmed and diced
- ✓ 4 tbsp vegan butter
- ✓ 1 tsp dried oregano
- ✓ 1/2 tsp dried dill weed
- ✓ 1/2 tsp dried marjoram
- ✓ 1 tsp dried basil

Directions:

- ❖ Cover the vegetables with the water by 1 inch. Bring to a boil and cook for about 25 minutes until they've softened; drain.
- ❖ Mash the vegetables with the remaining ingredients, adding cooking liquid, as needed.
- ❖ Serve warm and enjoy

157) ROASTED BUTTERNUT SQUASH

Preparation Time: 25 minutes

Servings: 4

Ingredients:

- ✓ 4 tbsp olive oil
- ✓ 1/2 tsp ground cumin
- ✓ 1/2 tsp ground allspice
- ✓ 1 ½ pounds butternut squash, peeled, seeded and diced
- ✓ 1/4 cup dry white wine
- ✓ 2 tbsp dark soy sauce
- ✓ 1 tsp mustard seeds
- ✓ 1 tsp paprika
- ✓ Sea salt and ground black pepper, to taste

Directions:

- ❖ Start by preheating your oven to 420 degrees F. Toss the squash with the remaining ingredients.
- ❖ Roast the butternut squash for about 25 minutes or until tender and caramelized.
- ❖ Serve warm and enjoy

158) SAUTÉED CREMINI MUSHROOMS

Preparation Time: 10 minutes

Servings: 4

Ingredients:

- ✓ 4 tbsp olive oil
- ✓ 4 tbsp shallots, chopped
- ✓ 2 cloves garlic, minced
- ✓ 1 ½ pounds Cremini mushrooms, sliced
- ✓ 1/4 cup dry white wine
- ✓ Sea salt and ground black pepper, to taste

Directions:

- ❖ In a sauté pan, heat the olive oil over a moderately high heat.
- ❖ Now, sauté the shallot for 3 to 4 minutes or until tender and translucent. Add in the garlic and continue to cook for 30 seconds more or until aromatic.
- ❖ Stir in the Cremini mushrooms, wine, salt and black pepper; continue sautéing an additional 6 minutes, until your mushrooms are lightly browned.
- ❖ Enjoy

LUNCH

LUNCH

159) COUNTRY CORNBREAD WITH SPINACH

Preparation Time: 50 minutes

Servings: 8

Ingredients:

- ✓ 1 tbsp flaxseed meal
- ✓ 1 cup all-purpose flour
- ✓ 1 cup yellow cornmeal
- ✓ 1/2 tsp baking soda
- ✓ 1/2 tsp baking powder
- ✓ 1 tsp kosher salt
- ✓ 1 tsp brown sugar

- ✓ A pinch of grated nutmeg
- ✓ 1 ¼ cups oat milk, unsweetened
- ✓ 1 tsp white vinegar
- ✓ 1/2 cup olive oil
- ✓ 2 cups spinach, torn into pieces

Directions:

- ❖ Start by preheating your oven to 420 degrees F. Now, spritz a baking pan with a nonstick cooking spray.
- ❖ To make the flax eggs, mix flaxseed meal with 3 tbsp of the water. Stir and let it sit for about 15 minutes.
- ❖ In a mixing bowl, thoroughly combine the flour, cornmeal, baking soda, baking powder, salt, sugar and grated nutmeg.
- ❖ Gradually add in the flax egg, oat milk, vinegar and olive oil, whisking constantly to avoid lumps. Afterwards, fold in the spinach.
- ❖ Scrape the batter into the prepared baking pan. Bake your cornbread for about 25 minutes or until a tester inserted in the middle comes out dry and clean.
- ❖ Let it stand for about 10 minutes before slicing and serving. Enjoy

160) RICE PUDDING WITH CURRANTS

Preparation Time: 45 minutes

Servings: 4

Ingredients:

- ✓ 1 ½ cups water
- ✓ 1 cup white rice
- ✓ 2 ½ cups oat milk, divided
- ✓ 1/2 cup white sugar

- ✓ A pinch of salt
- ✓ A pinch of grated nutmeg
- ✓ 1 tsp ground cinnamon
- ✓ 1/2 tsp vanilla extract
- ✓ 1/2 cup dried currants

Directions:

- ❖ In a saucepan, bring the water to a boil over medium-high heat. Immediately turn the heat to a simmer, add in the rice and let it cook for about 20 minutes.
- ❖ Add in the milk, sugar and spices and continue to cook for 20 minutes more, stirring constantly to prevent the rice from sticking to the pan.
- ❖ Top with dried currants and serve at room temperature. Enjoy

161) MILLET PORRIDGE WITH SULTANAS

Preparation Time: 25 minutes

Servings: 3

Ingredients:

- ✓ 1 cup water
- ✓ 1 cup coconut milk
- ✓ 1 cup millet, rinsed
- ✓ 1/4 tsp grated nutmeg
- ✓ 1⁄4 tsp ground cinnamon

- ✓ 1 tsp vanilla paste
- ✓ 1/4 tsp kosher salt
- ✓ 2 tbsp agave syrup
- ✓ 4 tbsp sultana raisins

Directions:

- ❖ Place the water, milk, millet, nutmeg, cinnamon, vanilla and salt in a saucepan; bring to a boil.
- ❖ Turn the heat to a simmer and let it cook for about 20 minutes; fluff the millet with a fork and spoon into individual bowls.
- ❖ Serve with agave syrup and sultanas. Enjoy

162) QUINOA PORRIDGE WITH DRIED FIGS

Preparation Time: 25 minutes

Servings: 3

Ingredients:

- ✓ 1 cup white quinoa, rinsed
- ✓ 2 cups almond milk
- ✓ 4 tbsp brown sugar
- ✓ A pinch of salt
- ✓ 1/4 tsp grated nutmeg

- ✓ 1/2 tsp ground cinnamon
- ✓ 1/2 tsp vanilla extract
- ✓ 1/2 cup dried figs, chopped

Directions:

- ❖ Place the quinoa, almond milk, sugar, salt, nutmeg, cinnamon and vanilla extract in a saucepan.
- ❖ Bring it to a boil over medium-high heat. Turn the heat to a simmer and let it cook for about 20 minutes; fluff with a fork.
- ❖ Divide between three serving bowls and garnish with dried figs. Enjoy

163)   BREAD PUDDING WITH RAISINS

Preparation Time: 1 hour

Servings: 4

Ingredients:

- ✓ 4 cups day-old bread, cubed
- ✓ 1 cup brown sugar
- ✓ 4 cups coconut milk
- ✓ 1/2 tsp vanilla extract
- ✓ 1 tsp ground cinnamon
- ✓ 2 tbsp rum
- ✓ 1/2 cup raisins

Directions:

- ❖ Start by preheating your oven to 360 degrees F. Lightly oil a casserole dish with a nonstick cooking spray.
- ❖ Place the cubed bread in the prepared casserole dish.
- ❖ In a mixing bowl, thoroughly combine the sugar, milk, vanilla, cinnamon, rum and raisins. Pour the custard evenly over the bread cubes.
- ❖ Let it soak for about 15 minutes.
- ❖ Bake in the preheated oven for about 45 minutes or until the top is golden and set. Enjoy

164)   BULGUR WHEAT SALAD

Preparation Time: 25 minutes

Servings: 4

Ingredients:

- ✓ 1 cup bulgur wheat
- ✓ 1 ½ cups vegetable broth
- ✓ 1 tsp sea salt
- ✓ 1 tsp fresh ginger, minced
- ✓ 4 tbsp olive oil
- ✓ 1 onion, chopped
- ✓ 8 ounces canned garbanzo beans, drained
- ✓ 2 large roasted peppers, sliced
- ✓ 2 tbsp fresh parsley, roughly chopped

Directions:

- ❖ In a deep saucepan, bring the bulgur wheat and vegetable broth to a simmer; let it cook, covered, for 12 to 13 minutes.
- ❖ Let it stand for about 10 minutes and fluff with a fork.
- ❖ Add the remaining ingredients to the cooked bulgur wheat; serve at room temperature or well-chilled. Enjoy

165)   RYE PORRIDGE WITH BLUEBERRY TOPPING

Preparation Time: 15 minutes

Servings: 3

Ingredients:

- ✓ 1 cup rye flakes
- ✓ 1 cup water
- ✓ 1 cup coconut milk
- ✓ 1 cup fresh blueberries
- ✓ 1 tbsp coconut oil
- ✓ 6 dates, pitted

Directions:

- ❖ Add the rye flakes, water and coconut milk to a deep saucepan; bring to a boil over medium-high. Turn the heat to a simmer and let it cook for 5 to 6 minutes.
- ❖ In a blender or food processor, puree the blueberries with the coconut oil and dates.
- ❖ Ladle into three bowls and garnish with the blueberry topping.
- ❖ Enjoy

166)   COCONUT SORGHUM PORRIDGE

Preparation Time: 15 minutes

Servings: 2

Ingredients:

- ✓ 1/2 cup sorghum
- ✓ 1 cup water
- ✓ 1/2 cup coconut milk
- ✓ 1/4 tsp grated nutmeg
- ✓ 1/4 tsp ground cloves
- ✓ 1/2 tsp ground cinnamon
- ✓ Kosher salt, to taste
- ✓ 2 tbsp agave syrup
- ✓ 2 tbsp coconut flakes

Directions:

- ❖ Place the sorghum, water, milk, nutmeg, cloves, cinnamon and kosher salt in a saucepan; simmer gently for about 15 minutes.
- ❖ Spoon the porridge into serving bowls. Top with agave syrup and coconut flakes. Enjoy

167) MUM'S AROMATIC RICE

Preparation Time: 20 minutes

Servings: 4

Ingredients:

- ✓ 3 tbsp olive oil
- ✓ 1 tsp garlic, minced
- ✓ 1 tsp dried oregano
- ✓ 1 tsp dried rosemary
- ✓ 1 bay leaf
- ✓ 1 ½ cups white rice
- ✓ 2 ½ cups vegetable broth
- ✓ Sea salt and cayenne pepper, to taste

Directions:

- ❖ In a saucepan, heat the olive oil over a moderately high flame. Add in the garlic, oregano, rosemary and bay leaf; sauté for about 1 minute or until aromatic.
- ❖ Add in the rice and broth. Bring to a boil; immediately turn the heat to a gentle simmer.
- ❖ Cook for about 15 minutes or until all the liquid has absorbed. Fluff the rice with a fork, season with salt and pepper and serve immediately.
- ❖ Enjoy

168) EVERYDAY SAVORY GRITS

Preparation Time: 35 minutes

Servings: 4

Ingredients:

- ✓ 2 tbsp vegan butter
- ✓ 1 sweet onion, chopped
- ✓ 1 tsp garlic, minced
- ✓ 4 cups water
- ✓ 1 cup stone-ground grits
- ✓ Sea salt and cayenne pepper, to taste

Directions:

- ❖ In a saucepan, melt the vegan butter over medium-high heat. Once hot, cook the onion for about 3 minutes or until tender.
- ❖ Add in the garlic and continue to sauté for 30 seconds more or until aromatic; reserve.
- ❖ Bring the water to a boil over a moderately high heat. Stir in the grits, salt and pepper. Turn the heat to a simmer, cover and continue to cook, for about 30 minutes or until cooked through.
- ❖ Stir in the sautéed mixture and serve warm. Enjoy

169) GREEK-STYLE BARLEY SALAD

Preparation Time: 35 minutes

Servings: 4

Ingredients:

- ✓ 1 cup pearl barley
- ✓ 2 ¾ cups vegetable broth
- ✓ 2 tbsp apple cider vinegar
- ✓ 4 tbsp extra-virgin olive oil
- ✓ 2 bell peppers, seeded and diced
- ✓ 1 shallot, chopped
- ✓ 2 ounces sun-dried tomatoes in oil, chopped
- ✓ 1/2 green olives, pitted and sliced
- ✓ 2 tbsp fresh cilantro, roughly chopped

Directions:

- ❖ Bring the barley and broth to a boil over medium-high heat; now, turn the heat to a simmer.
- ❖ Continue to simmer for about 30 minutes until all the liquid has absorbed; fluff with a fork.
- ❖ Toss the barley with the vinegar, olive oil, peppers, shallots, sun-dried tomatoes and olives; toss to combine well.
- ❖ Garnish with fresh cilantro and serve at room temperature or well-chilled. Enjoy

170) SWEET MAIZE MEAL PORRIDGE

Preparation Time: 15 minutes

Servings: 2

Ingredients:

- ✓ 2 cups water
- ✓ 1/2 cup maize meal
- ✓ 1/4 tsp ground allspice
- ✓ 1/4 tsp salt
- ✓ 2 tbsp brown sugar
- ✓ 2 tbsp almond butter

Directions:

- ❖ In a saucepan, bring the water to a boil; then, gradually add in the maize meal and turn the heat to a simmer.
- ❖ Add in the ground allspice and salt. Let it cook for 10 minutes.
- ❖ Add in the brown sugar and almond butter and gently stir to combine. Enjoy

171)   DAD'S MILLET MUFFINS

Preparation Time: 20 minutes

Servings: 8

Ingredients:

- ✓ 2 cup whole-wheat flour
- ✓ 1/2 cup millet
- ✓ 2 tsp baking powder
- ✓ 1/2 tsp salt
- ✓ 1 cup coconut milk
- ✓ 1/2 cup coconut oil, melted
- ✓ 1/2 cup agave nectar
- ✓ 1/2 tsp ground cinnamon
- ✓ 1/4 tsp ground cloves
- ✓ A pinch of grated nutmeg
- ✓ 1/2 cup dried apricots, chopped

Directions:

- ❖ Begin by preheating your oven to 400 degrees F. Lightly oil a muffin tin with a nonstick oil.
- ❖ In a mixing bowl, mix all dry ingredients. In a separate bowl, mix the wet ingredients. Stir the milk mixture into the flour mixture; mix just until evenly moist and do not overmix your batter.
- ❖ Fold in the apricots and scrape the batter into the prepared muffin cups.
- ❖ Bake the muffins in the preheated oven for about 15 minutes, or until a tester inserted in the center of your muffin comes out dry and clean.
- ❖ Let it stand for 10 minutes on a wire rack before unmolding and serving. Enjoy

172)   GINGER BROWN RICE

Preparation Time: 30 minutes

Servings: 4

Ingredients:

- ✓ 1 ½ cups brown rice, rinsed
- ✓ 2 tbsp olive oil
- ✓ 1 tsp garlic, minced
- ✓ 1 (1-inch) piece ginger, peeled and minced
- ✓ 1/2 tsp cumin seeds
- ✓ Sea salt and ground black pepper, to taste

Directions:

- ❖ Place the brown rice in a saucepan and cover with cold water by 2 inches. Bring to a boil.
- ❖ Turn the heat to a simmer and continue to cook for about 30 minutes or until tender.
- ❖ In a sauté pan, heat the olive oil over medium-high heat. Once hot, cook the garlic, ginger and cumin seeds until aromatic.
- ❖ Stir the garlic/ginger mixture into the hot rice; season with salt and pepper and serve immediately

173)   CHILI BEAN AND BROWN RICE TORTILLAS

Preparation Time: 50 minutes

Servings: 4

Ingredients:

- ✓ 1 cups brown rice
- ✓ Salt and black pepper to taste
- ✓ 1 tbsp olive oil
- ✓ 1 medium red onion, chopped
- ✓ 1 green bell pepper, diced
- ✓ 2 garlic cloves, minced
- ✓ 1 tbsp chili powder
- ✓ 1 tsp cumin powder
- ✓ 1/8 tsp red chili flakes
- ✓ 1 (15 oz) can black beans, rinsed
- ✓ 4 whole-wheat flour tortillas, warmed
- ✓ 1 cup salsa
- ✓ 1 cup coconut cream for topping
- ✓ 1 cup grated plant-based cheddar

Directions:

- ❖ Add 2 cups of water and brown rice to a medium pot, season with some salt, and cook over medium heat until the water absorbs and the rice is tender, 15 to 20 minutes.
- ❖ Heat the olive oil in a medium skillet over medium heat and sauté the onion, bell pepper, and garlic until softened and fragrant, 3 minutes.
- ❖ Mix in the chili powder, cumin powder, red chili flakes, and season with salt and black pepper. Cook for 1 minute or until the food releases fragrance. Stir in the brown rice, black beans, and allow warming through, 3 minutes. Lay the tortillas on a clean, flat surface and divide the rice mixture in the center of each. Top with the salsa, coconut cream, and plant cheddar cheese. Fold the sides and ends of the tortillas over the filling to secure. Serve immediately

174) CASHEW BUTTERED QUESADILLAS WITH LEAFY GREENS

Preparation Time: 30 minutes

Servings: 4

Ingredients:

- ✓ 3 tbsp flax seed powder
- ✓ ½ cup cashew cream cheese
- ✓ 1 ½ tsp psyllium husk powder
- ✓ 1 tbsp coconut flour
- ✓ ½ tsp salt
- ✓ 1 tbsp cashew butter
- ✓ 5 oz grated plant-based cheddar
- ✓ 1 oz leafy greens

Directions:

- ❖ Preheat oven to 400 F.
- ❖ In a bowl, mix flax seed powder with ½ cup water and allow sitting to thicken for 5 minutes. Whisk cashew cream cheese into the vegan "flax egg" until the batter is smooth. In another bowl, combine psyllium husk powder, coconut flour, and salt. Add the flour mixture to the flax egg batter and fold in until incorporated. Allow sitting for a few minutes. Line a baking sheet with wax paper and pour in the mixture. Spread and bake for 5-7 minutes. Slice into 8 pieces. Set aside.
- ❖ For the filling, spoon a little cashew butter into a skillet and place a tortilla in the pan. Sprinkle with some plant-based cheddar cheese, leafy greens, and cover with another tortilla. Brown each side of the quesadilla for 1 minute or until the cheese melts. Transfer to a plate. Repeat assembling the quesadillas using the remaining cashew butter. Serve

175) ASPARAGUS WITH CREAMY PUREE

Preparation Time: 15 minutes

Servings: 4

Ingredients:

- ✓ 4 tbsp flax seed powder
- ✓ 2 oz plant butter, melted
- ✓ 3 oz cashew cream cheese
- ✓ ½ cup coconut cream
- ✓ Powdered chili pepper to taste
- ✓ 1 tbsp olive oil
- ✓ ½ lb asparagus, hard stalks removed
- ✓ 3 oz plant butter
- ✓ Juice of ½ a lemon

Directions:

- ❖ In a safe microwave bowl, mix the flax seed powder with ½ cup water and set aside to thicken for 5 minutes. Warm the vegan "flax egg" in the microwave for 1-2 minutes, then pour it into a blender. Add in plant butter, cashew cream cheese, coconut cream, salt, and chili pepper. Puree until smooth.
- ❖ Heat olive oil in a saucepan and roast the asparagus until lightly charred. Season with salt and black pepper and set aside. Melt plant butter in a frying pan until nutty and golden brown. Stir in lemon juice and pour the mixture into a sauce cup. Spoon the creamy blend into the center of four serving plates and use the back of the spoon to spread out lightly. Top with the asparagus and drizzle the lemon butter on top. Serve immediately

176) KALE MUSHROOM GALETTE

Preparation Time: 35 minutes

Servings: 4

Ingredients:

- ✓ 1 tbsp flax seed powder
- ✓ ½ cup grated plant-based mozzarella
- ✓ 1 tbsp plant butter
- ✓ ½ cup almond flour
- ✓ ¼ cup coconut flour
- ✓ ½ tsp onion powder
- ✓ 1 tsp baking powder
- ✓ 3 oz cashew cream cheese, softened
- ✓ 1 garlic clove, finely minced
- ✓ Salt and black pepper to taste
- ✓ 1 cup kale, chopped
- ✓ 2 oz cremini mushrooms, sliced
- ✓ 2 oz grated plant-based mozzarella
- ✓ 1 oz grated plant-based Parmesan
- ✓ Olive oil for brushing

Directions:

- ❖ Preheat oven to 375 F. Line a baking sheet with parchment paper and grease with cooking spray.
- ❖ In a bowl, mix flax seed powder with 3 tbsp water and allow sitting to thicken for 5 minutes. Place a pot over low heat, add in plant-based mozzarella and plant butter, and melt both whiles stirring continuously; remove. Stir in almond and coconut flours, onion powder, baking powder, and ¼ tsp salt. Pour in the vegan "flax egg" and combine until a quite sticky dough forms. Transfer dough to the baking sheet and cover with another parchment paper. Use a rolling pin to flatten into a 12-inch circle.
- ❖ After, remove the parchment paper and spread the cashew cream cheese on the dough, leaving about a 2-inch border around the edges. Sprinkle with garlic, salt, and black pepper. Spread kale on top of the cheese, followed by the mushrooms. Sprinkle the plant-based mozzarella and plant-based Parmesan cheese on top. Fold the ends of the crust over the filling and brush with olive oil. Bake until the cheese has melted and the crust golden brown, about 25-30 minutes. Slice and serve with arugula salad

DINNER

177)   POWERFUL TEFF BOWL WITH TAHINI SAUCE

Preparation Time: 20 minutes + chilling time   **Servings: 4**

Ingredients:

- ✓ 3 cups water
- ✓ 1 cup teff
- ✓ 2 garlic cloves, pressed
- ✓ 4 tbsp tahini
- ✓ 2 tbsp tamari sauce
- ✓ 2 tbsp white vinegar
- ✓ 1 tsp agave nectar

- ✓ 1 tsp deli mustard
- ✓ 1 tsp Italian herb mix
- ✓ 1 cup canned chickpeas, drained
- ✓ 2 cups mixed greens
- ✓ 1 cup grape tomatoes, halved
- ✓ 1 Italian peppers, seeded and diced

Directions:

- ❖ In a deep saucepan, bring the water to a boil over high heat. Add in the teff grain and turn the heat to a simmer.
- ❖ Continue to cook, covered, for about 20 minutes or until tender. Let it cool completely and transfer to a salad bowl.
- ❖ In the meantime, mix the garlic, tahini, tamari sauce, vinegar, agave nectar, mustard and Italian herb mix; whisk until everything is well incorporated.
- ❖ Add the canned chickpeas, mixed greens, tomatoes and peppers to the salad bowl; toss to combine. Dress the salad and toss again. Serve at room temperature. Enjoy

178)   POLENTA TOASTS WITH BALSAMIC ONIONS

Preparation Time: 25 minutes + chilling time   **Servings: 5**

Ingredients:

- ✓ 3 cups vegetable broth
- ✓ 1 cup yellow cornmeal
- ✓ 4 tbsp vegan butter, divided
- ✓ 2 tbsp olive oil

- ✓ 2 large onions, sliced
- ✓ Sea salt and ground black pepper, to taste
- ✓ 1 thyme sprig, chopped
- ✓ 1 tbsp balsamic vinegar

Directions:

- ❖ In a medium saucepan, bring the vegetable broth to a boil over medium-high heat. Now, add in the cornmeal, whisking continuously to prevent lumps.
- ❖ Reduce the heat to a simmer. Continue to simmer, whisking periodically, for about 18 minutes, until the mixture has thickened. Stir the vegan butter into the cooked polenta.
- ❖ Spoon the cooked polenta into a lightly greased square baking dish. Cover with the plastic wrap and chill for about 2 hours or until firm.
- ❖ Meanwhile, heat the olive oil in a nonstick skillet over a moderately high heat. Cook the onions for about 3 minutes or until just tender and fragrant.
- ❖ Stir in the salt, black pepper, thyme and balsamic vinegar and continue to sauté for 1 minute or so; remove from the heat.
- ❖ Cut your polenta into squares. Spritz a nonstick skillet with a cooking spray. Fry the polenta squares for about 5 minutes per side or until golden brown.
- ❖ Top each polenta toast with the balsamic onion and serve. Enjoy

179)   FREEKEH PILAF WITH CHICKPEAS

Preparation Time: 40 minutes   **Servings: 4**

Ingredients:

- ✓ 4 tbsp olive oil
- ✓ 1 cup shallots, chopped
- ✓ 1 celery stalks, chopped
- ✓ 1 carrot, chopped
- ✓ 1 tsp garlic, minced
- ✓ Sea salt and ground black pepper, to taste

- ✓ 1 tsp cayenne pepper
- ✓ 1 tsp dried basil
- ✓ 1 tsp dried oregano
- ✓ 1 cup freekeh
- ✓ 2 ½ cups water
- ✓ 1 cup boiled chickpeas, drained
- ✓ 2 tbsp roasted peanuts, roughly chopped
- ✓ 2 tbsp fresh mint, chopped

Directions:

- ❖ Heat the olive oil in a heavy-bottomed pot over medium-high heat. Once hot, sauté the shallot, celery and carrot for about 3 minutes until just tender.
- ❖ Then, add in the garlic and continue to sauté for 30 seconds more or until aromatic. Add in the spices, freekeh and water.
- ❖ Turn the heat to a simmer for 30 to 35 minutes, stirring occasionally to promote even cooking. Fold in the boiled chickpeas.
- ❖ To serve, spoon into individual bowls and garnish with roasted peanuts and fresh mint. Enjoy

180) GRANDMA'S PILAU WITH GARDEN VEGETABLES

Preparation Time: 45 minutes

Servings: 4

Ingredients:

- ✓ 2 tbsp olive oil
- ✓ 1 onion, chopped
- ✓ 1 carrot, trimmed and grated
- ✓ 1 parsnip, trimmed and grated
- ✓ 1 celery with leaves, chopped
- ✓ 1 tsp garlic, chopped
- ✓ 1 cup brown rice
- ✓ 2 cups vegetable broth
- ✓ 2 tbsp fresh parsley, chopped
- ✓ 2 tbsp finely basil, chopped

Directions:

- ❖ Heat the olive oil in a saucepan over medium-high heat.
- ❖ Once hot, cook the onion, carrot, parsnip and celery for about 3 minutes until just tender. Add in the garlic and continue to sauté for 1 minute or so until aromatic.
- ❖ In a lightly oiled casserole dish, place the rice, flowed by the sautéed vegetables and broth.
- ❖ Bake, covered, at 375 degrees F for about 40 minutes, stirring after 20 minutes.
- ❖ Garnish with fresh parsley and basil and serve warm. Enjoy

181) EASY BARLEY RISOTTO

Preparation Time: 35 minutes

Servings: 4

Ingredients:

- ✓ 2 tbsp vegan butter
- ✓ 1 medium onion, chopped
- ✓ 1 bell pepper, seeded and chopped
- ✓ 2 garlic cloves, minced
- ✓ 1 tsp ginger, minced
- ✓ 2 cups vegetable broth
- ✓ 2 cups water
- ✓ 1 cup medium pearl barley
- ✓ 1/2 cup white wine
- ✓ 2 tbsp fresh chives, chopped

Directions:

- ❖ Melt the vegan butter in a saucepan over medium-high heat.
- ❖ Once hot, cook the onion and pepper for about 3 minutes until just tender.
- ❖ Add in the garlic and ginger and continue to sauté for 2 minutes or until aromatic.
- ❖ Add in the vegetable broth, water, barley and wine; cover and continue to simmer for about 30 minutes. Once all the liquid has been absorbed; fluff the barley with a fork.
- ❖ Garnish with fresh chives and serve warm. Enjoy

182) TRADITIONAL PORTUGUESE PAPAS

Preparation Time: 35 minutes

Servings: 4

Ingredients:

- ✓ 4 cups water
- ✓ 2 cups rice milk
- ✓ 1 cup grits
- ✓ 1/4 tsp grated nutmeg
- ✓ 1/4 tsp kosher salt
- ✓ 4 tbsp vegan butter
- ✓ 1/4 cup maple syrup

Directions:

- ❖ Bring the water and milk to a boil over a moderately high heat.
- ❖ Stir in the grits, nutmeg and salt. Turn the heat to a simmer, cover and continue to cook, for about 30 minutes or until cooked through.
- ❖ Stir in the vegan butter and maple syrup. Enjoy

183) THE BEST MILLET PATTIES EVER

Preparation Time: 40 minutes

Servings: 4

Ingredients:

- ✓ 1 cup millet
- ✓ 3 cups water
- ✓ 2 tbsp olive oil
- ✓ 1 onion, finely chopped
- ✓ 2 cloves garlic, crushed
- ✓ 1 tsp smoked paprika
- ✓ 1/2 tsp ground cumin
- ✓ Sea salt and ground black pepper, to taste

Directions:

- ❖ Bring the millet and water to a boil; turn the heat to a simmer and continue to cook for 30 minutes.
- ❖ Fluff your millet with a fork and combine it with the remaining ingredients, except for the oil. Shape the mixture into patties.
- ❖ Heat the olive oil in a nonstick skillet over medium-high heat. Fry the patties for 5 minutes per side or until golden-brown and cooked through. Enjoy

184) ITALIAN RICE WITH BROCCOLI

Preparation Time: 30 minutes

Servings: 4

Ingredients:

- 2 tbsp olive oil
- 1 shallot, chopped
- 1 tsp ginger, minced
- 1 tsp garlic, minced
- 1/2 pound broccoli florets
- 1 cup Arborio rice
- 4 cups roasted vegetable broth

Directions:

- ❖ In a medium-sized pot, heat the olive oil over a moderately high flame. Add in the shallot and cook for about 3 minutes or until tender and translucent.
- ❖ Then, add in the ginger and garlic and continue to cook for 30 seconds more. Add in the broccoli and rice and continue to cook for 4 minutes more.
- ❖ Pour the vegetable broth into the saucepan and bring to a boil; immediately turn the heat to a gentle simmer.
- ❖ Cook for about 20 minutes or until all the liquid has absorbed. Taste and adjust the seasonings. Enjoy

185) OVERNIGHT OATMEAL WITH PRUNES

Preparation Time: 5 minutes + chilling time

Servings: 2

Ingredients:

- 1 cup hemp milk
- 1 tbsp flax seed, ground
- 2/3 cup rolled oats
- 2 ounces prunes, sliced
- 2 tbsp agave syrup
- A pinch of salt
- 1/2 tsp ground cinnamon

Directions:

- ❖ Divide the ingredients, except for the prunes, between two mason jars.
- ❖ Cover and shake to combine well. Let them sit overnight in your refrigerator.
- ❖ Garnish with sliced prunes just before serving. Enjoy

186) MINI CORNBREAD PUDDINGS

Preparation Time: 30 minutes

Servings: 8

Ingredients:

- 1 cup all-purpose flour
- 1 cup yellow cornmeal
- 1 tsp baking powder
- 1 tsp baking soda
- 1 tsp sea salt
- 2 tbsp brown sugar
- 1/2 tsp ground allspice
- 1 cup soy yogurt
- 1/4 cup vegan butter, melted
- 1 tsp apple cider vinegar
- 1 red bell pepper, seeded and chopped
- 1 green bell pepper, seeded and chopped
- 1 cup marinated mushrooms, chopped
- 2 small pickled cucumbers, chopped
- 1 tbsp fresh basil, chopped
- 1 tbsp fresh cilantro, chopped
- 1 tbsp fresh chives, chopped

Directions:

- ❖ Start by preheating your oven to 420 degrees F. Now, spritz a muffin tin with a non-stick cooking spray.
- ❖ In a mixing bowl, thoroughly combine the flour, cornmeal, baking soda, baking powder, salt, sugar and ground allspice.
- ❖ Gradually add in the yogurt, vegan butter and apple cider vinegar, whisking constantly to avoid lumps. Fold in the vegetables and herbs.
- ❖ Scrape the batter into the prepared muffin tin. Bake your muffins for about 25 minutes or until a toothpick inserted in the middle comes out dry and clean.
- ❖ Transfer them to a wire rack to rest for 5 minutes before unmolding and serving. Enjoy

187) SHERRY SHALLOT BEANS

Preparation Time: 25 minutes

Servings: 4

Ingredients:

- 2 tsp olive oil
- 4 shallots, chopped
- 1 tsp ground cumin
- 1 (14.5-oz) cans black beans
- 1 cup vegetable broth
- 2 tbsp sherry vinegar

Directions:

- ❖ Heat the oil in a pot over medium heat. Place in shallots and cumin and cook for 3 minutes until soft. Stir in beans and broth. Bring to a boil, then lower the heat and simmer for 10 minutes. Add in sherry vinegar, increase the heat and cook for an additional 3 minutes. Serve warm

188) CELERY BUCKWHEAT CROQUETTES

Preparation Time: 25 minute

Servings: 6

Ingredients:

- ✓ ¾ cup cooked buckwheat groats
- ✓ ½ cup cooked brown rice
- ✓ 3 tbsp olive oil
- ✓ ¼ cup minced onion
- ✓ 1 celery stalk, chopped
- ✓ ¼ cup shredded carrots
- ✓ 1/3 cup whole-wheat flour
- ✓ ¼ cup chopped fresh parsley
- ✓ Salt and black pepper to taste

Directions:

- ❖ Combine the groats and rice in a bowl. Set aside. Heat 1 tbsp of oil in a skillet over medium heat. Place in onion, celery, and carrot and cook for 5 minutes. Transfer to the rice bowl.
- ❖ Mix in flour, parsley, salt, and pepper. Place in the fridge for 20 minutes. Mold the mixture into cylinder-shaped balls. Heat the remaining oil in a skillet over medium heat. Fry the croquettes for 8 minutes, turning occasionally until golden

189) OREGANO CHICKPEAS

Preparation Time: 5 minutes

Servings: 6

Ingredients:

- ✓ 1 tsp olive oil
- ✓ 1 onion, cut into half-moon slices
- ✓ 2 (14.5-oz) cans chickpeas
- ✓ ½ cup vegetable broth
- ✓ 2 tsp dried oregano
- ✓ Salt and black pepper to taste

Directions:

- ❖ Heat the oil in a skillet over medium heat. Cook the onion for 3 minutes. Stir in chickpeas, broth, oregano, salt, and pepper. Bring to a boil, then lower the heat and simmer for 10 minutes. Serve

190) MATCHA-INFUSED TOFU RICE

Preparation Time: 35 minutes

Servings: 4

Ingredients:

- ✓ 4 matcha tea bags
- ✓ 1 ½ cups brown rice
- ✓ 2 tbsp canola oil
- ✓ 8 oz extra-firm tofu, chopped
- ✓ 3 green onions, minced
- ✓ 2 cups snow peas, cut diagonally
- ✓ 1 tbsp fresh lemon juice
- ✓ 1 tsp grated lemon zest
- ✓ Salt and black pepper to taste

Directions:

- ❖ Boil 3 cups water in a pot. Place in the tea bags and turn the heat off. Let sit for 7 minutes. Discard the bags. Wash the rice and put it into the tea. Cook for 20 minutes over medium heat. Drain and set aside.
- ❖ Heat the oil in a skillet over medium heat. Fry the tofu for 5 minutes until golden. Stir in green onions and snow peas and cook for another 3 minutes. Mix in lemon juice and lemon zest. Place the rice in a serving bowl and mix in the tofu mixture. Adjust the seasoning with salt and pepper. Serve right away

191) CHINESE FRIED RICE

Preparation Time: 20 minutes

Servings: 4

Ingredients:

- ✓ 2 tbsp canola oil
- ✓ 1 onion, chopped
- ✓ 1 large carrot, chopped
- ✓ 1 head broccoli, cut into florets
- ✓ 2 garlic cloves, minced
- ✓ 2 tsp grated fresh ginger
- ✓ 3 green onions, minced
- ✓ 3 ½ cups cooked brown rice
- ✓ 1 cup frozen peas, thawed
- ✓ 3 tbsp soy sauce
- ✓ 2 tsp dry white wine
- ✓ 1 tbsp toasted sesame oil

Directions:

- ❖ Heat the oil in a skillet over medium heat. Place in onion, carrot, and broccoli, sauté for 5 minutes until tender. Add in garlic, ginger, and green onions and sauté for another 3 minutes. Stir in rice, peas, soy sauce, and white wine and cook for 5 minutes. Add in sesame oil, toss to combine. Serve right away

192)   SAVORY SEITAN XAND BELL PEPPER RICE

Preparation Time: 35 minutes   Servings: 4

Ingredients:

- ✓ 2 cups water
- ✓ 1 cup long-grain brown rice
- ✓ 2 tbsp olive oil
- ✓ 1 onion, chopped
- ✓ 2 garlic cloves, minced
- ✓ 8 oz seitan, chopped
- ✓ 1 green bell pepper, chopped
- ✓ 1 tsp dried basil
- ✓ ½ tsp ground fennel seeds
- ✓ ¼ tsp crushed red pepper
- ✓ Salt and black pepper to taste

Directions:

- ❖ Bring water to a boil in a pot. Place in rice and lower the heat. Simmer for 20 minutes.
- ❖ Heat the oil in a skillet over medium heat. Sauté the onion for 3 minutes until translucent. Add in the seitan and bell pepper and cook for another 5 minutes. Stir in basil, fennel, red pepper, salt, and black pepper. Once the rice is ready, remove it to a bowl. Add in seitan mixture and toss to combine. Serve

193)   ASPARAGUS AND MUSHROOMS WITH MASHED POTATOES

Preparation Time: 60 minutes   Servings: 4

Ingredients:

- ✓ 5 large portobello mushrooms, stems removed
- ✓ 6 potatoes, chopped
- ✓ 4 garlic cloves, minced
- ✓ 2 tsp olive oil
- ✓ ½ cup non-dairy milk
- ✓ 2 tbsp nutritional yeast
- ✓ Sea salt to taste
- ✓ 7 cups asparagus, chopped
- ✓ 3 tsp coconut oil
- ✓ 2 tbsp nutritional yeast

Directions:

- ❖ Place the chopped potatoes in a pot and cover with salted water. Cook for 20 minutes.
- ❖ Heat oil in a skillet and sauté garlic for 1 minute. Once the potatoes are ready, drain them and reserve the water. Transfer to a bowl and mash them with some hot water, garlic, milk, yeast, and salt.
- ❖ Preheat your grill to medium. Grease the mushrooms with cooking spray and season with salt. Arrange the mushrooms face down and grill for 10 minutes. After, grill the asparagus for about 10 minutes, turning often. Arrange the veggies in a serving platter. Add in the potato mash and serve

194)   GREEN PEA AND LEMON COUSCOUS

Preparation Time: 15 minutes   Servings: 6

Ingredients:

- ✓ 1 cup green peas
- ✓ 2 ¾ cups vegetable stock
- ✓ Juice and zest of 1 lemon
- ✓ 2 tbsp chopped fresh thyme
- ✓ 1 ½ cups couscous
- ✓ ¼ cup chopped fresh parsley

Directions:

- ❖ Pour the vegetable stock, lemon juice, thyme, salt, and pepper in a pot. Bring to a boil, then add in green peas and couscous. Turn the heat off and let sit covered for 5 minutes, until the liquid has absorbed. Fluff the couscous using a fork and mix in the lemon and parsley. Serve immediately

195)   CHIMICHURRI FUSILI WITH NAVY BEANS

Preparation Time: 25 minutes   Servings: 4

Ingredients:

- ✓ 8 oz whole-wheat fusilli
- ✓ 1 ½ cups canned navy beans
- ✓ ½ cup chimichurri salsa
- ✓ 1 cup chopped tomatoes
- ✓ 1 red onion, chopped
- ✓ ½ cup chopped pitted black olives

Directions:

- ❖ n a large pot over medium heat, pour 8 cups of salted water. Bring to a boil and add in the pasta. Cook for 8-10 minutes, drain and let cool. Combine the pasta, beans, and chimichurri in a bowl. Toss to coat. Stir in tomato, red onion, and olives

196) QUINOA AND CHICKPEA POT

Preparation Time: 15 minutes

Servings: 2

Ingredients:

- ✓ 2 tsp olive oil
- ✓ 1 cup cooked quinoa
- ✓ 1 (15-oz) can chickpeas
- ✓ 1 bunch arugula chopped
- ✓ 1 tbsp soy
- ✓ Sea salt and black pepper to taste

Directions:

- ❖ Heat the oil in a skillet over medium heat. Stir in quinoa, chickpeas, and arugula and cook for 3-5 minutes until the arugula wilts. Pour in soy sauce, salt, and pepper. Toss to coat. Serve immediately

197) BUCKWHEAT PILAF WITH PINE NUTS

Preparation Time: 25 minutes

Servings: 4

Ingredients:

- ✓ 1 cup buckwheat groats
- ✓ 2 cups vegetable stock
- ✓ ¼ cup pine nuts
- ✓ 2 tbsp olive oil
- ✓ ½ onion, chopped
- ✓ ⅓ cup chopped fresh parsley

Directions:

- ❖ Put the groats and vegetable stock in a pot. Bring to a boil, then lower the heat and simmer for 15 minutes. Heat a skillet over medium heat. Place in the pine nuts and toast for 2-3 minutes, shaking often. Heat the oil in the same skillet and sauté the onion for 3 minutes until translucent.
- ❖ Once the groats are ready, fluff them using a fork. Mix in pine nuts, onion, and parsley. Sprinkle with salt and pepper. Serve

198)

199) ITALIAN HOLIDAY STUFFING

Preparation Time: 25 minutes

Servings: 4

Ingredients:

- ✓ ¼ cup plant butter
- ✓ 1 onion, chopped
- ✓ 2 celery stalks, sliced
- ✓ 1 cup button mushrooms, sliced
- ✓ 3 garlic cloves, minced
- ✓ ½ cup vegetable broth
- ✓ ½ cup raisins
- ✓ ½ cup chopped walnuts
- ✓ 2 cups cooked quinoa
- ✓ 1 tsp Italian seasoning
- ✓ Sea salt to taste
- ✓ Chopped fresh parsley

Directions:

- ❖ In a skillet over medium heat, melt the butter. Sauté the onion, garlic, celery, and mushrooms for 5 minutes until tender, stirring occasionally. Pour in broth, raisins, and walnuts. Bring to a boil, then lower the heat and simmer for 5 minutes. Stir in quinoa, Italian seasoning, and salt. Cook for another 4 minutes. Serve garnished with parsley

200) PRESSURE COOKER GREEN LENTILS

Preparation Time: 30 minutes

Servings: 6

Ingredients:

- ✓ 3 tbsp coconut oil
- ✓ 2 tbsp curry powder
- ✓ 1 tsp ground ginger
- ✓ 1 onion, chopped
- ✓ 2 garlic cloves, sliced
- ✓ 1 cup dried green lentils
- ✓ 3 cups water
- ✓ Salt and black pepper to taste

Directions:

- ❖ Set your IP to Sauté. Add in coconut oil, curry powder, ginger, onion, and garlic. Cook for 3 minutes. Stir in green lentils. Pour in water. Lock the lid and set the time to 10 minutes on High. Once ready, perform a natural pressure release for 10 minutes. Unlock the lid and season with salt and pepper. Serve

201) CURRY CAULI RICE WITH MUSHROOMS

Preparation Time: 15 minutes

Servings: 4

Ingredients:

- ✓ 8 oz baby Bella mushrooms, stemmed and sliced
- ✓ 2 large heads cauliflower
- ✓ 2 tbsp toasted sesame oil, divided
- ✓ 1 onion, chopped
- ✓ 3 garlic cloves, minced
- ✓ Salt and black pepper to taste
- ✓ ½ tsp curry powder
- ✓ 1 tsp freshly chopped parsley
- ✓ 2 scallions, thinly sliced

Directions:

- ❖ Use a knife to cut the entire cauliflower head into 6 pieces and transfer to a food processor. With the grater attachment, shred the cauliflower into a rice-like consistency.
- ❖ Heat half of the sesame oil in a large skillet over medium heat and then add the onion and mushrooms. Sauté for 5 minutes or until the mushrooms are soft.
- ❖ Add the garlic and sauté for 2 minutes or until fragrant. Pour in the cauliflower and cook until the rice has slightly softened, about 10 minutes.
- ❖ Season with salt, black pepper, and curry powder; then, mix the ingredients to be well combined. After, turn the heat off and stir in the parsley and scallions. Dish the cauli rice into serving plates and serve warm

202) MIXED SEED CRACKERS

Preparation Time: 57 minutes

Servings: 6

Ingredients:

- ✓ 1/3 cup sesame seed flour
- ✓ 1/3 cup pumpkin seeds
- ✓ 1/3 cup sunflower seeds
- ✓ 1/3 cup sesame seeds
- ✓ 1/3 cup chia seeds
- ✓ 1 tbsp psyllium husk powder
- ✓ 1 tsp salt
- ✓ ¼ cup plant butter, melted
- ✓ 1 cup boiling water

Directions:

- ❖ Preheat oven to 300 F.
- ❖ Combine the sesame seed flour with the pumpkin seeds, sunflower seeds, sesame seeds, chia seeds, psyllium husk powder, and salt. Pour in the plant butter and hot water and mix the ingredients until a dough forms with a gel-like consistency.
- ❖ Line a baking sheet with parchment paper and place the dough on the sheet. Cover the dough with another parchment paper and, with a rolling pin, flatten the dough into the baking sheet. Remove the parchment paper on top.
- ❖ Tuck the baking sheet in the oven and bake for 45 minutes. Allow the crackers to cool and dry in the oven, about 10 minutes. After, remove the sheet and break the crackers into small pieces. Serve

203) GRILLED TOFU MAYO SANDWICHES

Preparation Time: 15 minutes

Servings: 2

Ingredients:

- ✓ ¼ cup tofu mayonnaise
- ✓ 2 slices whole-grain bread
- ✓ ¼ cucumber, sliced
- ✓ ½ cup lettuce, chopped
- ✓ ½ tomato, sliced
- ✓ 1 tsp olive oil, divided

Directions:

- ❖ Spread the vegan mayonnaise over a bread slice, top with the cucumber, lettuce, and tomato, and finish with the other slice. Heat the oil in a skillet over medium heat. Place the sandwich and grill for 3 minutes, then flip over and cook for a further 3 minutes. Cut the sandwich in half and serve

204) MUSHROOM BROCCOLI FAUX RISOTTO

Preparation Time: 25 minutes

Servings: 4

Ingredients:

- ✓ 4 oz plant butter
- ✓ 1 cup cremini mushrooms, chopped
- ✓ 2 garlic cloves, minced
- ✓ 1 small red onion, finely chopped
- ✓ 1 large head broccoli, grated
- ✓ ¾ cup white wine
- ✓ 1 cup coconut whipping cream
- ✓ ¾ cup grated plant-based Parmesan
- ✓ Freshly chopped thyme

Directions:

- ❖ Place a pot over medium heat, add, and melt the plant butter. Sauté the mushrooms in the pot until golden, about 5 minutes. Add the garlic and onions and cook for 3 minutes or until fragrant and soft. Mix in the broccoli, 1 cup water, and half of the white wine. Season with salt and black pepper and simmer the ingredients (uncovered) for 8 to 10 minutes or until the broccoli is soft.
- ❖ Mix in the coconut whipping cream and simmer until most of the cream has evaporated. Turn the heat off and stir in the parmesan cheese and thyme until well incorporated. Dish the risotto and serve warm.

205) **BAKED SPICY EGGPLANT**

Preparation Time: 30 minutes

Servings: 4

Ingredients:

- ✓ 2 large eggplants
- ✓ Salt and black pepper to taste
- ✓ 2 tbsp plant butter
- ✓ 1 tsp red chili flakes
- ✓ 4 oz raw ground almonds

Directions:

- ❖ Preheat oven to 400 F.
- ❖ Cut off the head of the eggplants and slice the body into 2-inch rounds. Season with salt and black pepper and arrange on a parchment paper-lined baking sheet.
- ❖ Drop thin slices of the plant butter on each eggplant slice, sprinkle with red chili flakes, and bake in the oven for 20 minutes.
- ❖ Slide the baking sheet out and sprinkle with the almonds. Roast further for 5 minutes or until golden brown. Dish the eggplants and serve with arugula salad

206) **MASHED BROCCOLI WITH ROASTED GARLIC**

Preparation Time: 45 minutes

Servings: 4

Ingredients:

- ✓ ½ head garlic
- ✓ 2 tbsp olive oil + for garnish
- ✓ 1 head broccoli, cut into florets
- ✓ 1 tsp salt
- ✓ 4 oz plant butter
- ✓ ¼ tsp dried thyme
- ✓ Juice and zest of half a lemon
- ✓ 4 tbsp coconut cream

Directions:

- ❖ Preheat oven to 400 F.
- ❖ Use a knife to cut a ¼ inch off the top of the garlic cloves, drizzle with olive oil, and wrap in aluminum foil. Place on a baking sheet and roast for 30 minutes. Remove and set aside when ready.
- ❖ Pour the broccoli into a pot, add 3 cups of water, and 1 tsp of salt. Bring to a boil until tender, about 7 minutes. Drain and transfer the broccoli to a bowl. Add the plant butter, thyme, lemon juice and zest, coconut cream, and olive oil. Use an immersion blender to puree the ingredients until smooth and nice. Spoon the mash into serving bowls and garnish with some olive oil. Serve

207) **SPICY PISTACHIO DIP**

Preparation Time: 10 minutes

Servings: 4

Ingredients:

- ✓ 3 oz toasted pistachios + for garnish
- ✓ 3 tbsp coconut cream
- ✓ ¼ cup water
- ✓ Juice of half a lemon
- ✓ ½ tsp smoked paprika
- ✓ Cayenne pepper to taste
- ✓ ½ tsp salt
- ✓ ½ cup olive oil

Directions:

- ❖ Pour the pistachios, coconut cream, water, lemon juice, paprika, cayenne pepper, and salt. Puree the ingredients at high speed until smooth. Add the olive oil and puree a little further. Manage the consistency of the dip by adding more oil or water. Spoon the dip into little bowls, garnish with some pistachios, and serve with julienned celery and carrots

208) **PAPRIKA ROASTED NUTS**

Preparation Time: 10 minutes

Servings: 4

Ingredients:

- ✓ 8 oz walnuts and pecans
- ✓ 1 tsp salt
- ✓ 1 tbsp coconut oil
- ✓ 1 tsp cumin powder
- ✓ 1 tsp paprika powder

Directions:

- ❖ In a bowl, mix walnuts, pecans, salt, coconut oil, cumin powder, and paprika powder until the nuts are well coated with spice and oil. Pour the mixture into a pan and toast while stirring continually. Once the nuts are fragrant and brown, transfer to a bowl. Allow cooling and serve with a chilled berry juice

209) BAKED APPLES FILLED WITH NUTS

Preparation Time: 35 minutes + cooling time

Servings: 4

Ingredients:

- ✓ 4 gala apples
- ✓ 3 tbsp pure maple syrup
- ✓ 4 tbsp almond flour
- ✓ 6 tbsp pure date sugar
- ✓ 6 tbsp plant butter, cold and cubed
- ✓ 1 cup chopped mixed nuts

Directions:

- ❖ Preheat the oven the 400 F.
- ❖ Slice off the top of the apples and use a melon baller or spoon to scoop out the cores of the apples. In a bowl, mix the maple syrup, almond flour, date sugar, butter, and nuts. Spoon the mixture into the apples and then bake in the oven for 25 minutes or until the nuts are golden brown on top and the apples soft. Remove the apples from the oven, allow cooling, and serve

210) MINT ICE CREAM

Preparation Time: 10 minutes + chilling time

Servings: 4

Ingredients:

- ✓ 2 avocados, pitted
- ✓ 1 ¼ cups coconut cream
- ✓ ½ tsp vanilla extract
- ✓ 2 tbsp erythritol
- ✓ 2 tsp chopped mint leaves

Directions:

- ❖ Into a blender, spoon the avocado pulps, pour in the coconut cream, vanilla extract, erythritol, and mint leaves. Process until smooth. Pour the mixture into your ice cream maker and freeze according to the manufacturer's instructions. When ready, remove and scoop the ice cream into bowls. Serve

211) CARDAMOM COCONUT FAT BOMBS

Preparation Time: 10 minutes

Servings: 6

Ingredients:

- ✓ ½ cup grated coconut
- ✓ 3 oz plant butter, softened
- ✓ ¼ tsp green cardamom powder
- ✓ ½ tsp vanilla extract
- ✓ ¼ tsp cinnamon powder

Directions:

- ❖ Pour the grated coconut into a skillet and roast until lightly brown. Set aside to cool. In a bowl, combine butter, half of the coconut, cardamom, vanilla, and cinnamon. Form balls from the mixture and roll each one in the remaining coconut. Refrigerate until ready to serve

212) CINNAMON FAUX RICE PUDDING

Preparation Time: 25 minutes

Servings: 6

Ingredients:

- ✓ 1 ¼ cups coconut cream
- ✓ 1 tsp vanilla extract
- ✓ 1 tsp cinnamon powder
- ✓ 1 cup mashed tofu
- ✓ 2 oz fresh strawberries

Directions:

- ❖ Pour the coconut cream into a bowl and whisk until a soft peak forms. Mix in the vanilla and cinnamon. Lightly fold in the vegan cottage cheese and refrigerate for 10 to 15 minutes to set. Spoon into serving glasses, top with the strawberries and serve immediately

213) WHITE CHOCOLATE FUDGE

Preparation Time: 20 minutes + chilling time

Servings: 6

Ingredients:

- ✓ 2 cups coconut cream
- ✓ 1 tsp vanilla extract
- ✓ 3 oz plant butter
- ✓ 3 oz vegan white chocolate
- ✓ Swerve sugar for sprinkling

Directions:

- ❖ Pour coconut cream and vanilla into a saucepan and bring to a boil over medium heat, then simmer until reduced by half, 15 minutes. Stir in plant butter until the batter is smooth. Chop white chocolate into bits and stir in the cream until melted. Pour the mixture into a baking sheet; chill in the fridge for 3 hours. Cut into squares, sprinkle with swerve sugar, and serve

214) MACEDONIA SALAD WITH COCONUT AND PECANS

Preparation Time: 15 minutes + cooling time

Servings: 4

Ingredients:

- ✓ 1 cup pure coconut cream
- ✓ ½ tsp vanilla extract
- ✓ 2 bananas, cut into chunks
- ✓ 1 ½ cups coconut flakes
- ✓ 4 tbsp toasted pecans, chopped
- ✓ 1 cup pineapple tidbits, drained
- ✓ 1 (11-oz) can mandarin oranges
- ✓ ¾ cup maraschino cherries, stems removed

Directions:

- ❖ In a medium bowl, mix the coconut cream and vanilla extract until well combined.
- ❖ In a larger bowl, combine the bananas, coconut flakes, pecans, pineapple, oranges, and cherries until evenly distributed. Pour on the coconut cream mixture and fold well into the salad. Chill in the refrigerator for 1 hour and serve afterward

215) BERRY HAZELNUT TRIFLE

Preparation Time: 10 minutes

Servings: 4

Ingredients:

- ✓ 1 ½ ripe avocados
- ✓ ¾ cup coconut cream
- ✓ Zest and juice of ½ a lemon
- ✓ 1 tbsp vanilla extract
- ✓ 3 oz fresh strawberries
- ✓ 2 oz toasted hazelnuts

Directions:

- ❖ In a bowl, add avocado pulp, coconut cream, lemon zest and juice, and half of the vanilla extract. Mix with an immersion blender. Put the strawberries and remaining vanilla in another bowl and use a fork to mash the fruits. In a tall glass, alternate layering the cream and strawberry mixtures. Drop a few hazelnuts on each and serve the dessert immediately

216) AVOCADO TRUFFLES WITH CHOCOLATE COATING

Preparation Time: 5 minutes

Servings: 6

Ingredients:

- ✓ 1 ripe avocado, pitted
- ✓ ½ tsp vanilla extract
- ✓ ½ tsp lemon zest
- ✓ 5 oz dairy-free dark chocolate
- ✓ 1 tbsp coconut oil
- ✓ 1 tbsp unsweetened cocoa powder

Directions:

- ❖ Scoop the pulp of the avocado into a bowl and mix with the vanilla using an immersion blender. Stir in the lemon zest and a pinch of salt. Pour the chocolate and coconut oil into a safe microwave bowl and melt in the microwave for 1 minute. Add to the avocado mixture and stir. Allow cooling to firm up a bit. Form balls out of the mix. Roll each ball in the cocoa powder and serve immediately

217) VANILLA BERRY TARTS

Preparation Time: 35 minutes + cooling time

Servings: 4

Ingredients:

- ✓ 4 tbsp flaxseed powder
- ✓ 1/3 cup whole-wheat flour
- ✓ ½ tsp salt
- ✓ ¼ cup plant butter, crumbled
- ✓ 3 tbsp pure malt syrup
- ✓ 6 oz cashew cream
- ✓ 6 tbsp pure date sugar
- ✓ ¾ tsp vanilla extract
- ✓ 1 cup mixed frozen berries

Directions:

- ❖ Preheat oven to 350 F and grease mini pie pans with cooking spray. In a bowl, mix flaxseed powder with 12 tbsp water and allow soaking for 5 minutes. In a large bowl, combine flour and salt. Add in butter and whisk until crumbly. Pour in the vegan "flax egg" and malt syrup and mix until smooth dough forms. Flatten the dough on a flat surface, cover with plastic wrap, and refrigerate for 1 hour.
- ❖ Dust a working surface with some flour, remove the dough onto the surface, and using a rolling pin, flatten the dough into a 1-inch diameter circle. Use a large cookie cutter, cut out rounds of the dough and fit into the pie pans. Use a knife to trim the edges of the pan. Lay a parchment paper on the dough cups, pour on some baking beans, and bake in the oven until golden brown, 15-20 minutes. Remove the pans from the oven, pour out the baking beans, and allow cooling. In a bowl, mix cashew cream, date sugar, and vanilla extract. Divide the mixture into the tart cups and top with berries. Serve

218) HOMEMADE CHOCOLATES WITH COCONUT AND RAISINS

Preparation Time: 10 minutes + chilling time

Servings: 20

Ingredients:

- ✓ 1/2 cup cacao butter, melted
- ✓ 1/3 cup peanut butter
- ✓ 1/4 cup agave syrup
- ✓ A pinch of grated nutmeg
- ✓ A pinch of coarse salt
- ✓ 1/2 tsp vanilla extract
- ✓ 1 cup dried coconut, shredded
- ✓ 6 ounces dark chocolate, chopped
- ✓ 3 ounces raisins

Directions:

- ❖ Thoroughly combine all the ingredients, except for the chocolate, in a mixing bowl.
- ❖ Spoon the mixture into molds. Leave to set hard in a cool place.
- ❖ Melt the dark chocolate in your microwave. Pour in the melted chocolate until the fillings are covered. Leave to set hard in a cool place.
- ❖ Enjoy

219) MOCHA FUDGE

Preparation Time: 1 hour 10 minutes

Servings: 20

Ingredients:

- ✓ 1 cup cookies, crushed
- ✓ 1/2 cup almond butter
- ✓ 1/4 cup agave nectar
- ✓ 6 ounces dark chocolate, broken into chunks
- ✓ 1 tsp instant coffee
- ✓ A pinch of grated nutmeg
- ✓ A pinch of salt

Directions:

- ❖ Line a large baking sheet with parchment paper.
- ❖ Melt the chocolate in your microwave and add in the remaining ingredients; stir to combine well.
- ❖ Scrape the batter into a parchment-lined baking sheet. Place it in your freezer for at least 1 hour to set.
- ❖ Cut into squares and serve. Enjoy

220) ALMOND AND CHOCOLATE CHIP BARS

Preparation Time: 40 minutes

Servings: 10

Ingredients:

- ✓ 1/2 cup almond butter
- ✓ 1/4 cup coconut oil, melted
- ✓ 1/4 cup agave syrup
- ✓ 1 tsp vanilla extract
- ✓ 1/4 tsp sea salt
- ✓ 1/4 tsp grated nutmeg
- ✓ 1/2 tsp ground cinnamon
- ✓ 2 cups almond flour
- ✓ 1/4 cup flaxseed meal
- ✓ 1 cup vegan chocolate, cut into chunks
- ✓ 1 1/3 cups almonds, ground
- ✓ 2 tbsp cacao powder
- ✓ 1/4 cup agave syrup

Directions:

- ❖ In a mixing bowl, thoroughly combine the almond butter, coconut oil, 1/4 cup of agave syrup, vanilla, salt, nutmeg and cinnamon.
- ❖ Gradually stir in the almond flour and flaxseed meal and stir to combine. Add in the chocolate chunks and stir again.
- ❖ In a small mixing bowl, combine the almonds, cacao powder and agave syrup. Now, spread the ganache onto the cake. Freeze for about 30 minutes, cut into bars and serve well chilled. Enjoy

221) ALMOND BUTTER COOKIES

Preparation Time: 45 minutes

Servings: 10

Ingredients:

- ✓ 3/4 cup all-purpose flour
- ✓ 1/2 tsp baking soda
- ✓ 1/4 tsp kosher salt
- ✓ 1 flax egg
- ✓ 1/4 cup coconut oil, at room temperature
- ✓ 2 tbsp almond milk
- ✓ 1/2 cup brown sugar
- ✓ 1/2 cup almond butter
- ✓ 1/2 tsp ground cinnamon
- ✓ 1/2 tsp vanilla

Directions:

- ❖ In a mixing bowl, combine the flour, baking soda and salt.
- ❖ In another bowl, combine the flax egg, coconut oil, almond milk, sugar, almond butter, cinnamon and vanilla. Stir the wet mixture into the dry ingredients and stir until well combined.
- ❖ Place the batter in your refrigerator for about 30 minutes. Shape the batter into small cookies and arrange them on a parchment-lined cookie pan.
- ❖ Bake in the preheated oven at 350 degrees F for approximately 12 minutes. Transfer the pan to a wire rack to cool at room temperature. Enjoy

222)   PEANUT BUTTER OATMEAL BARS

Preparation Time: 25 minutes

Servings: 20

Ingredients:

- ✓ 1 cup vegan butter
- ✓ 3/4 cup coconut sugar
- ✓ 2 tbsp applesauce
- ✓ 1 ¾ cups old-fashioned oats
- ✓ 1 tsp baking soda
- ✓ A pinch of sea salt
- ✓ A pinch of grated nutmeg
- ✓ 1 tsp pure vanilla extract
- ✓ 1 cup oat flour
- ✓ 1 cup all-purpose flour

Directions:

- ❖ Begin by preheating your oven to 350 degrees F.
- ❖ In a mixing bowl, thoroughly combine the dry ingredients. In another bowl, combine the wet ingredients.
- ❖ Then, stir the wet mixture into the dry ingredients; mix to combine well.
- ❖ Spread the batter mixture in a parchment-lined square baking pan. Bake in the preheated oven for about 20 minutes. Enjoy

223)   VANILLA HALVAH FUDGE

Preparation Time: 10 minutes + chilling time

Servings: 16

Ingredients:

- ✓ 1/2 cup cocoa butter
- ✓ 1/2 cup tahini
- ✓ 8 dates, pitted
- ✓ 1/4 tsp ground cloves
- ✓ A pinch of grated nutmeg
- ✓ A pinch coarse salt
- ✓ 1 tsp vanilla extract

Directions:

- ❖ Line a square baking pan with parchment paper.
- ❖ Mix the ingredients until everything is well incorporated.
- ❖ Scrape the batter into the parchment-lined pan. Place in your freezer until ready to serve. Enjoy

224)   RAW CHOCOLATE MANGO PIE

Preparation Time: 10 minutes + chilling time

Servings: 16

Ingredients:

- ✓ Avocado layer:
- ✓ 3 ripe avocados, pitted and peeled
- ✓ A pinch of sea salt
- ✓ A pinch of ground anise
- ✓ 1/2 tsp vanilla paste
- ✓ 2 tbsp coconut milk
- ✓ 5 tbsp agave syrup
- ✓ 1/3 cup cocoa powder
- ✓ Crema layer:
- ✓ 1/3 cup almond butter
- ✓ 1/2 cup coconut cream
- ✓ 1 medium mango, peeled
- ✓ 1/2 coconut flakes
- ✓ 2 tbsp agave syrup

Directions:

- ❖ In your food processor, blend the avocado layer until smooth and uniform, reserve.
- ❖ Then, blend the other layer in a separate bowl. Spoon the layers in a lightly oiled baking pan.
- ❖ Transfer the cake to your freezer for about 3 hours. Store in your freezer. Enjoy

225)   CHOCOLATE N'ICE CREAM

Preparation Time: 10 minutes

Servings: 1

Ingredients:

- ✓ 2 frozen bananas, peeled and sliced
- ✓ 2 tbsp coconut milk
- ✓ 1 tsp carob powder
- ✓ 1 tsp cocoa powder
- ✓ A pinch of grated nutmeg
- ✓ 1/8 tsp ground cardamom
- ✓ 1/8 tsp ground cinnamon
- ✓ 1 tbsp chocolate curls

Directions:

- ❖ Place all the ingredients in the bowl of your food processor or high-speed blender.
- ❖ Blitz the ingredients until creamy or until your desired consistency is achieved.
- ❖ Serve immediately or store in your freezer.
- ❖ Enjoy

PART 3: INTRODUCTION TO THE PLANT-BASED DIET

Vegan athletes need to be aware of what they eat and how much they eat to absorb the necessary nutrition that supports muscle function, repair, endurance, strength, and motivation. These are qualities that professional athlete's treasure. Protein is at the top of the list of things to eat. You should also consider your caloric intake, macro and micro nutritional sources, and amino acids, some of which may need to be supplemented. Protein and carbohydrates average four calories per gram, while fat averages nine calories per gram. Following this, you can calculate how much of each type of nutrient to consume per day.

When planning a vegan diet, an athlete may need to consider their exercise routines, as those who work out may have high-impact days (like the dreaded "leg-day") and low-impact days where their body needs more nutrients geared toward repair work. Their eating plan will be based solely on their age, weight, activity level, food availability (vegetables and fruits tend to be seasonal), and personal taste for each athlete. It is certainly not necessary to eat buckets of beans to be vegan.

Converting to a vegetarian diet from an omnivorous diet can, surprisingly, be a vast mental shock; however, there are also some changes to your digestive system to consider. Vegans consume more dietary fiber than most omnivores, so your intestines may go through phases where you feel a bit bloated. You will need to consume more water. There are many suggested ratios, but the simplest is to work on a per calorie basis. A quick rule of 1 milliliter of water per calorie seems easy enough to follow. Keeping in mind that your food volume may increase, you may also need to eat a little earlier than an omnivore would before exercising. So, the usual rule of one hour of fasting before eating may need to be extended to 90 minutes of fasting before exercising.

Always consider adding variety to your vegan diet, as this increases your body's ability to consume all the vital amino acids, leading to better protein synthesis (which is essential for developing muscle tone and recovering from injuries). Plant-based meals are very satiating due to their high fiber content, but you need to consume more of them to meet your calorie needs. To avoid feeling too full, you can get extra carbs by eating nuts and seeds throughout the day as snacks.

Finally, when adding the finishing touches to your workout program, it's essential to intersperse your training sessions with enough time to ensure your muscles have time to rest and recover (where you rebuild your energy reserves, hydrate your body, and restore your metabolism's normal chemical balance). Short-term rest periods can be anything from taking a break for a few minutes before moving on to the next training activity or even taking the rest of the day off after a particularly strenuous session. Professional athletes know that the body may be a machine, but it's a machine that needs to have "downtime" as well. It would be best to make a training journal in which you record what you ate, how long you fasted before your workout, and how you felt during and after your training session. This will help you assess whether you need to add more carbs or protein to your diet and whether you need a longer rest period before moving on to the next training activity.

If you struggle with fatigue (or shakes) after strenuous activities, you may need to increase your amino acid intake or get more zinc and iron into your system. We are all unique, and what works for another vegan athlete may not work for you. This training log can also allow you to experiment by perhaps switching to shorter training sessions with more frequent rest periods to achieve the same fitness and muscle-building level. No two professional athletes train the same way. Listen to your body and your instincts to find a way that works for you.

Finally, don't forget to get enough sleep. Mental fatigue can easily translate into physical symptoms. A magnesium deficiency can also cause insomnia. This could be caused by strenuous activity that uses up the body's natural minerals. Taking a magnesium supplement or eating some dark chocolate or half a banana before bed can help create restful sleep.

Fortunately, the Internet allows for the development of support networks for vegan athletes. What we eat says a lot about us, and vegans can be successful, high-level athletes with planning and experimentation to find what works for their unique bodies.

THE BENEFITS OF THE PLANT-BASED DIET

A plant-based diet has proven health effects due to its food composition. Reduced saturated fat consumption prevents various diseases, including cardiovascular problems, high cholesterol levels, and obesity. The following are other guaranteed benefits of this diet:

WEIGHT AND BMI CONTROL

Research studies conducted on the plant-based diet have revealed that people who follow it tend to have a lower BMI or body mass index, reduced risk of obesity, and a lower likelihood of heart disease and diabetes. This is mainly because plant-based diets provide more fiber, water, and carbohydrates to the body. This can keep the body's metabolism active and functioning properly while providing a good boost of continuous energy.

In 2018, a study was conducted on this diet plan, and it was found to be the most effective in treating obesity. In that study, 75 people with obesity or weight issues were given a completely vegan plant-based diet, and their results were compared to those consuming animal-based diets. After four months of this experiment, the plant-based diet group showed a significant decrease in their body weight (up to 6.5 kilograms). Everyone lost more fat mass and demonstrated improved insulin sensitivity. Another study involving 60,000 individuals showed similar results, with people following a vegan diet recording lower body mass index than vegetarians and those following a plant-based diet.

Lower risk of heart disease and other conditions

The American Heart Association recently conducted a study in which middle-aged adults who followed a plant-based diet were studied. All of the subjects showed a decrease in their rate of heart disease. Based on the results of this research, the association listed the following illnesses that can be prevented through a plant-based diet:

- Heart attack
- High blood pressure
- High cholesterol levels
- Certain types of cancer
- Type II diabetes
- Obesity
- Diabetes

Plant-based diets also help manage diabetes because they improve insulin sensitivity and combat insulin resistance. Of all 60,000 study participants, about 2.9% on the vegan diet had type II diabetes, while 7.6% of participants on non-vegetarian diets had type II diabetes. From this observation, the researchers confirmed that a plant-based diet could help in the treatment of diabetes. It has also been proposed that this diet may help diabetic patients lose weight, improve metabolic rate and decrease their need for medical treatment.

It has also been suggested that doctors recommend this diet as part of treating people with type II diabetes or prediabetes. While medical treatments ensure short-term results, the plant-based dietary approach offers long-term results.

HOW TO START TO LOSE WEIGHT

Collect recipes for the meals you will be making.

Organize your list. You can divide the meals into groups, for example, soups, meat dishes, vegetarian dishes and so on, so that it is easy to manage them.

Find the recipes you need and write them down or print them on sheets of paper. Also, you can consider buying a special notebook for recipes. The most important thing is to have easy access to them because you will need them often.

Write your menu on paper

You have many ways to do this. You can use a notebook. On the other side, write a list of your meals, and on the right side, write down all the ingredients needed to prepare this meal (at once, you will have a meal plan and shopping list).

Regardless of which method you choose, put your plan in a visible place for everyone in the house. The best site is in the kitchen.

Adapt the menu according to your family's eventualities

When planning your meals, consider your daily activities and those of your family. Did your children eat lunch at school? Plan a more modest lunch at home that day. Are you coming home late from work? Think about a dinner that takes little time to prepare. Has the family been invited to a Sunday dinner? You don't have to prepare dinner that day. It is good to consider all related factors and take them into account when creating the menu.

Make a list of 15-20 of your favorite foods.

To make this list, sit down with your whole family and ask everyone what their favorite foods are. Once you've done that, look at the list and select those quick and easy to prepare and don't need too many ingredients. Best if they are healthy meals.

Check what you have in your pantry

Before you put your menu in place, it's a good idea to check your pantry, refrigerator, and freezer. Organize all the food you have there: throw away what is already expired, and sort everything else into appropriate groups (go to the shopping list template to see an example of groups)

Plan meals based on the products you already have. For example, do you have pasta? Put the pasta on your grocery list for the next day. If you like chicken pasta but don't have it, write "chicken" on your grocery list.

This way, you'll cut down on your grocery bill and also avoid unnecessary purchases of products you already have at home. Plus, it's the first step to keeping your refrigerator and pantry in order.

Use seasonal products

Depending on the season, the availability of individual fruits and vegetables can change drastically. As a result, their prices change as well. The best prices are found during the harvest, which becomes saving. The bottom line is that it's normal for your menu to change throughout the year.

I recommend using fresh ingredients from your garden season or those available in the market this season.

Plan meals throughout the day

Don't just create a list of lunches. It is advisable to eat 3-5 times a day, so think about planning all your breakfasts, lunches, and dinners.

This will prevent you from eating out, help you plan and make better use of your cooking time. You will also have the opportunity to use better leftover food (this is important if you want to maximize the savings effect).

Plan your food clean-up day

If you ever collect all the leftovers from your refrigerator at the end of the week, you can plan an evening when you and your family will dine on only the leftovers.

On that day, you should also check which products are close to the expiration date, and these are the products to be used in the following days' meals. This will reduce food waste and save you money.

Prepare multiple meals at once

Are you planning to eat the same dish more than once during the week? Try preparing a more significant amount of this meal for today and the next few days. If you do, put the food separately in containers and put them in the refrigerator or freezer; you can also bottle the food in jars.

Another example: you make chicken breast chops for lunch, and you also like a salad with chicken breast. Cook more than a single chicken breast at a time and then store some in the refrigerator. As a result, you will prepare the salad much faster in the afternoon or the next day.

Review your daily plan

Your meal plan should be flexible. If necessary, don't be afraid to make adjustments and take advantage of opportunities.

Many people consider themselves picky about food before they switch to a plant-based diet. However, then you find foods that they couldn't even think. Beans, tofu, different kinds of sweets from plants - such a meal for a meat lover seems tasteless. So, try a new dish and let your taste buds decide for themselves what they like best.

THE FUNDAMENTAL FACTORS FOR BEING FIT

It is not easy to make a change in any diet that you quickly embrace. The decision to embark on a plant-based eating plan is based on a desire to live a healthier life. Change may be inevitable later, after many realizations of what we get when we eventually abandon what we prefer to consume.

1. The first tip is about creating a consistent trend towards plant-based meals. Make a plan to cook this food more often within a week. Don't wait until ages have passed since you are inducing yourself to start your plant-based diet. Practice makes perfect, and within a long time, your skills, especially the necessary ones, will improve. Your experience will be a notch higher, and this will be reflected in your habits. Making it a point to cook plant-based meals frequently is one of the most excellent tips to start your plant-based meal. Along the way, you will adapt to it. You'll also find that you've changed your approach from how you've always thought about other types of food, such as diets filled with meat and junk food.

2. One tip that will help you start a plant-based diet meal is the use of whole grains during breakfast. Use them in large quantities, as they will help you to adopt this type of diet in a short period. It is not always easy to use all these whole grains. The best way to go about it is to choose meals that can satisfy you and the rest of your family at first. Good examples will be highly recommended. These could include oats, barley, or even buckwheat. Here, you can add some flavors provided by different types of nuts and other seeds. Don't forget to include fresh fruit alongside your entree.

3. The next tip is about making rules and making sure you are initiated into new plant-based meal recipes even twice a week. Regulations created by yourself will be followed quickly than those formed and forced on you. In this plant-based diet, it is all about loving what you are doing. The recipes you create will always be easy to follow, and once you master them, you will only get better at them. One rule that can be created here is the setting of a day. This day is kept mainly for one purpose, and that is to make a plant-based meal. Do this to the family and get their final verdict on what you did. Ask them to comment on the tastes and the food in general. The result will help you a lot, especially in your next meal.

4. Another tip is about food pairing. You can use this tool to have a more excellent knowledge of what types of plant-based foods can be paired and good taste results. You can do this pairing by combining different flavors. The result should give you a strong feeling that works for you.

5. As a beginner in this diet, the best tip for starting a plant-based eating plan will be, to begin with, vegetables. Try your best to eat vegetables. The act can be during lunch and dinner or rather a dinner. Make sure that your plate is always filled with plants from different categories. The different colors can help you choose the different types that you want to learn. Vegetables can also be eaten as snacks, especially when combined with hummus or salsa. You can also use guacamole in this combination, and rest assured you will love it.

BREAKFAST

226)   KID-FRIENDLY CEREAL

Preparation Time: 15 minutes

Servings: 5

Ingredients:

- ✓ 1 ½ cups spelt flour
- ✓ 1/2 tsp baking powder
- ✓ 1 tsp cinnamon
- ✓ 1/2 tsp cardamom
- ✓ 1/4 tsp ground cloves
- ✓ 1/2 cup brown sugar
- ✓ 1/3 cup almond milk
- ✓ 2 tsp coconut oil, melted

Directions:

- ❖ Begin by preheating your oven to 350 degrees F.
- ❖ In a mixing bowl, thoroughly combine all the dry ingredients. Gradually, pour in the milk and coconut oil and mix to combine well.
- ❖ Fill the pastry bag with the batter. Now, pipe 1/4-inch balls onto parchment-lined cookie sheets.
- ❖ Bake in the preheated oven for about 13 minutes. Serve with your favorite plant-based milk.
- ❖ Store in an air-thigh container for about 1 month. Enjoy

227)   ORIGINAL BREAKFAST BURRITO

Preparation Time: 15 minutes

Servings: 4

Ingredients:

- ✓ 1 tbsp olive oil
- ✓ 16 ounces tofu, pressed
- ✓ 4 (6-inch) whole-wheat tortillas
- ✓ 1 ½ cups canned chickpeas, drained
- ✓ 1 medium-sized avocado, pitted and sliced
- ✓ 1 tbsp lemon juice
- ✓ 1 tsp garlic, pressed
- ✓ 2 bell peppers, sliced
- ✓ Sea salt and ground black pepper, to taste
- ✓ 1/2 tsp red pepper flakes

Directions:

- ❖ Heat the olive oil in a frying skillet over medium heat. When it's hot, add the tofu and sauté for about 10 minutes, stirring occasionally to promote even cooking.
- ❖ Divide the fried tofu between warmed tortillas; place the remaining ingredients on your tortillas, roll them up and serve immediately.
- ❖ Enjoy

228)   HOMEMADE TOAST CRUNCH

Preparation Time: 15 minutes

Servings: 8

Ingredients:

- ✓ 1 cup almond flour
- ✓ 1 cup coconut flour
- ✓ 1/2 cup all-purpose flour
- ✓ 1 cup sugar
- ✓ 1 tsp kosher salt
- ✓ 1 tsp cardamom
- ✓ 1/4 tsp grated nutmeg
- ✓ 1 tbsp cinnamon
- ✓ 3 tbsp flax seeds, ground
- ✓ 1/2 cup coconut oil, melted
- ✓ 8 tbsp coconut milk

Directions:

- ❖ Begin by preheating the oven to 340 degrees F. In a mixing bowl, thoroughly combine all the dry ingredients.
- ❖ Gradually pour in the oil and milk; mix to combine well.
- ❖ Shape the dough into a ball and roll out between 2 sheets of a parchment paper. Cut into small squares and prick them with a fork to prevent air bubbles.
- ❖ Bake in the preheated oven for about 15 minutes. They will continue to crisp as they cool. Enjoy!

229)   CINNAMON AND APPLE OATMEAL CUPS

Preparation Time: 30 minutes

Servings: 9

Ingredients:

- ✓ 2 cups old-fashioned oats
- ✓ 1/2 tsp baking powder
- ✓ 1 tsp cinnamon
- ✓ 1/4 tsp grated nutmeg
- ✓ 1/4 tsp sea salt
- ✓ 1 cup almond milk
- ✓ 1/4 cup agave syrup
- ✓ 1/2 cup applesauce
- ✓ 2 tbsp coconut oil
- ✓ 2 tbsp peanut butter
- ✓ 1 tbsp chia seeds
- ✓ 1 small apple, cored and diced

Directions:

- ❖ Begin by preheating your oven to 360 degrees F. Spritz a muffin tin with a nonstick cooking oil.
- ❖ In a mixing bowl, thoroughly combine all the ingredients, except for the apples.
- ❖ Fold in the apples and scrape the batter into the prepared muffin tin.
- ❖ Bake your muffins for about 25 minutes or until a toothpick comes out dry and clean. Enjoy

230) CHICKPEA TOFU SCRAMBLE WITH SPICY VEGETABLES

Preparation Time: 15 minutes

Servings: 2

Ingredients:

- ✓ 2 tbsp oil
- ✓ 1 bell pepper, seeded and sliced
- ✓ 2 tbsp scallions, chopped
- ✓ 6 ounces cremini button mushrooms, sliced
- ✓ 1/2 tsp garlic, minced
- ✓ 1 jalapeno pepper, seeded and chopped
- ✓ 6 ounces firm tofu, pressed
- ✓ 1 tbsp nutritional yeast
- ✓ 1/4 tsp turmeric powder
- ✓ Kala namak and ground black pepper, to taste
- ✓ 6 ounces chickpeas, drained

Directions:

- ❖ Heat the olive oil in a nonstick skillet over a moderate flame. Once hot, sauté the pepper for about 2 minutes.
- ❖ Now, add in the scallions, mushrooms and continue sautéing for a further 3 minutes or until the mushrooms release the liquid.
- ❖ Then, add in the garlic, jalapeno and tofu and sauté for 5 minutes more, crumbling the tofu with a fork.
- ❖ Add in the nutritional yeast, turmeric, salt, pepper and chickpeas; continue sautéing an additional 2 minutes or until cooked through. Enjoy

231) COCONUT PRUNES GRANOLA

Preparation Time: 1 hour

Servings: 10

Ingredients:

- ✓ 1/3 cup coconut oil
- ✓ 1/2 cup maple syrup
- ✓ 1 tsp sea salt
- ✓ 1/4 tsp grated nutmeg
- ✓ 1/2 tsp cinnamon powder
- ✓ 1/2 tsp vanilla extract
- ✓ 4 cups old-fashioned oats
- ✓ 1/2 cup almonds, chopped
- ✓ 1/2 cup pecans, chopped
- ✓ 1/2 coconut, shredded
- ✓ 1 cup prunes, chopped

Directions:

- ❖ Begin by preheating your oven to 260 degrees F; line two rimmed baking sheets with a piece of parchment paper.
- ❖ Then, thoroughly combine the coconut oil, maple syrup, salt, nutmeg, cinnamon and vanilla.
- ❖ Gradually add in the oats, almonds, pecans and coconut; toss to coat well.
- ❖ Spread the mixture out onto the prepared baking sheets.
- ❖ Bake in the middle of the oven, stirring halfway through the cooking time, for about 1 hour or until golden brown.
- ❖ Stir in the prunes and let your granola cool completely before storing. Store in an airtight container.
- ❖ Enjoy

232) THYME PUMPKIN FRY

Preparation Time: 25 minutes

Servings: 2

Ingredients:

- ✓ 1 cup pumpkin, shredded
- ✓ 1 tbsp olive oil
- ✓ ½ onion, chopped
- ✓ 1 carrot, peeled and chopped
- ✓ 2 garlic cloves, minced
- ✓ ½ tsp dried thyme
- ✓ 1 cup chopped kale
- ✓ Salt and black pepper to taste

Directions:

- ❖ Heat the oil in a skillet over medium heat. Sauté onion and carrot for 5 minutes. Add in garlic and thyme, cook for 30 seconds until the garlic is fragrant. Place in the pumpkin and cook for 10 minutes until tender. Stir in kale, cook for 4 minutes until the kale wilts. Season with salt and pepper. Serve hot

233) ALMOND RASPBERRY SMOOTHIE

Preparation Time: 5 minutes

Servings: 4

Ingredients:

- ✓ 1 ½ cups almond milk
- ✓ ½ cup raspberries
- ✓ Juice from half lemon
- ✓ ½ tsp almond extract

Directions:

- ❖ In a blender or smoothie maker, pour the almond milk, raspberries, lemon juice, and almond extract. Puree the ingredients at high speed until the raspberries have blended almost entirely into the liquid. Pour the smoothie into serving glasses. Stick in some straws and serve immediately

234)   KIWI OATMEAL BARS

Preparation Time: 50 minutes

Servings: 12

Ingredients:

- ✓ 2 cups uncooked rolled oats
- ✓ 2 cups all-purpose flour
- ✓ 1 ½ cups pure date sugar
- ✓ 1 ½ tsp baking soda
- ✓ ½ tsp ground cinnamon
- ✓ 1 cup plant butter, melted
- ✓ 4 cups kiwi, chopped
- ✓ ¼ cup organic cane sugar
- ✓ 2 tbsp corn-starch

Directions:

- ❖ Preheat oven to 380 F. Grease a baking dish.
- ❖ In a bowl, mix the oats, flour, date sugar, baking soda, salt, and cinnamon. Put in butter and whisk to combine. In another bowl, combine the kiwis, cane sugar, and corn-starch until the kiwis are coated. Spread 3 cups of oatmeal mixture on a greased baking dish and top with kiwi mixture and finally put the remaining oatmeal mixture on top. Bake for 40 minutes. Allow cooling and slice into bars

235)   APPLE SPICY PANCAKES

Preparation Time: 30 minutes

Servings: 4

Ingredients:

- ✓ 2 cups almond milk
- ✓ 1 tsp apple cider vinegar
- ✓ 2 ½ cups whole-wheat flour
- ✓ 2 tbsp baking powder
- ✓ ½ tsp baking soda
- ✓ 1 tsp sea salt
- ✓ ½ tsp ground cinnamon
- ✓ ¼ tsp grated nutmeg
- ✓ ¼ tsp ground allspice
- ✓ ½ cup applesauce
- ✓ 1 cup water
- ✓ 1 tbsp coconut oil

Directions:

- ❖ Whisk the almond milk and apple cider vinegar in a bowl and set aside. In another bowl, combine the flour, baking powder, baking soda, salt, cinnamon, nutmeg, and allspice. Transfer the almond mixture to another bowl and beat with the applesauce and water.
- ❖ Pour in the dry ingredients and stir. Melt some coconut oil in a skillet over medium heat. Pour a ladle of the batter and cook for 5 minutes, flipping once until golden. Repeat the process until the batter is exhausted. Serve

236)   ALMOND AND COCONUT GRANOLA WITH CHERRIES

Preparation Time: 45 minutes

Servings: 6

Ingredients:

- ✓ ½ cup coconut oil, melted
- ✓ ½ cup maple syrup
- ✓ 1 tsp vanilla extract
- ✓ 3 tsp pumpkin pie spice
- ✓ 4 cups rolled oats
- ✓ ⅓ cup whole-wheat flour
- ✓ ¼ cup ground flaxseed
- ✓ ½ cup sunflower seeds
- ✓ ½ cup slivered almonds
- ✓ ½ cup shredded coconut
- ✓ ½ cup dried cherries
- ✓ ½ cup dried apricots, chopped

Directions:

- ❖ Preheat oven to 350 F.
- ❖ In a bowl, combine the coconut oil, maple syrup, and vanilla. Add in the pumpkin pie spice. Put oats, flour, flaxseed, sunflower seeds, almonds, and coconut in a baking sheet and toss to combine. Coat with the oil mixture. Spread the granola out evenly. Bake for 25 minutes. Once ready, break the granola into chunks and stir in the cherries and apricots. Bake another 5 minutes. Allow cooling and serve

237)   ALMONDS CINNAMON BUCKWHEAT

Preparation Time: 20 minutes

Servings: 4

Ingredients:

- ✓ 1 cup almond milk
- ✓ 1 cup water
- ✓ 1 cup buckwheat groats, rinsed
- ✓ 1 tsp cinnamon
- ✓ ¼ cup chopped almonds
- ✓ 2 tbsp pure date syrup

Directions:

- ❖ Place almond milk, water, and buckwheat in a pot over medium heat and bring to a boil. Lower the heat and simmer covered for 15 minutes. Allow sitting covered for 5 minutes. Mix in the cinnamon, almonds, and date syrup. Serve warm

238)   YELLOW SMOOTHIE

Preparation Time: 5 minutes

Servings: 4

Ingredients:

- ✓ 1 banana
- ✓ 1 cup chopped mango
- ✓ 1 cup chopped apricots
- ✓ 1 cup strawberries
- ✓ 1 carrot, peeled and chopped
- ✓ 1 cup water

Directions:

- ❖ Put the banana, mango, apricots, strawberries, carrot, and water in a food processor. Pulse until smooth; add more water if needed. Divide between glasses and serve

239)   HEARTY SMOOTHIE

Preparation Time: 5 minutes

Servings: 3

Ingredients:

- ✓ 1 banana
- ✓ ½ cup coconut milk
- ✓ 1 cup water
- ✓ 1 cup broccoli sprouts
- ✓ 2 cherries, pitted
- ✓ 1 tbsp hemp hearts
- ✓ ¼ tsp ground cinnamon
- ✓ ¼ tsp ground cardamom
- ✓ 1 tbsp grated fresh ginger

Directions:

- ❖ In a food processor, place banana, coconut milk, water, broccoli, cherries, hemp hearts, cinnamon, cardamom, and ginger. Blitz until smooth. Divide between glasses and serve

240)   CARROT AND STRAWBERRY SMOOTHIE

Preparation Time: 5 minutes

Servings: 2

Ingredients:

- ✓ 1 cup peeled and diced carrots
- ✓ 1 cup strawberries
- ✓ 1 apple, chopped
- ✓ 2 tbsp maple syrup
- ✓ 2 cups unsweetened almond milk

Directions:

- ❖ Place in a food processor all the ingredients. Blitz until smooth. Pour in glasses and serve

241)   SUPER GREEN SMOOTHIE

Preparation Time: 10 minutes

Servings: 2

Ingredients:

- ✓ 1 banana, sliced
- ✓ 2 cups kale
- ✓ 1 cup sliced kiwi
- ✓ 1 orange, cut into segments
- ✓ 1 cup unsweetened coconut milk

Directions:

- ❖ In a food processor, put the banana, kale, kiwi, orange, and coconut milk. Pulse until smooth. Serve right away in glasses

242)   BLUEBERRY MAPLE SMOOTHIE

Preparation Time: 5 minutes

Servings: 4

Ingredients:

- ✓ 4 cups chopped arugula
- ✓ 2 cups frozen blueberries
- ✓ 4 cups unsweetened almond milk
- ✓ Juice of 2 limes
- ✓ 4 tbsp maple syrup

Directions:

- ❖ In a food processor, blitz the arugula, blueberries, almond milk, lime juice, and maple syrup until smooth. Serve

243)   POWER CHIA-PEACH SMOOTHIE

Preparation Time: 5 minutes

Servings: 2

Ingredients:

- ✓ 1 banana, sliced
- ✓ 1 peach, chopped
- ✓ 1 cup almond milk
- ✓ 1 scoop plant-based protein powder
- ✓ 1 tbsp chia seeds
- ✓ 1 cucumber, chopped

Directions:

- ❖ Purée the banana, peach, almond milk, protein powder, chia seeds, and cucumber for 50 seconds until smooth in a food processor. Serve immediately in glasses

244)   PORRIDGE WITH STRAWBERRIES AND COCONUT

Preparation Time: 12 minutes

Servings: 2

Ingredients:

- ✓ 1 tbsp flax seed powder
- ✓ 1 oz olive oil
- ✓ 1 tbsp coconut flour
- ✓ 1 pinch ground chia seeds
- ✓ 5 tbsp coconut cream
- ✓ Thawed frozen strawberries

Directions:

- ❖ In a small bowl, mix the flax seed powder with the 3 tbsp water, and allow soaking for 5 minutes.
- ❖ Place a non-stick saucepan over low heat and pour in the olive oil, vegan "flax egg," coconut flour, chia seeds, and coconut cream.
- ❖ Cook the mixture while stirring continuously until your desired consistency is achieved. Turn the heat off and spoon the porridge into serving bowls.
- ❖ Top with 4 to 6 strawberries and serve immediately.

245)   BROCCOLI BROWNS

Preparation Time: 35 minutes

Servings: 4

Ingredients:

- ✓ 3 tbsp flax seed powder
- ✓ 1 head broccoli, cut into florets
- ✓ ½ white onion, grated
- ✓ 1 tsp salt
- ✓ 1 tbsp freshly ground black pepper
- ✓ 5 tbsp plant butter, for frying

Directions:

- ❖ In a small bowl, mix the flax seed powder with 9 tbsp water, and allow soaking for 5 minutes. Pour the broccoli into a food processor and pulse a few times until smoothly grated.
- ❖ Transfer the broccoli into a bowl, add the vegan "flax egg," white onion, salt, and black pepper. Use a spoon to mix the ingredients evenly and set aside 5 to 10 minutes to firm up a bit. Place a large non-stick skillet over medium heat and drop 1/3 of the plant butter to melt until no longer shimmering.
- ❖ Ladle scoops of the broccoli mixture into the skillet (about 3 to 4 hash browns per batch). Flatten the pancakes to measure 3 to 4 inches in diameter, and fry until golden brown on one side, 4 minutes. Turn the pancakes with a spatula and cook the other side to brown too, another 5 minutes.
- ❖ Transfer the hash browns to a serving plate and repeat the frying process for the remaining broccoli mixture. Serve the hash browns warm with green salad.

SOUPS, STEW, AND SALADS

SOUPS, STEW AND SALADS

246) ROASTED CARROT SOUP

Preparation Time: 50 minutes

Servings: 4

Ingredients:

- ✓ 1 ½ pounds carrots
- ✓ 4 tbsp olive oil
- ✓ 1 yellow onion, chopped
- ✓ 2 cloves garlic, minced
- ✓ 1/3 tsp ground cumin
- ✓ Sea salt and white pepper, to taste
- ✓ 1/2 tsp turmeric powder
- ✓ 4 cups vegetable stock
- ✓ 2 tsp lemon juice
- ✓ 2 tbsp fresh cilantro, roughly chopped

Directions:

- ❖ Start by preheating your oven to 400 degrees F. Place the carrots on a large parchment-lined baking sheet; toss the carrots with 2 tbsp of the olive oil.
- ❖ Roast the carrots for about 35 minutes or until they've softened.
- ❖ In a heavy-bottomed pot, heat the remaining 2 tbsp of the olive oil. Now, sauté the onion and garlic for about 3 minutes or until aromatic.
- ❖ Add in the cumin, salt, pepper, turmeric, vegetable stock and roasted carrots. Continue to simmer for 12 minutes more.
- ❖ Puree your soup with an immersion blender. Drizzle lemon juice over your soup and serve garnished with fresh cilantro leaves. Enjoy

247) ITALIAN PENNE PASTA SALAD

Preparation Time: 15 minutes + chilling time

Servings: 3

Ingredients:

- ✓ 9 ounces penne pasta
- ✓ 9 ounces canned Cannellini bean, drained
- ✓ 1 small onion, thinly sliced
- ✓ 1/3 cup Niçoise olives, pitted and sliced
- ✓ 2 Italian peppers, sliced
- ✓ 1 cup cherry tomatoes, halved
- ✓ 3 cups arugula
- ✓ Dressing:
- ✓ 3 tbsp extra-virgin olive oil
- ✓ 1 tsp lemon zest
- ✓ 1 tsp garlic, minced
- ✓ 3 tbsp balsamic vinegar
- ✓ 1 tsp Italian herb mix
- ✓ Sea salt and ground black pepper, to taste

Directions:

- ❖ Cook the penne pasta according to the package directions. Drain and rinse the pasta. Let it cool completely and then, transfer it to a salad bowl.
- ❖ Then, add the beans, onion, olives, peppers, tomatoes and arugula to the salad bowl.
- ❖ Mix all the dressing ingredients until everything is well incorporated. Dress your salad and serve well

248) CHANA CHAAT INDIAN SALAD

Preparation Time: 45 minutes + chilling time

Servings: 4

Ingredients:

- ✓ 1 pound dry chickpeas, soaked overnight
- ✓ 2 San Marzano tomatoes, diced
- ✓ 1 Persian cucumber, sliced
- ✓ 1 onion, chopped
- ✓ 1 bell pepper, seeded and thinly sliced
- ✓ 1 green chili, seeded and thinly sliced
- ✓ 2 handfuls baby spinach
- ✓ 1/2 tsp Kashmiri chili powder
- ✓ 4 curry leaves, chopped
- ✓ 1 tbsp chaat masala
- ✓ 2 tbsp fresh lemon juice, or to taste
- ✓ 4 tbsp olive oil
- ✓ 1 tsp agave syrup
- ✓ 1/2 tsp mustard seeds
- ✓ 1/2 tsp coriander seeds
- ✓ 2 tbsp sesame seeds, lightly toasted
- ✓ 2 tbsp fresh cilantro, roughly chopped

Directions:

- ❖ Drain the chickpeas and transfer them to a large saucepan. Cover the chickpeas with water by 2 inches and bring it to a boil.
- ❖ Immediately turn the heat to a simmer and continue to cook for approximately 40 minutes.
- ❖ Toss the chickpeas with the tomatoes, cucumber, onion, peppers, spinach, chili powder, curry leaves and chaat masala.
- ❖ In a small mixing dish, thoroughly combine the lemon juice, olive oil, agave syrup, mustard seeds and coriander seeds.
- ❖ Garnish with sesame seeds and fresh cilantro. Enjoy

249) TEMPEH AND NOODLE SALAD THAI-STYLE

Preparation Time: 45 minutes

Servings: 3

Ingredients:

- 6 ounces tempeh
- 4 tbsp rice vinegar
- 4 tbsp soy sauce
- 2 garlic cloves, minced
- 1 small-sized lime, freshly juiced
- 5 ounces rice noodles
- 1 carrot, julienned
- 1 shallot, chopped
- 3 handfuls Chinese cabbage, thinly sliced
- 3 handfuls kale, torn into pieces
- 1 bell pepper, seeded and thinly sliced
- 1 bird's eye chili, minced
- 1/4 cup peanut butter
- 2 tbsp agave syrup

Directions:

- ❖ Place the tempeh, 2 tbsp of the rice vinegar, soy sauce, garlic and lime juice in a ceramic dish; let it marinate for about 40 minutes.
- ❖ Meanwhile, cook the rice noodles according to the package directions. Drain your noodles and transfer them to a salad bowl.
- ❖ Add the carrot, shallot, cabbage, kale and peppers to the salad bowl. Add in the peanut butter, the remaining 2 tbsp of the rice vinegar and agave syrup and toss to combine well.
- ❖ Top with the marinated tempeh and serve immediately. Enjoy

250) TYPICAL CREAM OF BROCCOLI SOUP

Preparation Time: 35 minutes

Servings: 4

Ingredients:

- 2 tbsp olive oil
- 1 pound broccoli florets
- 1 onion, chopped
- 1 celery rib, chopped
- 1 parsnip, chopped
- 1 tsp garlic, chopped
- 3 cups vegetable broth
- 1/2 tsp dried dill
- 1/2 tsp dried oregano
- Sea salt and ground black pepper, to taste
- 2 tbsp flaxseed meal
- 1 cup full-fat coconut milk

Directions:

- ❖ In a heavy-bottomed pot, heat the olive oil over medium-high heat. Now, sauté the broccoli onion, celery and parsnip for about 5 minutes, stirring periodically.
- ❖ Add in the garlic and continue sautéing for 1 minute or until fragrant.
- ❖ Then, stir in the vegetable broth, dill, oregano, salt and black pepper; bring to a boil. Immediately reduce the heat to a simmer and let it cook for about 20 minutes.
- ❖ Puree the soup using an immersion blender until creamy and uniform.
- ❖ Return the pureed mixture to the pot. Fold in the flaxseed meal and coconut milk; continue to simmer until heated through or about 5 minutes.
- ❖ Ladle into four serving bowls and enjoy

251) RAISIN MOROCCAN LENTIL SALAD

Preparation Time: 20 minutes + chilling time

Servings: 4

Ingredients:

- 1 cup red lentils, rinsed
- 1 large carrot, julienned
- 1 Persian cucumber, thinly sliced
- 1 sweet onion, chopped
- 1/2 cup golden raisins
- 1/4 cup fresh mint, snipped
- 1/4 cup fresh basil, snipped
- 1/4 cup extra-virgin olive oil
- 1/4 cup lemon juice, freshly squeezed
- 1 tsp grated lemon peel
- 1/2 tsp fresh ginger root, peeled and minced
- 1/2 tsp granulated garlic
- 1 tsp ground allspice
- Sea salt and ground black pepper, to taste

Directions:

- ❖ In a large-sized saucepan, bring 3 cups of the water and 1 cup of the lentils to a boil.
- ❖ Immediately turn the heat to a simmer and continue to cook your lentils for a further 15 to 17 minutes or until they've softened but are not mushy yet. Drain and let it cool completely.
- ❖ Transfer the lentils to a salad bowl; add in the carrot, cucumber and sweet onion. Then, add the raisins, mint and basil to your salad.
- ❖ In a small mixing dish, whisk the olive oil, lemon juice, lemon peel, ginger, granulated garlic, allspice, salt and black pepper.
- ❖ Dress your salad and serve well-chilled. Enjoy

252)   CHICKPEA AND ASPARAGUS SALAD

Preparation Time: 10 minutes + chilling time   **Servings: 5**

Ingredients:

- ✓ 1 ¼ pounds asparagus, trimmed and cut into bite-sized pieces
- ✓ 5 ounces canned chickpeas, drained and rinsed
- ✓ 1 chipotle pepper, seeded and chopped
- ✓ 1 Italian pepper, seeded and chopped
- ✓ 1/4 cup fresh basil leaves, chopped
- ✓ 1/4 cup fresh parsley leaves, chopped
- ✓ 2 tbsp fresh mint leaves
- ✓ 2 tbsp fresh chives, chopped
- ✓ 1 tsp garlic, minced
- ✓ 1/4 cup extra-virgin olive oil
- ✓ 1 tbsp balsamic vinegar
- ✓ 1 tbsp fresh lime juice
- ✓ 2 tbsp soy sauce
- ✓ 1/4 tsp ground allspice
- ✓ 1/4 tsp ground cumin
- ✓ Sea salt and freshly cracked peppercorns, to taste

Directions:

- ❖ Bring a large pot of salted water with the asparagus to a boil; let it cook for 2 minutes; drain and rinse.
- ❖ Transfer the asparagus to a salad bowl.
- ❖ Toss the asparagus with the chickpeas, peppers, herbs, garlic, olive oil, vinegar, lime juice, soy sauce and spices.
- ❖ Toss to combine and serve immediately. Enjoy

253)   OLD-FASHIONED GREEN BEAN SALAD

Preparation Time: 10 minutes + chilling time   **Servings: 4**

Ingredients:

- ✓ 1 ½ pounds green beans, trimmed
- ✓ 1/2 cup scallions, chopped
- ✓ 1 tsp garlic, minced
- ✓ 1 Persian cucumber, sliced
- ✓ 2 cups grape tomatoes, halved
- ✓ 1/4 cup olive oil
- ✓ 1 tsp deli mustard
- ✓ 2 tbsp tamari sauce
- ✓ 2 tbsp lemon juice
- ✓ 1 tbsp apple cider vinegar
- ✓ 1/4 tsp cumin powder
- ✓ 1/2 tsp dried thyme
- ✓ Sea salt and ground black pepper, to taste

Directions:

- ❖ Boil the green beans in a large saucepan of salted water until they are just tender or about 2 minutes.
- ❖ Drain and let the beans cool completely; then, transfer them to a salad bowl. Toss the beans with the remaining ingredients.
- ❖ Enjoy

254)   WINTER BEAN SOUP

Preparation Time: 25 minutes   **Servings: 4**

Ingredients:

- ✓ 1 tbsp olive oil
- ✓ 2 tbsp shallots, chopped
- ✓ 1 carrot, chopped
- ✓ 1 parsnip, chopped
- ✓ 1 celery stalk, chopped
- ✓ 1 tsp fresh garlic, minced
- ✓ 4 cups vegetable broth
- ✓ 2 bay leaves
- ✓ 1 rosemary sprig, chopped
- ✓ 16 ounces canned navy beans
- ✓ Flaky sea salt and ground black pepper, to taste

Directions:

- ❖ In a heavy-bottomed pot, heat the olive over medium-high heat. Now, sauté the shallots, carrot, parsnip and celery for approximately 3 minutes or until the vegetables are just tender.
- ❖ Add in the garlic and continue to sauté for 1 minute or until aromatic.
- ❖ Then, add in the vegetable broth, bay leaves and rosemary and bring to a boil. Immediately reduce the heat to a simmer and let it cook for 10 minutes.
- ❖ Fold in the navy beans and continue to simmer for about 5 minutes longer until everything is thoroughly heated. Season with salt and black pepper to taste.
- ❖ Ladle into individual bowls, discard the bay leaves and serve hot. Enjoy

255) ITALIAN-STYLE CREAM MUSHROOMS SOUP

Preparation Time: 15 minutes

Servings: 3

Ingredients:

- ✓ 3 tbsp vegan butter
- ✓ 1 white onion, chopped
- ✓ 1 red bell pepper, chopped
- ✓ 1/2 tsp garlic, pressed
- ✓ 3 cups Cremini mushrooms, chopped
- ✓ 2 tbsp almond flour
- ✓ 3 cups water
- ✓ 1 tsp Italian herb mix
- ✓ Sea salt and ground black pepper, to taste
- ✓ 1 heaping tbsp fresh chives, roughly chopped

Directions:

- ❖ In a stockpot, melt the vegan butter over medium-high heat. Once hot, sauté the onion and pepper for about 3 minutes until they have softened.
- ❖ Add in the garlic and Cremini mushrooms and continue sautéing until the mushrooms have softened. Sprinkle almond meal over the mushrooms and continue to cook for 1 minute or so.
- ❖ Add in the remaining ingredients. Let it simmer, covered and continue to cook for 5 to 6 minutes more until the liquid has thickened slightly.
- ❖ Ladle into three soup bowls and garnish with fresh chives. Enjoy

256) ROASTED BASIL AND TOMATO SOUP

Preparation Time: 60 minutes

Servings: 4

Ingredients:

- ✓ 2 lb tomatoes, halved
- ✓ 2 tsp garlic powder
- ✓ 3 tbsp olive oil
- ✓ 1 tbsp balsamic vinegar
- ✓ Salt and black pepper to taste
- ✓ 4 shallots, chopped
- ✓ 2 cups vegetable broth
- ✓ ½ cup basil leaves, chopped

Directions:

- ❖ Preheat oven to 450 F.
- ❖ In a bowl, mix tomatoes, garlic, 2 tbsp of oil, vinegar, salt, and pepper. Arrange the tomatoes onto a baking dish. Sprinkle with some olive oil, garlic powder, balsamic vinegar, salt, and pepper. Bake for 30 minutes until the tomatoes get dark brown color. Take out from the oven; reserve.
- ❖ Heat the remaining oil in a pot over medium heat. Place the shallots and cook for 3 minutes, stirring often. Add in roasted tomatoes and broth. Bring to a boil, then lower the heat and simmer for 10 minutes. Transfer to a food processor and blitz the soup until smooth. Serve topped with basil

257) UNDER PRESSURE COOKER GREEN ONION AND POTATO SOUP

Preparation Time: 25 minutes

Servings: 5

Ingredients:

- ✓ 3 green onions, chopped
- ✓ 4 garlic cloves, minced
- ✓ 1 tbsp olive oil
- ✓ 6 russet potatoes, chopped
- ✓ ½ (13.5-oz) can coconut milk
- ✓ 5 cups vegetable broth
- ✓ Salt and black pepper to taste

Directions:

- ❖ Set your IP to Sauté. Place in green onions, garlic, and olive oil. Cook for 3 minutes until softened. Add in potatoes, coconut milk, broth, and salt. Lock the lid in place, set time to 6 minutes on High. Once ready, perform a natural pressure release for 10 minutes. Allow cooling for a few minutes. Using an immersion blender, blitz the soup until smooth. Serve

258) BELL PEPPER AND MUSHROOM SOUP

Preparation Time: 45 minutes

Servings: 6

Ingredients:

- ✓ 3 tbsp olive oil
- ✓ 1 onion, chopped
- ✓ 1 large carrot, chopped
- ✓ 1 lb mixed bell peppers, chopped
- ✓ 1 cup cremini mushrooms, quartered
- ✓ 1 cup white mushrooms, quartered
- ✓ 6 cups vegetable broth
- ✓ ¼ cup chopped fresh parsley
- ✓ 1 tsp minced fresh thyme
- ✓ Salt and black pepper to taste

Directions:

- ❖ Heat the oil in a pot over medium heat. Place onion, carrot, and celery and cook for 5 minutes. Add in bell peppers and broth and stir. Bring to a boil, lower the heat, and simmer for 20 minutes. Adjust the seasoning with salt and black pepper. Serve in soup bowls topped with parsley and thyme

259)   PUMPKIN CAYENNE SOUP

Preparation Time: 55 minutes

Servings: 6

Ingredients:

- ✓ 1 (2-pound) pumpkin, sliced
- ✓ 3 tbsp olive oil
- ✓ 1 tsp salt
- ✓ 2 red bell peppers
- ✓ 1 onion, halved
- ✓ 1 head garlic
- ✓ 6 cups water
- ✓ Zest and juice of 1 lime
- ✓ ¼ tsp cayenne pepper
- ✓ ½ tsp ground coriander
- ✓ ½ tsp ground cumin
- ✓ Toasted pumpkin seeds

Directions:

- ❖ Preheat oven to 350 F.
- ❖ Brush the pumpkin slices with oil and sprinkle with salt. Arrange the slices skin-side-down and on a greased baking dish and bake for 20 minutes. Brush the onion with oil. Cut the top of the garlic head and brush with oil.
- ❖ When the pumpkin is ready, add in bell peppers, onion, and garlic, and bake for another 10 minutes. Allow cooling.
- ❖ Take out the flesh from the pumpkin skin and transfer to a food processor. Cut the pepper roughly, peel and cut the onion, and remove the cloves from the garlic head. Transfer to the food processor and pour in the water, lime zest, and lime juice.
- ❖ Blend the soup until smooth. If it's very thick, add a bit of water to reach your desired consistency. Sprinkle with salt, cayenne, coriander, and cumin. Serve

260)   ZUCCHINI CREAM SOUP WITH WALNUTS

Preparation Time: 45 minutes

Servings: 4

Ingredients:

- ✓ 3 zucchinis, chopped
- ✓ 2 tsp olive oil
- ✓ Sea salt and black pepper to taste
- ✓ 1 onion, diced
- ✓ 4 cups vegetable stock
- ✓ 3 tsp ground sage
- ✓ 3 tbsp nutritional yeast
- ✓ 1 cup non-dairy milk
- ✓ ¼ cup toasted walnuts

Directions:

- ❖ Heat the oil in a skillet and place zucchini, onion, salt, and pepper; cook for 5 minutes. Pour in vegetable stock and bring to a boil. Lower the heat and simmer for 15 minutes. Stir in sage, nutritional yeast, and milk. Purée the soup with a blender until smooth. Serve garnished with toasted walnuts and pepper

261)   RAMEN SOUP

Preparation Time: 25 minutes

Servings: 4

Ingredients:

- ✓ 7 oz Japanese buckwheat noodles
- ✓ 4 tbsp sesame paste
- ✓ 1 cup canned pinto beans, drained
- ✓ 2 tbsp fresh cilantro, chopped
- ✓ 2 scallions, thinly sliced

Directions:

- ❖ In boiling salted water, add in the noodles and cook for 5 minutes over low heat. Remove a cup of the noodle water to a bowl and add in the sesame paste; stir until it has dissolved. Pour the sesame mix in the pot with the noodles, add in pinto beans, and stir until everything is hot. Serve topped with cilantro and scallions in individual bowls

262)   BLACK-EYED PEA SOUP

Preparation Time: 45 minutes

Servings: 6

Ingredients:

- ✓ 2 carrots, chopped
- ✓ 1 onion, chopped
- ✓ 2 cups canned dried black-eyed peas
- ✓ 1 tbsp soy sauce
- ✓ 3 tsp dried thyme
- ✓ 1 tsp onion powder
- ✓ ½ tsp garlic powder
- ✓ Salt and black pepper to taste
- ✓ ¼ cup chopped pitted black olives

Directions:

- ❖ Place carrots, onion, black-eyed peas, 3 cups water, soy sauce, thyme, onion powder, garlic powder, and pepper in a pot. Bring to a boil, then reduce the heat to low. Cook for 20 minutes. Allow cooling for a few minutes. Transfer to a food processor and blend until smooth. Stir in black olives. Serve

VEGETABLES
AND SIDE
DISHES

263)   ROASTED KOHLRABI

Preparation Time: 30 minutes   **Servings:** 4

Ingredients:

✓ 1 pound kohlrabi bulbs, peeled and sliced
✓ 4 tbsp olive oil
✓ 1/2 tsp mustard seeds
✓ 1 tsp celery seeds
✓ 1 tsp dried marjoram
✓ 1 tsp granulated garlic, minced
✓ Sea salt and ground black pepper, to taste
✓ 2 tbsp nutritional yeast

Directions:

❖ Start by preheating your oven to 450 degrees F.
❖ Toss the kohlrabi with the olive oil and spices until well coated. Arrange the kohlrabi in a single layer on a parchment-lined roasting pan.
❖ Bake the kohlrabi in the preheated oven for about 15 minutes; stir them and continue to cook an additional 15 minutes.
❖ Sprinkle nutritional yeast over the warm kohlrabi and serve immediately. Enjoy

264)   CAULIFLOWER WITH TAHINI SAUCE

Preparation Time: 10 minutes   **Servings:** 4

Ingredients:

✓ 1 cup water
✓ 2 pounds cauliflower florets
✓ Sea salt and ground black pepper, to taste
✓ 3 tbsp soy sauce
✓ 5 tbsp tahini
✓ 2 cloves garlic, minced
✓ 2 tbsp lemon juice

Directions:

❖ In a large saucepan, bring the water to a boil; then, add in the cauliflower and cook for about 6 minutes or until fork-tender; drain, season with salt and pepper and reserve.
❖ In a mixing bowl, thoroughly combine the soy sauce, tahini, garlic and lemon juice. Spoon the sauce over the cauliflower florets and serve.
❖ Enjoy

265)   HERB CAULIFLOWER MASH

Preparation Time: 25 minutes   **Servings:** 4

Ingredients:

✓ 1 ½ pounds cauliflower florets
✓ 4 tbsp vegan butter
✓ 4 cloves garlic, sliced
✓ Sea salt and ground black pepper, to taste
✓ 1/4 cup plain oat milk, unsweetened
✓ 2 tbsp fresh parsley, roughly chopped

Directions:

❖ Steam the cauliflower florets for about 20 minutes; set it aside to cool.
❖ In a saucepan, melt the vegan butter over a moderately high heat; now, sauté the garlic for about 1 minute or until aromatic.
❖ Add the cauliflower florets to your food processor followed by the sautéed garlic, salt, black pepper and oat milk. Puree until everything is well incorporated.
❖ Garnish with fresh parsley leaves and serve hot. Enjoy

266)   GARLIC AND HERB MUSHROOM SKILLET

Preparation Time: 10 minutes   **Servings:** 4

Ingredients:

✓ 4 tbsp vegan butter
✓ 1 ½ pounds oyster mushrooms halved
✓ 3 cloves garlic, minced
✓ 1 tsp dried oregano
✓ 1 tsp dried rosemary
✓ 1 tsp dried parsley flakes
✓ 1 tsp dried marjoram
✓ 1/2 cup dry white wine
✓ Kosher salt and ground black pepper, to taste

Directions:

❖ In a sauté pan, heat the olive oil over a moderately high heat.
❖ Now, sauté the mushrooms for 3 minutes or until they release the liquid. Add in the garlic and continue to cook for 30 seconds more or until aromatic.
❖ Stir in the spices and continue sautéing an additional 6 minutes, until your mushrooms are lightly browned.
❖ Enjoy

267) PAN-FRIED ASPARAGUS

Preparation Time: 10 minutes

Servings: 4

Ingredients:

- ✓ 4 tbsp vegan butter
- ✓ 1 ½ pounds asparagus spears, trimmed
- ✓ 1/2 tsp cumin seeds, ground
- ✓ 1/4 tsp bay leaf, ground
- ✓ Sea salt and ground black pepper, to taste
- ✓ 1 tsp fresh lime juice

Directions:

- ❖ Melt the vegan butter in a saucepan over medium-high heat.
- ❖ Sauté the asparagus for about 3 to 4 minutes, stirring periodically to promote even cooking.
- ❖ Add in the cumin seeds, bay leaf, salt and black pepper and continue to cook the asparagus for 2 minutes more until crisp-tender.
- ❖ Drizzle lime juice over the asparagus and serve warm. Enjoy

268) GINGERY CARROT MASH

Preparation Time: 25 minutes

Servings: 4

Ingredients:

- ✓ 2 pounds carrots, cut into rounds
- ✓ 2 tbsp olive oil
- ✓ 1 tsp ground cumin
- ✓ Salt ground black pepper, to taste
- ✓ 1/2 tsp cayenne pepper
- ✓ 1/2 tsp ginger, peeled and minced
- ✓ 1/2 cup whole milk

Directions:

- ❖ Begin by preheating your oven to 400 degrees F.
- ❖ Toss the carrots with the olive oil, cumin, salt, black pepper and cayenne pepper. Arrange them in a single layer on a parchment-lined roasting sheet.
- ❖ Roast the carrots in the preheated oven for about 20 minutes, until crisp-tender.
- ❖ Add the roasted carrots, ginger and milk to your food processor; puree the ingredients until everything is well blended.
- ❖ Enjoy

269) MEDITERRANEAN-STYLE ROASTED ARTICHOKES

Preparation Time: 50 minutes

Servings: 4

Ingredients:

- ✓ 4 artichokes, trimmed, tough outer leaves and chokes removed, halved
- ✓ 2 lemons, freshly squeezed
- ✓ 4 tbsp extra-virgin olive oil
- ✓ 4 cloves garlic, chopped
- ✓ 1 tsp fresh rosemary
- ✓ 1 tsp fresh basil
- ✓ 1 tsp fresh parsley
- ✓ 1 tsp fresh oregano
- ✓ Flaky sea salt and ground black pepper, to taste
- ✓ 1 tsp red pepper flakes
- ✓ 1 tsp paprika

Directions:

- ❖ Start by preheating your oven to 395 degrees F. Rub the lemon juice all over the entire surface of your artichokes.
- ❖ In a small mixing bowl, thoroughly combine the garlic with herbs and spices
- ❖ Place the artichoke halves in a parchment-lined baking dish, cut-side-up. Brush the artichokes evenly with the olive oil. Fill the cavities with the garlic/herb mixture.
- ❖ Bake for about 20 minutes. Now, cover them with aluminum foil and bake for a further 30 minutes. Serve warm and enjoy

270) THAI-STYLE BRAISED KALE

Preparation Time: 10 minutes

Servings: 4

Ingredients:

- ✓ 1 cup water
- ✓ 1 ½ pounds kale, tough stems and ribs removed, torn into pieces
- ✓ 2 tbsp sesame oil
- ✓ 1 tsp fresh garlic, pressed
- ✓ 1 tsp ginger, peeled and minced
- ✓ 1 Thai chili, chopped
- ✓ 1/2 tsp turmeric powder
- ✓ 1/2 cup coconut milk
- ✓ Kosher salt and ground black pepper, to taste

Directions:

- ❖ In a large saucepan, bring the water to a rapid boil. Add in the kale and let it cook until bright, about 3 minutes. Drain, rinse and squeeze dry.
- ❖ Wipe the saucepan with paper towels and preheat the sesame oil over a moderate heat. Once hot, cook the garlic, ginger and chili for approximately 1 minute or so, until fragrant.
- ❖ Add in the kale and turmeric powder and continue to cook for a further 1 minute or until heated through.
- ❖ Gradually pour in the coconut milk, salt and black pepper; continue to simmer until the liquid has thickened. Taste, adjust the seasonings and serve hot. Enjoy

271) SILKY KOHLRABI PUREE

Preparation Time: 30 minutes

Servings: 4

Ingredients:

- ✓ 1 ½ pounds kohlrabi, peeled and cut into pieces
- ✓ 4 tbsp vegan butter
- ✓ Sea salt and freshly ground black pepper, to taste
- ✓ 1/2 tsp cumin seeds
- ✓ 1/2 tsp coriander seeds
- ✓ 1/2 cup soy milk
- ✓ 1 tsp fresh dill
- ✓ 1 tsp fresh parsley

Directions:

- ❖ Cook the kohlrabi in boiling salted water until soft, about 30 minutes; drain.
- ❖ Puree the kohlrabi with the vegan butter, salt, black pepper, cumin seeds and coriander seeds.
- ❖ Puree the ingredients with an immersion blender, gradually adding the milk. Top with fresh dill and parsley. Enjoy

272) CREAMY SAUTÉED SPINACH

Preparation Time: 15 minutes

Servings: 4

Ingredients:

- ✓ 2 tbsp vegan butter
- ✓ 1 onion, chopped
- ✓ 1 tsp garlic, minced
- ✓ 1 ½ cups vegetable broth
- ✓ 2 pounds spinach, torn into pieces
- ✓ Sea salt and ground black pepper, to taste
- ✓ 1/4 tsp dried dill
- ✓ 1/4 tsp mustard seeds
- ✓ 1/2 tsp celery seeds
- ✓ 1 tsp cayenne pepper
- ✓ 1/2 cup oat milk

Directions:

- ❖ In a saucepan, melt the vegan butter over medium-high heat.
- ❖ Then, sauté the onion for about 3 minutes or until tender and translucent. Then, sauté the garlic for about 1 minute until aromatic.
- ❖ Add in the broth and spinach and bring to a boil.
- ❖ Turn the heat to a simmer. Add in the spices and continue to cook for 5 minutes longer.
- ❖ Add in the milk and continue to cook for 5 minutes more. Enjoy

273) ROASTED CARROTS WITH HERBS

Preparation Time: 25 minute

Servings: 4

Ingredients:

- ✓ 2 pounds carrots, trimmed and halved lengthwise
- ✓ 4 tbsp olive oil
- ✓ 1 tsp granulated garlic
- ✓ 1 tsp paprika
- ✓ Sea salt and freshly ground black pepper
- ✓ 2 tbsp fresh cilantro, chopped
- ✓ 2 tbsp fresh parsley, chopped
- ✓ 2 tbsp fresh chives, chopped

Directions:

- ❖ Start by preheating your oven to 400 degrees F.
- ❖ Toss the carrots with the olive oil, granulated garlic, paprika, salt and black pepper. Arrange them in a single layer on a parchment-lined roasting sheet.
- ❖ Roast the carrots in the preheated oven for about 20 minutes, until fork-tender.
- ❖ Toss the carrots with the fresh herbs and serve immediately. Enjoy

274) BRAISED GREEN BEANS

Preparation Time: 15 minutes

Servings: 4

Ingredients:

- ✓ 4 tbsp olive oil
- ✓ 1 carrot, cut into matchsticks
- ✓ 1 ½ pounds green beans, trimmed
- ✓ 4 garlic cloves, peeled
- ✓ 1 bay laurel
- ✓ 1 ½ cups vegetable broth
- ✓ Sea salt and ground black pepper, to taste
- ✓ 1 lemon, cut into wedges

Directions:

- ❖ Heat the olive oil in a saucepan over medium flame. Once hot, fry the carrots and green beans for about 5 minutes, stirring periodically to promote even cooking.
- ❖ Add in the garlic and bay laurel and continue sautéing an additional 1 minute or until fragrant.
- ❖ Add in the broth, salt and black pepper and continue to simmer, covered, for about 9 minutes or until the green beans are tender.
- ❖ Taste, adjust the seasonings and serve with lemon wedges. Enjoy

LUNCH

275) JALAPEÑO QUINOA BOWL WITH LIMA BEANS

Preparation Time: 30 minutes

Servings: 4

Ingredients:

- ✓ 1 tbsp olive oil
- ✓ 1 lb extra firm tofu, cubed
- ✓ Salt and black pepper to taste
- ✓ 1 medium yellow onion, finely diced
- ✓ ½ cup cauliflower florets
- ✓ 1 jalapeño pepper, minced
- ✓ 2 garlic cloves, minced
- ✓ 1 tbsp red chili powder
- ✓ 1 tsp cumin powder
- ✓ 1 (8 oz) can sweet corn kernels
- ✓ 1 (8 oz) can lima beans, rinsed
- ✓ 1 cup quick-cooking quinoa
- ✓ 1 (14 oz) can diced tomatoes
- ✓ 2 ½ cups vegetable broth
- ✓ 1 cup grated plant-based cheddar
- ✓ 2 tbsp chopped fresh cilantro
- ✓ 2 limes, cut into wedges
- ✓ 1 avocado, pitted, sliced, and peeled

Directions:

- ❖ Heat olive oil in a pot and cook the tofu until golden brown, 5 minutes. Season with salt, pepper, and mix in onion, cauliflower, and jalapeño pepper. Cook until the vegetables soften, 3 minutes.
- ❖ Stir in garlic, chili powder, and cumin powder; cook for 1 minute. Mix in sweet corn kernels, lima beans, quinoa, tomatoes, and vegetable broth. Simmer until the quinoa absorbs all the liquid, 10 minutes. Fluff quinoa. Top with the plant-based cheddar cheese, cilantro, lime wedges, and avocado. Serve

276) AVOCADO COCONUT PIE

Preparation Time: 80 minutes

Servings: 4

Ingredients:

- ✓ Piecrust:
- ✓ 1 tbsp flax seed powder + 3 tbsp water
- ✓ 1 cup coconut flour
- ✓ 4 tbsp chia seeds
- ✓ 1 tbsp psyllium husk powder
- ✓ 1 tsp baking soda
- ✓ 1 pinch salt
- ✓ 3 tbsp coconut oil
- ✓ 4 tbsp water
- ✓ Filling:
- ✓ 2 ripe avocados, chopped
- ✓ 1 cup tofu mayonnaise
- ✓ 3 tbsp flax seed powder + 9 tbsp water
- ✓ 2 tbsp fresh parsley, chopped
- ✓ 1 jalapeno, finely chopped
- ✓ ½ tsp onion powder
- ✓ ¼ tsp salt
- ✓ ½ cup cream cheese
- ✓ 1 ¼ cups grated plant-based Parmesan

Directions:

- ❖ In 2 separate bowls, mix the different portions of flax seed powder with the respective quantity of water. Allow absorbing for 5 minutes.
- ❖ Preheat oven to 350 F. In a food processor, add the piecrust ingredients and the smaller portion of the vegan "flax egg." Blend until the resulting dough forms into a ball. Line a springform pan with parchment paper and spread the dough in the pan. Bake for 10-15 minutes.
- ❖ Put the avocado in a bowl and add the tofu mayonnaise, remaining vegan "flax egg," parsley, jalapeno, onion powder, salt, cream cheese, and plant-based Parmesan. Combine well. Remove the piecrust when ready and fill with the creamy mixture. Bake for 35 minutes. Cool before slicing and serving

277) GREEN AVOCADO CARBONARA

Preparation Time: 30 minutes

Servings: 4

Ingredients:

- ✓ 8 tbsp flax seed powder
- ✓ 1 ½ cups cashew cream cheese
- ✓ 5 ½ tbsp psyllium husk powder
- ✓ 1 avocado, chopped
- ✓ 1 ¾ cups coconut cream
- ✓ Juice of ½ lemon
- ✓ 1 tsp onion powder
- ✓ ½ tsp garlic powder
- ✓ ¼ cup olive oil
- ✓ Salt and black pepper to taste
- ✓ ½ cup grated plant-based Parmesan
- ✓ 4 tbsp toasted pecans

Directions:

- ❖ Preheat oven to 300 F.
- ❖ In a medium bowl, mix the flax seed powder with 1 ½ cups water and allow sitting to thicken for 5 minutes. Add the cashew cream cheese, salt, and psyllium husk powder. Whisk until smooth batter forms. Line a baking sheet with parchment paper, pour in the batter, and cover with another parchment paper. Use a rolling pin to flatten the dough into the sheet. Bake for 10-12 minutes. Remove, take off the parchment papers and use a sharp knife to slice the pasta into thin strips lengthwise. Cut each piece into halves, pour into a bowl, and set aside.
- ❖ In a blender, combine avocado, coconut cream, lemon juice, onion powder, and garlic powder; puree until smooth. Pour the olive oil over the pasta and stir to coat properly. Pour the avocado sauce on top and mix. Season with salt and black pepper. Divide the pasta into serving plates, garnish with Parmesan cheese and pecans, and serve immediately

278)   MUSHROOM AND GREEN BEAN BIRYANI

Preparation Time: 50 minutes

Servings: 4

Ingredients:

- ✓ 1 cup brown rice
- ✓ 3 tbsp plant butter
- ✓ 3 medium white onions, chopped
- ✓ 6 garlic cloves, minced
- ✓ 1 tsp ginger puree
- ✓ 1 tbsp turmeric powder + for dusting
- ✓ ¼ tsp cinnamon powder
- ✓ 2 tsp garam masala
- ✓ ½ tsp cardamom powder
- ✓ ½ tsp cayenne powder
- ✓ ½ tsp cumin powder
- ✓ 1 tsp smoked paprika
- ✓ 3 large tomatoes, diced
- ✓ 2 green chilies, minced
- ✓ 1 tbsp tomato puree
- ✓ 1 cup chopped cremini mushrooms
- ✓ 1 cup chopped mustard greens
- ✓ 1 cup plant-based yogurt

Directions:

- ❖ Melt the butter in a large pot and sauté the onions until softened, 3 minutes. Mix in the garlic, ginger, turmeric, cardamom powder, garam masala, cardamom powder, cayenne pepper, cumin powder, paprika, and salt. Stir-fry for 1-2 minutes.
- ❖ Stir in the tomatoes, green chili, tomato puree, and mushrooms. Once boiling, mix in the rice and cover with water. Cover the pot and cook over medium heat until the liquid absorbs and the rice is tender, 15-20 minutes. Open the lid and fluff in the mustard greens and half of the parsley. Dish the food, top with the coconut yogurt, garnish with the remaining parsley, and serve warm

279)   MUSHROOM LETTUCE WRAPS

Preparation Time: 25 minutes

Servings: 4

Ingredients:

- ✓ 2 tbsp plant butter
- ✓ 4 oz baby Bella mushrooms, sliced
- ✓ 1 ½ lb tofu, crumbled
- ✓ 1 iceberg lettuce, leaves extracted
- ✓ 1 cup grated plant-based cheddar
- ✓ 1 large tomato, sliced

Directions:

- ❖ Melt the plant butter in a skillet, add in mushrooms and sauté until browned and tender, about 6 minutes. Transfer to a plate. Add the tofu to the skillet and cook until brown, about 10 minutes. Spoon the tofu and mushrooms into the lettuce leaves, sprinkle with the plant-based cheddar cheese, and share the tomato slices on top. Serve the burger immediately

280)   CLASSIC GARLICKY RICE

Preparation Time: 20 minutes

Servings: 4

Ingredients:

- ✓ 4 tbsp olive oil
- ✓ 4 cloves garlic, chopped
- ✓ 1 ½ cups white rice
- ✓ 2 ½ cups vegetable broth

Directions:

- ❖ In a saucepan, heat the olive oil over a moderately high flame. Add in the garlic and sauté for about 1 minute or until aromatic.
- ❖ Add in the rice and broth. Bring to a boil; immediately turn the heat to a gentle simmer.
- ❖ Cook for about 15 minutes or until all the liquid has absorbed. Fluff the rice with a fork, season with salt and pepper and serve hot

281)   BROWN RICE WITH VEGETABLES AND TOFU

Preparation Time: 45 minutes

Servings: 4

Ingredients:

- ✓ 4 tsp sesame seeds
- ✓ 2 spring garlic stalks, minced
- ✓ 1 cup spring onions, chopped
- ✓ 1 carrot, trimmed and sliced
- ✓ 1 celery rib, sliced
- ✓ 1/4 cup dry white wine
- ✓ 10 ounces tofu, cubed
- ✓ 1 ½ cups long-grain brown rice, rinsed thoroughly
- ✓ 2 tbsp soy sauce
- ✓ 2 tbsp tahini
- ✓ 1 tbsp lemon juice

Directions:

- ❖ In a wok or large saucepan, heat 2 tsp of the sesame oil over medium-high heat. Now, cook the garlic, onion, carrot and celery for about 3 minutes, stirring periodically to ensure even cooking.
- ❖ Add the wine to deglaze the pan and push the vegetables to one side of the wok. Add in the remaining sesame oil and fry the tofu for 8 minutes, stirring occasionally.
- ❖ Bring 2 ½ cups of water to a boil over medium-high heat. Bring to a simmer and cook the rice for about 30 minutes or until it is tender; fluff the rice and stir it with the soy sauce and tahini.
- ❖ Stir the vegetables and tofu into the hot rice; add a few drizzles of the fresh lemon juice and serve warm. Enjoy

282) AMARANTH PORRIDGE

Preparation Time: 35 minutes

Servings: 4

Ingredients:

- ✓ 3 cups water
- ✓ 1 cup amaranth
- ✓ 1/2 cup coconut milk
- ✓ 4 tbsp agave syrup
- ✓ A pinch of kosher salt
- ✓ A pinch of grated nutmeg

Directions:

- ❖ Bring the water to a boil over medium-high heat; add in the amaranth and turn the heat to a simmer.
- ❖ Let it cook for about 30 minutes, stirring periodically to prevent the amaranth from sticking to the bottom of the pan.
- ❖ Stir in the remaining ingredients and continue to cook for 1 to 2 minutes more until cooked through. Enjoy

283) MUM'S AROMATIC RICE

Preparation Time: 20 minutes

Servings: 4

Ingredients:

- ✓ 3 tbsp olive oil
- ✓ 1 tsp garlic, minced
- ✓ 1 tsp dried oregano
- ✓ 1 tsp dried rosemary
- ✓ 1 bay leaf
- ✓ 1 ½ cups white rice
- ✓ 2 ½ cups vegetable broth
- ✓ Sea salt and cayenne pepper, to taste

Directions:

- ❖ In a saucepan, heat the olive oil over a moderately high flame. Add in the garlic, oregano, rosemary and bay leaf; sauté for about 1 minute or until aromatic.
- ❖ Add in the rice and broth. Bring to a boil; immediately turn the heat to a gentle simmer.
- ❖ Cook for about 15 minutes or until all the liquid has absorbed. Fluff the rice with a fork, season with salt and pepper and serve immediately.
- ❖ Enjoy

284) EVERYDAY SAVORY GRITS

Preparation Time: 35 minutes

Servings: 4

Ingredients:

- ✓ 2 tbsp vegan butter
- ✓ 1 sweet onion, chopped
- ✓ 1 tsp garlic, minced
- ✓ 4 cups water
- ✓ 1 cup stone-ground grits
- ✓ Sea salt and cayenne pepper, to taste

Directions:

- ❖ In a saucepan, melt the vegan butter over medium-high heat. Once hot, cook the onion for about 3 minutes or until tender.
- ❖ Add in the garlic and continue to sauté for 30 seconds more or until aromatic; reserve.
- ❖ Bring the water to a boil over a moderately high heat. Stir in the grits, salt and pepper. Turn the heat to a simmer, cover and continue to cook, for about 30 minutes or until cooked through.
- ❖ Stir in the sautéed mixture and serve warm. Enjoy

285) GREEK-STYLE BARLEY SALAD

Preparation Time: 35 minutes

Servings: 4

Ingredients:

- ✓ 1 cup pearl barley
- ✓ 2 ¾ cups vegetable broth
- ✓ 2 tbsp apple cider vinegar
- ✓ 4 tbsp extra-virgin olive oil
- ✓ 2 bell peppers, seeded and diced
- ✓ 1 shallot, chopped
- ✓ 2 ounces sun-dried tomatoes in oil, chopped
- ✓ 1/2 green olives, pitted and sliced
- ✓ 2 tbsp fresh cilantro, roughly chopped

Directions:

- ❖ Bring the barley and broth to a boil over medium-high heat; now, turn the heat to a simmer.
- ❖ Continue to simmer for about 30 minutes until all the liquid has absorbed; fluff with a fork.
- ❖ Toss the barley with the vinegar, olive oil, peppers, shallots, sun-dried tomatoes and olives; toss to combine well.
- ❖ Garnish with fresh cilantro and serve at room temperature or well-chilled. Enjoy

286)   SWEET MAIZE MEAL PORRIDGE

Preparation Time: 15 minutes

Servings: 2

Ingredients:

- ✓ 2 cups water
- ✓ 1/2 cup maize meal
- ✓ 1/4 tsp ground allspice
- ✓ 1/4 tsp salt
- ✓ 2 tbsp brown sugar
- ✓ 2 tbsp almond butter

Directions:

- ❖ In a saucepan, bring the water to a boil; then, gradually add in the maize meal and turn the heat to a simmer.
- ❖ Add in the ground allspice and salt. Let it cook for 10 minutes.
- ❖ Add in the brown sugar and almond butter and gently stir to combine. Enjoy

287)   FOCACCIA WITH MIXED MUSHROOMS

Preparation Time: 35 minutes

Servings: 4

Ingredients:

- ✓ 2 tbsp flax seed powder
- ✓ ½ cup tofu mayonnaise
- ✓ ¾ cup almond flour
- ✓ 1 tbsp psyllium husk powder
- ✓ 1 tsp baking powder
- ✓ 2 oz mixed mushrooms, sliced
- ✓ 1 tbsp plant-based basil pesto
- ✓ 2 tbsp olive oil
- ✓ Salt and black pepper to taste
- ✓ ½ cup coconut cream
- ✓ ¾ cup grated plant-based Parmesan

Directions:

- ❖ Preheat oven to 350 F.
- ❖ Combine flax seed powder with 6 tbsp water and allow sitting to thicken for 5 minutes. Whisk in tofu mayonnaise, almond flour, psyllium husk powder, baking powder, and salt. Allow sitting for 5 minutes. Pour the batter into a baking sheet and spread out with a spatula. Bake for 10 minutes.
- ❖ In a bowl, mix mushrooms with pesto, olive oil, salt, and black pepper. Remove the crust from the oven and spread the coconut cream on top. Add the mushroom mixture and plant-based Parmesan cheese. Bake the pizza further until the cheese has melted, 5-10 minutes. Slice and serve with salad

288)   SEITAN CAKES WITH BROCCOLI MASH

Preparation Time: 30 minutes

Servings: 4

Ingredients:

- ✓ 1 tbsp flax seed powder
- ✓ 1 ½ lb crumbled seitan
- ✓ ½ white onion
- ✓ 2 oz olive oil
- ✓ 1 lb broccoli
- ✓ 5 oz cold plant butter
- ✓ 2 oz grated plant-based Parmesan
- ✓ 4 oz plant butter, room temperature
- ✓ 2 tbsp lemon juice

Directions:

- ❖ Preheat oven to 220 F. In a bowl, mix the flax seed powder with 3 tbsp water and allow sitting to thicken for 5 minutes. When the vegan "flax egg" is ready, add in crumbled seitan, white onion, salt, and pepper. Mix and mold out 6-8 cakes out of the mixture. Melt plant butter in a skillet and fry the patties on both sides until golden brown. Remove onto a wire rack to cool slightly.
- ❖ Pour salted water into a pot, bring to a boil, and add in broccoli. Cook until the broccoli is tender but not too soft. Drain and transfer to a bowl. Add in cold plant butter, plant-based Parmesan, salt, and pepper. Puree the ingredients until smooth and creamy. Set aside. Mix the soft plant butter with lemon juice, salt, and pepper in a bowl. Serve the seitan cakes with the broccoli mash and lemon butter

289)   SPICY CHEESE WITH TOFU BALLS

Preparation Time: 40 minutes

Servings: 4

Ingredients:

- ✓ 1/3 cup tofu mayonnaise
- ✓ ¼ cup pickled jalapenos
- ✓ 1 tsp paprika powder
- ✓ 1 tbsp mustard powder
- ✓ 1 pinch cayenne pepper

- ✓ 4 oz grated plant-based cheddar
- ✓ 1 tbsp flax seed powder
- ✓ 2 ½ cup crumbled tofu
- ✓ 2 tbsp plant butter

Directions:

- ❖ In a bowl, mix tofu mayonnaise, jalapeños, paprika, mustard powder, cayenne powder, and plant-based cheddar cheese; set aside. In another bowl, combine flax seed powder with 3 tbsp water and allow absorbing for 5 minutes. Add the vegan "flax egg" to the cheese mixture, crumbled tofu, salt, and pepper and combine well. Form meatballs out of the mix. Melt plant butter in a skillet and fry the tofu balls until browned. Serve the tofu balls with roasted cauliflower mash

290) QUINOA ANDVEGGIE BURGERS

Preparation Time: 35 minutes

Servings: 4

Ingredients:

- ✓ 1 cup quick-cooking quinoa
- ✓ 1 tbsp olive oil
- ✓ 1 shallot, chopped
- ✓ 2 tbsp chopped fresh celery
- ✓ 1 garlic clove, minced
- ✓ 1 (15 oz) can pinto beans, drained

- ✓ 2 tbsp whole-wheat flour
- ✓ ¼ cup chopped fresh basil
- ✓ 2 tbsp pure maple syrup
- ✓ 4 whole-grain hamburger buns, split
- ✓ 4 small lettuce leaves for topping
- ✓ ½ cup tofu mayonnaise for topping

Directions:

- ❖ Cook the quinoa with 2 cups of water in a medium pot until the liquid absorbs, 10 to 15 minutes. Heat the olive oil in a medium skillet over medium heat and sauté the shallot, celery, and garlic until softened and fragrant, 3 minutes.
- ❖ Transfer the quinoa and shallot mixture to a medium bowl and add the pinto beans, flour, basil, maple syrup, salt, and black pepper. Mash and mold 4 patties out of the mixture and set aside.
- ❖ Heat a grill pan to medium heat and lightly grease with cooking spray. Cook the patties on both sides until light brown, compacted, and cooked through, 10 minutes. Place the patties between the burger buns and top with the lettuce and tofu mayonnaise. Serve

291) BAKED TOFU WITH ROASTED PEPPERS

Preparation Time: 20 minutes

Servings: 4

Ingredients:

- ✓ 3 oz cashew cream cheese
- ✓ ¾ cup tofu mayonnaise
- ✓ 2 oz cucumber, diced
- ✓ 1 large tomato, chopped

- ✓ 2 tsp dried parsley
- ✓ 4 medium orange bell peppers
- ✓ 2 ½ cups cubed tofu
- ✓ 1 tbsp melted plant butter
- ✓ 1 tsp dried basil

Directions:

- ❖ Preheat the oven's broiler to 450 F and line a baking sheet with parchment paper. In a salad bowl, combine cashew cream cheese, tofu mayonnaise, cucumber, tomato, salt, pepper, and parsley. Refrigerate.
- ❖ Arrange the bell peppers and tofu on the baking sheet, drizzle with melted plant butter, and season with basil, salt, and pepper. Bake for 10-15 minutes or until the peppers have charred lightly and the tofu browned. Remove from the oven and serve with the salad

292) ZOODLE BOLOGNESE

Preparation Time: 45 minutes

Servings: 4

Ingredients:

- ✓ 3 oz olive oil
- ✓ 1 white onion, chopped
- ✓ 1 garlic clove, minced
- ✓ 3 oz carrots, chopped
- ✓ 3 cups crumbled tofu

- ✓ 2 tbsp tomato paste
- ✓ 1 ½ cups crushed tomatoes
- ✓ Salt and black pepper to taste
- ✓ 1 tbsp dried basil
- ✓ 1 tbsp vegan Worcestershire sauce
- ✓ 2 lb zucchini, spiralized
- ✓ 2 tbsp plant butter

Directions:

- ❖ Pour olive oil into a saucepan and heat over medium heat. Add in onion, garlic, and carrots and sauté for 3 minutes or until the onions are soft and the carrots caramelized. Pour in tofu, tomato paste, tomatoes, salt, pepper, basil, and Worcestershire sauce. Stir and cook for 15 minutes. Mix in some water if the mixture is too thick and simmer further for 20 minutes. Melt plant butter in a skillet and toss in the zoodles quickly, about 1 minute. Season with salt and black pepper. Divide into serving plates and spoon the Bolognese on top. Serve immediately

293)   ZUCCHINI BOATS WITH VEGAN CHEESE

Preparation Time: 40 minutes

Servings: 2

Ingredients:

- ✓ 1 medium-sized zucchini
- ✓ 4 tbsp plant butter
- ✓ 2 garlic cloves, minced
- ✓ 1 ½ oz baby kale
- ✓ Salt and black pepper to taste
- ✓ 2 tbsp unsweetened tomato sauce
- ✓ 1 cup grated plant-based mozzarella
- ✓ Olive oil for drizzling

Directions:

- ❖ Preheat oven to 375 F.
- ❖ Use a knife to slice the zucchini in halves and scoop out the pulp with a spoon into a plate. Keep the flesh. Grease a baking sheet with cooking spray and place the zucchini boats on top. Put the plant butter in a skillet and melt over medium heat.
- ❖ Sauté the garlic for 1 minute. Add in kale and zucchini pulp. Cook until the kale wilts; season with salt and black pepper. Spoon tomato sauce into the boats and spread to coat the bottom evenly. Then, spoon the kale mixture into the zucchinis and sprinkle with the plant-based mozzarella cheese. Bake for 20-25 minutes. Serve immediately

294)   ROASTED BUTTERNUT SQUASH WITH CHIMICHURRI

Preparation Time: 15 minutes

Servings: 4

Ingredients:

- ✓ Zest and juice of 1 lemon
- ✓ ½ medium red bell pepper, chopped
- ✓ 1 jalapeno pepper, chopped
- ✓ 1 cup olive oil
- ✓ ½ cup chopped fresh parsley
- ✓ 2 garlic cloves, minced
- ✓ 1 lb butternut squash
- ✓ 1 tbsp plant butter, melted
- ✓ 3 tbsp toasted pine nuts

Directions:

- ❖ In a bowl, add the lemon zest and juice, red bell pepper, jalapeno, olive oil, parsley, garlic, salt, and black pepper. Use an immersion blender to grind the ingredients until your desired consistency is achieved; set aside the chimichurri.
- ❖ Slice the butternut squash into rounds and remove the seeds. Drizzle with the plant butter and season with salt and black pepper. Preheat a grill pan over medium heat and cook the squash for 2 minutes on each side or until browned. Remove the squash to serving plates, scatter the pine nuts on top, and serve with the chimichurri and red cabbage salad

295)   BLACK BEAN BURGERS WITH BBQ SAUCE

Preparation Time: 20 minutes

Servings: 4

- ✓ Salt and black pepper to taste
- ✓ 4 whole-grain hamburger buns, split
- ✓ For topping:
- ✓ Red onion slices
- ✓ Tomato slices
- ✓ Fresh basil leaves
- ✓ Additional barbecue sauce

Directions:

- ❖ In a medium bowl, mash the black beans and mix in the flour, oats, basil, barbecue sauce, garlic salt, and black pepper until well combined. Mold 4 patties out of the mixture and set aside.
- ❖ Heat a grill pan to medium heat and lightly grease with cooking spray. Cook the bean patties on both sides until light brown and cooked through, 10 minutes. Place the patties between the burger buns and top with the onions, tomatoes, basil, and some barbecue sauce. Serve warm

296)   CREAMY BRUSSELS SPROUTS BAKE

Preparation Time: 26 minutes

Servings: 4

- ✓ 1 ¼ cups coconut cream
- ✓ 10 oz grated plant-based mozzarella
- ✓ ¼ cup grated plant-based Parmesan
- ✓ Salt and black pepper to taste

Directions:

- ❖ Preheat oven to 400 F.
- ❖ Melt the plant butter in a large skillet over medium heat and fry the tempeh cubes until browned on both sides, about 6 minutes. Remove onto a plate and set aside. Pour the Brussels sprouts and garlic into the skillet and sauté until fragrant.
- ❖ Mix in coconut cream and simmer for 4 minutes. Add tempeh cubes and combine well. Pour the sauté into a baking dish, sprinkle with plant-based mozzarella cheese, and plant-based Parmesan cheese. Bake for 10 minutes or until golden brown on top. Serve with tomato salad

297)   BAKED CHEESY SPAGHETTI SQUASH

Preparation Time: 40 minutes

Servings: 4

Ingredients:

- ✓ 2 lb spaghetti squash
- ✓ 1 tbsp coconut oil
- ✓ Salt and black pepper to taste
- ✓ 2 tbsp melted plant butter
- ✓ ½ tbsp garlic powder
- ✓ 1/5 tsp chili powder
- ✓ 1 cup coconut cream
- ✓ 2 oz cashew cream cheese
- ✓ 1 cup plant-based mozzarella
- ✓ 2 oz grated plant-based Parmesan
- ✓ 2 tbsp fresh cilantro, chopped
- ✓ Olive oil for drizzling

Directions:

- ❖ Preheat oven to 350 F.
- ❖ Cut the squash in halves lengthwise and spoon out the seeds and fiber. Place on a baking dish, brush with coconut oil, and season with salt and pepper. Bake for 30 minutes. Remove and use two forks to shred the flesh into strands.
- ❖ Empty the spaghetti strands into a bowl and mix with plant butter, garlic and chili powders, coconut cream, cream cheese, half of the plant-based mozzarella and plant-based Parmesan cheeses. Spoon the mixture into the squash cups and sprinkle with the remaining mozzarella cheese. Bake further for 5 minutes. Sprinkle with cilantro and drizzle with some oil. Serve

298)   KALE AND MUSHROOM PIEROGIS

Preparation Time: 45 minutes

Servings: 4

Ingredients:

- ✓ Stuffing:
- ✓ 2 tbsp plant butter
- ✓ 2 garlic cloves, finely chopped
- ✓ 1 small red onion, finely chopped
- ✓ 3 oz baby Bella mushrooms, sliced
- ✓ 2 oz fresh kale
- ✓ ½ tsp salt
- ✓ ¼ tsp freshly ground black pepper
- ✓ ½ cup dairy-free cream cheese
- ✓ 2 oz plant-based Parmesan, grated
- ✓ Pierogi:
- ✓ 1 tbsp flax seed powder
- ✓ ½ cup almond flour
- ✓ 4 tbsp coconut flour
- ✓ ½ tsp salt
- ✓ 1 tsp baking powder
- ✓ 1 ½ cups grated plant-based Parmesan
- ✓ 5 tbsp plant butter
- ✓ Olive oil for brushing

Directions:

- ❖ Put the plant butter in a skillet and melt over medium heat, then add and sauté the garlic, red onion, mushrooms, and kale until the mushrooms brown. Season the mixture with salt and black pepper and reduce the heat to low. Stir in the cream cheese and plant-based Parmesan cheese and simmer for 1 minute. Turn the heat off and set the filling aside to cool.
- ❖ Make the pierogis: In a small bowl, mix the flax seed powder with 3 tbsp water and allow sitting for 5 minutes. In a bowl, combine almond flour, coconut flour, salt, and baking powder. Put a small pan over low heat, add, and melt the plant-based Parmesan cheese and plant butter while stirring continuously until smooth batter forms. Turn the heat off.
- ❖ Pour the vegan "flax egg" into the cream mixture, continue stirring while adding the flour mixture until a firm dough forms. Mold the dough into four balls, place on a chopping board, and use a rolling pin to flatten each into ½ inch thin round pieces. Spread a generous amount of stuffing on one-half of each dough, then fold over the filling, and seal the dough with your fingers. Brush with olive oil, place on a baking sheet, and bake for 20 minutes at 380 F. Serve with salad

299)   VEGAN MUSHROOM PIZZA

Preparation Time: 35 minutes

Servings: 4

Ingredients:

- ✓ 2 tsp plant butter
- ✓ 1 cup chopped button mushrooms
- ✓ ½ cup sliced mixed bell peppers
- ✓ Salt and black pepper to taste
- ✓ 1 pizza crust
- ✓ 1 cup tomato sauce
- ✓ 1 cup plant-based Parmesan cheese
- ✓ 5-6 basil leaves

Directions:

- ❖ Melt plant butter in a skillet and sauté mushrooms and bell peppers for 10 minutes until softened. Season with salt and black pepper. Put the pizza crust on a pizza pan, spread the tomato sauce all over, and scatter vegetables evenly on top. Sprinkle with plant-based Parmesan cheese. Bake for 20 minutes until the cheese has melted. Garnish with basil and serve

DINNER

300) PARSLEY CARROTS AND PARSNIPS

Preparation Time: 25 minutes

Servings: 4

Ingredients:

- ✓ 2 tbsp plant butter
- ✓ ½ lb carrots, cut lengthways
- ✓ ½ lb parsnips, cut lengthways
- ✓ Salt and black pepper to taste
- ✓ ½ cup Port wine
- ✓ ¼ cup chopped fresh parsley

Directions:

- ❖ Melt the butter in a skillet over medium heat. Place in carrots and parsnips and cook for 5 minutes, stirring occasionally. Sprinkle with salt and pepper. Pour in Port wine and ¼ cup water. Lower the heat and simmer for 15 minutes. Uncover and increase the heat. Cook until a syrupy sauce forms. Remove to a bowl and serve garnished with parsley

301) SESAME ROASTED BROCCOLI WITH BROWN RICE

Preparation Time: 30 minutes

Servings: 4

Ingredients:

- ✓ 1 head broccoli, cut into florets
- ✓ 2 tbsp olive oil
- ✓ ¾ cup pure date sugar
- ✓ ⅔ cup water
- ✓ ⅓ cup apple cider vinegar
- ✓ 1 tbsp ketchup
- ✓ ¼ cup soy sauce
- ✓ 2 tbsp corn-starch
- ✓ 4 cups cooked brown rice
- ✓ 2 scallions, chopped
- ✓ Sesame seeds

Directions:

- ❖ Preheat oven to 420 F. Line with parchment paper a baking sheet. Coat the broccoli with oil in a bowl. Spread on the baking sheet and roast for 20 minutes, turning once.
- ❖ Add the sugar, water, vinegar, and ketchup to a skillet and bring to a boil. Lower the heat and simmer for 5 minutes. In a bowl, whisk the soy sauce with corn-starch and pour it into the skillet. Stir for 2-4 minutes. Once the broccoli is ready, transfer into the skillet and toss to combine. Share the rice into 4 bowls and top with the broccoli. Serve garnished with scallions and sesame seeds

302) MATCHA-INFUSED TOFU RICE

Servings: 4

- ✓ 2 cups snow peas, cut diagonally
- ✓ 1 tbsp fresh lemon juice
- ✓ 1 tsp grated lemon zest
- ✓ Salt and black pepper to taste

Directions:

- ❖ Boil 3 cups water in a pot. Place in the tea bags and turn the heat off. Let sit for 7 minutes. Discard the bags. Wash the rice and put it into the tea. Cook for 20 minutes over medium heat. Drain and set aside.
- ❖ Heat the oil in a skillet over medium heat. Fry the tofu for 5 minutes until golden. Stir in green onions and snow peas and cook for another 3 minutes. Mix in lemon juice and lemon zest. Place the rice in a serving bowl and mix in the tofu mixture. Adjust the seasoning with salt and pepper. Serve right away

303) CHINESE FRIED RICE

Servings: 4

- ✓ 3 green onions, minced
- ✓ 3 ½ cups cooked brown rice
- ✓ 1 cup frozen peas, thawed
- ✓ 3 tbsp soy sauce
- ✓ 2 tsp dry white wine
- ✓ 1 tbsp toasted sesame oil

Directions:

- ❖ Heat the oil in a skillet over medium heat. Place in onion, carrot, and broccoli, sauté for 5 minutes until tender. Add in garlic, ginger, and green onions and sauté for another 3 minutes. Stir in rice, peas, soy sauce, and white wine and cook for 5 minutes. Add in sesame oil, toss to combine. Serve right away

304) PEPPERED PINTO BEANS

Preparation Time: 30 minutes

Servings: 6

Ingredients:

- ✓ 1 serrano pepper, cut into strips
- ✓ 1 red bell pepper, cut into strips
- ✓ 1 green bell pepper, cut into strips
- ✓ 1 onion, chopped
- ✓ 2 carrots, chopped
- ✓ 2 garlic cloves, minced
- ✓ 3 (15-oz) cans pinto beans
- ✓ 18-ounce bottle barbecue sauce
- ✓ ½ tsp chipotle powder

Directions:

- ❖ In a blender, place the serrano and bell peppers, onion, carrot, and garlic. Pulse until well mixed.
- ❖ Place the mixture in a pot with the beans, BBQ sauce, and chipotle powder. Cook for 15 minutes. Season with salt and pepper. Serve warm

305) BLACK-EYED PEAS WITH SUN-DRIED TOMATOES

Preparation Time: 35 minutes

Servings: 4

Ingredients:

- ✓ 1 cup black-eyed peas, soaked overnight
- ✓ ¼ cup sun-dried tomatoes, chopped
- ✓ 2 tbsp olive oil
- ✓ 2 tsp ground chipotle pepper
- ✓ 1 ½ tsp ground cumin
- ✓ 1 ½ tsp onion powder
- ✓ 1 tsp dried oregano
- ✓ ¾ tsp garlic powder
- ✓ ½ tsp smoked paprika

Directions:

- ❖ Place the black-eyed peas in a pot and add 2 cups of water, olive oil, chipotle pepper, cumin, onion powder, oregano, garlic powder, salt, and paprika. Cook for 20 minutes over medium heat. Mix in sun-dried tomatoes, let sit for a few minutes and serve

306) VEGETARIAN QUINOA CURRY

Preparation Time: 35 minutes

Servings: 4

Ingredients:

- ✓ 4 tsp olive oil
- ✓ 1 onion, chopped
- ✓ 2 tbsp curry powder
- ✓ 1 ½ cups quinoa
- ✓ 1 cup canned diced tomatoes
- ✓ 4 cups chopped spinach
- ✓ ½ cup non-dairy milk
- ✓ 2 tbsp soy sauce
- ✓ Salt to taste

Directions:

- ❖ Heat the oil in a pot over medium heat. Sauté the onion and ginger for 3 minutes until tender. Pour in curry powder, quinoa, and 3 cups of water. Bring to a boil, then lower the heat and simmer for 15-20 minutes. Mix in tomatoes, spinach, milk, soy sauce, and salt. Simmer for an additional 3 minutes

307) ALFREDO RICE WITH GREEN BEANS

Preparation Time: 25 minutes

Servings: 3

- ✓ **2 cups brown rice**

Ingredients:

- ✓ 1 cup Alfredo arugula vegan pesto
- ✓ 1 cup frozen green beans, thawed

Directions:

- ❖ Cook the rice in salted water in a pot over medium heat for 20 minutes. Drain and let it cool completely. Place the Alfredo sauce and beans in a skillet. Cook over low heat for 3-5 minutes. Stir in the rice to coat. Serve immediately

308) KOREAN-STYLE MILLET

Preparation Time: 30 minutes

Servings: 4

- ✓ **Salt and black pepper to taste**

Ingredients:

- ✓ 1 cup dried millet, drained
- ✓ 1 tsp gochugaru flakes

Directions:

- ❖ Place the millet and gochugaru flakes in a pot. Cover with enough water and bring to a boil. Lower the heat and simmer for 20 minutes. Drain and let cool. Transfer to a serving bowl and season with salt and pepper. Serve

309)   LEMONY CHICKPEAS WITH KALE

Preparation Time: 20 minutes

Servings: 4

Ingredients:

- ✓ 4 tbsp olive oil
- ✓ 1 (15-oz) can chickpeas
- ✓ 1 onion, chopped
- ✓ 2 garlic cloves, minced

- ✓ 1 tbsp Italian seasoning
- ✓ 2 cups kale, chopped
- ✓ Sea salt and black pepper to taste
- ✓ Juice and zest of 1 lemon

Directions:

- ❖ Heat the oil in a skillet over medium heat. Place in chickpeas and cook for 5 minutes. Add in onion, garlic, Italian seasoning, and kale and cook for 5 minutes until the kale wilts. Stir in salt, lemon juice, lemon zest, and pepper. Serve warm

310)   DINNER RICE AND LENTILS

Preparation Time: 25 minutes

Servings: 4

Ingredients:

- ✓ 2 tbsp olive oil
- ✓ 4 scallions, chopped
- ✓ 1 carrot, diced
- ✓ 1 celery stalk, chopped
- ✓ 2 (15-oz) cans lentils, drained
- ✓ 1 (15-oz) can diced tomatoes

- ✓ 1 tbsp dried rosemary
- ✓ 1 tsp ground coriander
- ✓ 1 tbsp garlic powder
- ✓ 2 cups cooked brown rice
- ✓ Sea salt and black pepper to taste

Directions:

- ❖ Heat the oil in a pot over medium heat. Place in scallions, carrot, and celery and cook for 5 minutes until tender. Stir in lentils, tomatoes, rosemary, coriander, and garlic powder. Lower the heat and simmer for 5-7 minutes. Mix in rice, salt, and pepper and cook another 2-3 minutes. Serve

311)   SESAME KALE SLAW

Preparation Time: 15 minutes

Servings: 4

Ingredients:

- ✓ ¼ cup tahini
- ✓ 2 tbsp white miso paste
- ✓ 1 tbsp rice vinegar
- ✓ 1 tbsp toasted sesame oil

- ✓ 2 tsp soy sauce
- ✓ 1 (12-oz) bag kale slaw
- ✓ 2 scallions, minced
- ✓ ¼ cup toasted sesame seeds

Directions:

- ❖ In a bowl, combine the tahini, miso, vinegar, oil, and soy sauce. Stir in kale slaw, scallions, and sesame seeds. Let sit for 20 minutes. Serve immediately

312)   SPICY STEAMED BROCCOLI

Preparation Time: 15 minutes

Servings: 6

Ingredients:

- ✓ 1 large head broccoli, into florets
- ✓ Salt to taste

- ✓ **1 tsp red pepper flakes**

Directions:

- ❖ Boil 1 cup water in a pot over medium heat. Place in a steamer basket and put in the florets. Steam covered for 5-7 minutes. In a bowl, toss the broccoli with red pepper flakes and salt. Serve

313)   GARLIC ROASTED CARROTS

Preparation Time: 35 minutes

Servings: 4

Ingredients:

- ✓ 2 lb carrots, chopped into ¾ inch cubes
- ✓ 2 tsp olive oil
- ✓ ½ tsp chili powder
- ✓ ½ tsp smoked paprika

- ✓ ½ tsp dried oregano
- ✓ ½ tsp dried thyme
- ✓ ½ tsp garlic powder
- ✓ Salt to taste

Directions:

- ❖ Preheat oven to 400 F. Line with parchment paper a baking sheet. Rinse the carrots and pat dry. Chop into ¾ inch cubes. Place in a bowl and toss with olive oil.
- ❖ In a bowl, mix chili powder, paprika, oregano, thyme, olive oil, salt, and garlic powder. Pour over the carrots and toss to coat. Transfer to a greased baking sheet and bake for 30 minutes, turn once by half

314)   EGGPLANT AND HUMMUS PIZZA

Preparation Time: 25 minutes

Servings: 2

Ingredients:

- ✓ ½ eggplant, sliced
- ✓ ½ red onion, sliced
- ✓ 1 cup cherry tomatoes, halved
- ✓ 3 tbsp chopped black olives
- ✓ Salt to taste

- ✓ Drizzle olive oil
- ✓ 2 prebaked pizza crusts
- ✓ ½ cup hummus
- ✓ 2 tbsp oregano

Directions:

- ❖ Preheat oven to 390 F,
- ❖ In a bowl, combine the eggplant, onion, tomatoes, olives, and salt. Toss to coat. Sprinkle with some olive oil. Arrange the crusts on a baking sheet and spread the hummus on each pizza. Top with the eggplant mixture. Bake for 20-30 minutes. Serve warm

315)   MISO GREEN CABBAGE

Preparation Time: 50 minutes

Servings: 4

Ingredients:

- ✓ 1 lb green cabbage, halved
- ✓ 2 tsp olive
- ✓ 3 tsp miso paste

- ✓ 1 tsp dried oregano
- ✓ ½ tsp dried rosemary
- ✓ 1 tbsp balsamic vinegar

Directions:

- ❖ Preheat oven to 390 F. Line with parchment paper a baking sheet.
- ❖ Put the green cabbage in a bowl. Coat with olive oil, miso, oregano, rosemary, salt, and pepper. Remove to the baking sheet and bake for 35-40 minutes, shaking every 5 minutes until tender. Remove from the oven to a plate. Drizzle with balsamic vinegar and serve

316)   STEAMED BROCCOLI WITH HAZELNUTS

Preparation Time: 20 minutes

Servings: 4

Ingredients:

- ✓ 1 lb broccoli, cut into florets
- ✓ 2 tbsp olive oil
- ✓ 3 garlic cloves, minced
- ✓ 1 cup sliced white mushrooms

- ✓ ¼ cup dry white wine
- ✓ 2 tbsp minced fresh parsley
- ✓ Salt and black pepper to taste
- ✓ ½ cup slivered toasted hazelnuts

Directions:

- ❖ Steam the broccoli for 8 minutes or until tender. Remove and set aside.
- ❖ Heat 1 tbsp of oil in a skillet over medium heat. Add in garlic and mushrooms and sauté for 5 minutes until tender. Pour in the wine and cook for 1 minute. Stir in broccoli, parsley, salt, and pepper. Cook for 3 minutes, until the liquid has reduced. Remove to a bowl and add in the remaining oil and hazelnuts and toss to coat. Serve warm

317)   CILANTRO OKRA

Preparation Time: 10 minutes

Servings: 4

Ingredients:

- ✓ 2 tbsp olive oil
- ✓ 4 cups okra, halved

- ✓ Sea salt and black pepper to taste
- ✓ 3 tbsp chopped fresh cilantro

Directions:

- ❖ Heat the oil in a skillet over medium heat. Place in the okra, cook for 5 minutes. Turn the heat off and mix in salt, pepper, and cilantro. Serve immediately

318)   CITRUS ASPARAGUS

Preparation Time: 15 minutes

Servings: 4

Ingredients:

- ✓ 1 onion, minced
- ✓ 2 tsp lemon zest
- ✓ 1/3 cup fresh lemon juice

- ✓ 1 tbsp olive oil
- ✓ Salt and black pepper to taste
- ✓ 1 lb asparagus, trimmed

Directions:

- ❖ Combine the onion, lemon zest, lemon juice, and oil in a bowl. Sprinkle with salt and pepper. Let sit for 5-10 minutes.
- ❖ Insert a steamer basket and 1 cup of water in a pot over medium heat. Place the asparagus on the basket and steam for 4-5 minutes until tender but crispy. Leave to cool for 10 minutes, then arrange on a plate. Serve drizzled with the dressing

SNACKS

319) SESAME CABBAGE SAUTÉ

Preparation Time: 15 minutes   Servings: 4

Ingredients:

- 2 tbsp soy sauce
- 1 tbsp toasted sesame oil
- 1 tbsp hot sauce
- ½ tbsp pure date sugar
- ½ tbsp olive oil
- 1 head green cabbage, shredded
- 2 carrots, julienned
- 3 green onions, thinly sliced
- 2 garlic cloves, minced
- 1 tbsp fresh grated ginger
- Salt and black pepper to taste
- 1 tbsp sesame seeds

Directions:

- In a small bowl, mix the soy sauce, sesame oil, hot sauce, and date sugar.
- Heat the olive oil in a large skillet and sauté the cabbage, carrots, green onion, garlic, and ginger until softened, 5 minutes. Mix in the prepared sauce and toss well. Cook for 1 to 2 minutes. Dish the food and garnish with the sesame seeds

320) TOMATOES STUFFED WITH CHICKPEAS AND QUINOA

Preparation Time: 50 minutes   Servings: 4

Ingredients:

- 8 medium tomatoes
- ¾ cup quinoa, rinsed and drained
- 1 ½ cups water
- 1 tbsp olive oil
- 1 small onion, diced
- 3 garlic cloves, minced
- 1 cup chopped spinach
- 1 (7 oz) can chickpeas, drained
- ½ cup chopped fresh basil

Directions:

- Preheat the oven to 400 F.
- Cut off the heads of tomatoes and use a paring knife to scoop the inner pulp of the tomatoes. Season with some olive oil, salt, and black pepper. Add the quinoa and water to a medium pot, season with salt, and cook until the quinoa is tender and the water absorbs, 10 to 15 minutes. Fluff and set aside.
- Heat the remaining olive oil in a skillet and sauté the onion and garlic for 30 seconds. Mix in the spinach and cook until wilted, 2 minutes. Stir in the basil, chickpeas, and quinoa; allow warming from 2 minutes.
- Spoon the mixture into the tomatoes, place the tomatoes into the baking dish and bake in the oven for 20 minutes or until the tomatoes soften. Remove the tomatoes from the oven and dish the food

321) HERBED VEGETABLE TRAYBAKE

Preparation Time: 85 minutes   Servings: 4

Ingredients:

- 2 tbsp plant butter
- 1 large onion, diced
- 1 cup celery, diced
- ½ cup carrots, diced
- ½ tsp dried marjoram
- 2 cups chopped cremini mushrooms
- 1 cup vegetable broth
- ¼ cup chopped fresh parsley
- 1 whole-grain bread loaf, cubed

Directions:

- Melt the butter in a large skillet and sauté onion, celery, mushrooms, and carrots for 5 minutes. Mix in marjoram, salt, and pepper. Pour in the vegetable broth and mix in parsley and bread. Cook until the broth reduces by half, 10 minutes. Pour the mixture into a baking dish and cover with foil. Bake in the oven at 375 F for 30 minutes. Uncover and bake further for 30 minutes or until golden brown on top, and the liquid absorbs. Remove the dish from the oven and serve the stuffing

322) LOUISIANA-STYLE SWEET POTATO CHIPS

Preparation Time: 55 minutes   Servings: 4

Ingredients:

- 2 sweet potatoes, peeled and sliced
- 2 tbsp melted plant butter

- **1 tbsp Cajun seasoning**

Directions:

- Preheat the oven to 400 F and line a baking sheet with parchment paper.
- In a medium bowl, add the sweet potatoes, salt, plant butter, and Cajun seasoning. Toss well. Spread the chips on the baking sheet, making sure not to overlap, and bake in the oven for 50 minutes to 1 hour or until crispy. Remove the sheet and pour the chips into a large bowl. Allow cooling and enjoy

323) BELL PEPPER AND SEITAN BALLS

Preparation Time: 25 minutes

Servings: 4

Ingredients:

- ✓ 1 tbsp flaxseed powder
- ✓ 1 lb seitan, crumbled
- ✓ ¼ cup chopped mixed bell peppers
- ✓ Salt and black pepper to taste
- ✓ 1 tbsp almond flour
- ✓ 1 tsp garlic powder
- ✓ 1 tsp onion powder
- ✓ 1 tsp tofu mayonnaise
- ✓ Olive oil for brushing

Directions:

- ❖ Preheat the oven to 400 F and line a baking sheet with parchment paper.
- ❖ In a bowl, mix flaxseed powder with 3 tbsp water and allow thickening for 5 minutes. Add in seitan, bell peppers, salt, pepper, almond flour, garlic powder, onion powder, and tofu mayonnaise. Mix and form 1-inch balls from the mixture. Arrange on the baking sheet, brush with cooking spray, and bake in the oven for 15 to 20 minutes or until brown and compacted. Remove from the oven and serve

324) PARMESAN BROCCOLI TOTS

Preparation Time: 30 minutes

Servings: 4

Ingredients:

- ✓ 1 tbsp flaxseed powder
- ✓ 1 head broccoli, cut into florets
- ✓ 2/3 cup toasted almond flour
- ✓ 2 garlic cloves, minced
- ✓ 2 cups grated plant-based Parmesan
- ✓ Salt to taste

Directions:

- ❖ Preheat the oven to 350 F and line a baking sheet with parchment paper.
- ❖ In a small bowl, mix the flaxseed powder with the 3 tbsp water and allow thickening for 5 minutes to make the vegan "flax egg". Place the broccoli in a safe microwave bowl, sprinkle with 2 tbsp of water, and steam in the microwave for 1 minute or until softened. Transfer the broccoli to a food processor and add the vegan "flax egg," almond flour, garlic, plant cheese, and salt. Blend until coarsely smooth.
- ❖ Pour the mixture into a bowl and form 2-inch oblong balls from the mixture. Place the tots on the baking sheet and bake in the oven for 15 to 20 minutes or until firm and compacted. Remove the tots from the oven and serve warm with tomato dipping sauce.

325) CHOCOLATE BARS WITH WALNUTS

Preparation Time: 60 minutes

Servings: 4

Ingredients:

- ✓ 1 cup walnuts
- ✓ 3 tbsp sunflower seeds
- ✓ 2 tbsp unsweetened chocolate chips
- ✓ 1 tbsp unsweetened cocoa powder
- ✓ 1 ½ tsp vanilla extract
- ✓ ¼ tsp cinnamon powder
- ✓ 2 tbsp melted coconut oil
- ✓ 2 tbsp toasted almond meal
- ✓ 2 tsp pure maple syrup

Directions:

- ❖ In a food processor, add the walnuts, sunflower seeds, chocolate chips, cocoa powder, vanilla extract, cinnamon powder, coconut oil, almond meal, maple syrup, and blitz a few times until combined.
- ❖ Line a flat baking sheet with plastic wrap, pour the mixture onto the sheet and place another plastic wrap on top. Use a rolling pin to flatten the batter and then remove the top plastic wrap. Freeze the snack until firm, 1 hour. Remove from the freezer, cut into 1 ½-inch sized bars and enjoy immediately

326) CARROT ENERGY BALLS

Preparation Time: 10 minutes + chilling time

Servings: 8

Ingredients:

- ✓ 1 large carrot, grated carrot
- ✓ 1 ½ cups old-fashioned oats
- ✓ 1 cup raisins
- ✓ 1 cup dates, pitied
- ✓ 1 cup coconut flakes
- ✓ 1/4 tsp ground cloves
- ✓ 1/2 tsp ground cinnamon

Directions:

- ❖ In your food processor, pulse all ingredients until it forms a sticky and uniform mixture.
- ❖ Shape the batter into equal balls.
- ❖ Place in your refrigerator until ready to serve. Enjoy

327) CRUNCHY SWEET POTATO BITES

Preparation Time: 25 minutes + chilling time

Servings: 4

Ingredients:

- ✓ 4 sweet potatoes, peeled and grated
- ✓ 2 chia eggs
- ✓ 1/4 cup nutritional yeast
- ✓ 2 tbsp tahini
- ✓ 2 tbsp chickpea flour
- ✓ 1 tsp shallot powder
- ✓ 1 tsp garlic powder
- ✓ 1 tsp paprika
- ✓ Sea salt and ground black pepper, to taste

Directions:

- ❖ Start by preheating your oven to 395 degrees F. Line a baking pan with parchment paper or Silpat mat.
- ❖ Thoroughly combine all the ingredients until everything is well incorporated.
- ❖ Roll the batter into equal balls and place them in your refrigerator for about 1 hour.
- ❖ Bake these balls for approximately 25 minutes, turning them over halfway through the cooking time. Enjoy

328) ROASTED GLAZED BABY CARROTS

Preparation Time: 30 minutes

Servings: 6

Ingredients:

- ✓ 2 pounds baby carrots
- ✓ 1/4 cup olive oil
- ✓ 1/4 cup apple cider vinegar
- ✓ 1/2 tsp red pepper flakes
- ✓ Sea salt and freshly ground black pepper, to taste
- ✓ 1 tbsp agave syrup
- ✓ 2 tbsp soy sauce
- ✓ 1 tbsp fresh cilantro, minced

Directions:

- ❖ Start by preheating your oven 395 degrees F.
- ❖ Then, toss the carrots with the olive oil, vinegar, red pepper, salt, black pepper, agave syrup and soy sauce.
- ❖ Roast the carrots for about 30 minutes, rotating the pan once or twice. Garnish with fresh cilantro and serve. Enjoy

329) OVEN-BAKED KALE CHIPS

Preparation Time: 20 minutes

Servings: 8

Ingredients:

- ✓ 2 bunches kale, leaves separated
- ✓ 2 tbsp olive oil
- ✓ 1/2 tsp mustard seeds
- ✓ 1/2 tsp celery seeds
- ✓ 1/2 tsp dried oregano
- ✓ 1/4 tsp ground cumin
- ✓ 1 tsp garlic powder
- ✓ Coarse sea salt and ground black pepper, to taste

Directions:

- ❖ Start by preheating your oven to 340 degrees F. Line a baking sheet with parchment paper or Silpat mar.
- ❖ Toss the kale leaves with the remaining ingredients until well coated.
- ❖ Bake in the preheated oven for about 13 minutes, rotating the pan once or twice. Enjoy

330) CHEESY CASHEW DIP

Preparation Time: 10 minutes

Servings: 8

Ingredients:

- ✓ 1 cup raw cashews
- ✓ 1 lemon, freshly squeezed
- ✓ 2 tbsp tahini
- ✓ 2 tbsp nutritional yeast
- ✓ 1/2 tsp turmeric powder
- ✓ 1/2 tsp red pepper flakes, crushed
- ✓ Sea salt and ground black pepper, to taste

Directions:

- ❖ Place all the ingredients in the bowl of your food processor. Blend until uniform, creamy and smooth. You can add a splash of water to thin it out, as needed.
- ❖ Spoon your dip into a serving bowl; serve with veggie sticks, chips, or crackers.
- ❖ Enjoy

331) PEPPERY HUMMUS DIP

Preparation Time: 10 minutes

Servings: 10

Ingredients:

- ✓ 20 ounces canned or boiled chickpeas, drained
- ✓ 1/4 cup tahini
- ✓ 2 garlic cloves, minced
- ✓ 2 tbsp lemon juice, freshly squeezed
- ✓ 1/2 cup chickpea liquid
- ✓ 2 red roasted peppers, seeded and sliced
- ✓ 1/2 tsp paprika
- ✓ 1 tsp dried basil
- ✓ Sea salt and ground black pepper, to taste
- ✓ 2 tbsp olive oil

Directions:

- ❖ Blitz all the ingredients, except for the oil, in your blender or food processor until your desired consistency is reached.
- ❖ Place in your refrigerator until ready to serve.
- ❖ Serve with toasted pita wedges or chips, if desired. Enjoy

332) TRADITIONAL LEBANESE MUTABAL

Preparation Time: 10 minutes

Servings: 6

Ingredients:

- ✓ 1 pound eggplant
- ✓ 1 onion, chopped
- ✓ 1 tbsp garlic paste
- ✓ 4 tbsp tahini
- ✓ 1 tbsp coconut oil
- ✓ 2 tbsp lemon juice
- ✓ 1/2 tsp ground coriander
- ✓ 1/4 cup ground cloves
- ✓ 1 tsp red pepper flakes
- ✓ 1 tsp smoked peppers
- ✓ Sea salt and ground black pepper, to taste

Directions:

- ❖ Roast the eggplant until the skin turns black; peel the eggplant and transfer it to the bowl of your food processor.
- ❖ Add in the remaining ingredients. Blend until everything is well incorporated.
- ❖ Serve with crostini or pita bread, if desired. Enjoy

333) INDIAN-STYLE ROASTED CHICKPEAS

Preparation Time: 10 minutes

Servings: 8

Ingredients:

- ✓ 2 cups canned chickpeas, drained
- ✓ 2 tbsp olive oil
- ✓ 1/2 tsp garlic powder
- ✓ 1/2 tsp paprika
- ✓ 1 tsp curry powder
- ✓ 1 tsp garam masala
- ✓ Sea salt and red pepper, to taste

Directions:

- ❖ Pat the chickpeas dry using paper towels. Drizzle olive oil over the chickpeas.
- ❖ Roast the chickpeas in the preheated oven at 400 degrees F for about 25 minutes, tossing them once or twice.
- ❖ Toss your chickpeas with the spices and enjoy

334) AVOCADO WITH TAHINI SAUCE

Preparation Time: 10 minutes

Servings: 4

Ingredients:

- ✓ 2 large-sized avocados, pitted and halved
- ✓ 4 tbsp tahini
- ✓ 4 tbsp soy sauce
- ✓ 1 tbsp lemon juice
- ✓ 1/2 tsp red pepper flakes
- ✓ Sea salt and ground black pepper, to taste
- ✓ 1 tsp garlic powder

Directions:

- ❖ Place the avocado halves on a serving platter.
- ❖ Mix the tahini, soy sauce, lemon juice, red pepper, salt, black pepper and garlic powder in a small bowl. Divide the sauce between the avocado halves.
- ❖ Enjoy

DESSERTS

335)   CHOCOLATE DREAM BALLS

Preparation Time: 10 minutes + chilling time

Servings: 8

Ingredients:

- ✓ 3 tbsp cocoa powder
- ✓ 8 fresh dates, pitted and soaked for 15 minutes
- ✓ 2 tbsp tahini, at room temperature
- ✓ 1/2 tsp ground cinnamon
- ✓ 1/2 cup vegan chocolate, broken into chunks
- ✓ 1 tbsp coconut oil, at room temperature

Directions:

- ❖ Add the cocoa powder, dates, tahini and cinnamon to the bowl of your food processor. Process until the mixture forms a ball.
- ❖ Use a cookie scoop to portion the mixture into 1-ounce portions. Roll the balls and refrigerate them for at least 30 minutes.
- ❖ Meanwhile, microwave the chocolate until melted; add in the coconut oil and whisk to combine well.
- ❖ Dip the chocolate balls in the coating and store them in your refrigerator until ready to serve. Enjoy

336)   LAST-MINUTE MACAROONS

Preparation Time: 15 minutes

Servings: 10

Ingredients:

- ✓ 3 cups coconut flakes, sweetened
- ✓ 9 ounces canned coconut milk, sweetened
- ✓ 1 tsp ground anise
- ✓ 1 tsp vanilla extract

Directions:

- ❖ Begin by preheating your oven to 325 degrees F. Line the cookie sheets with parchment paper.
- ❖ Thoroughly combine all the ingredients until everything is well incorporated.
- ❖ Use a cookie scoop to drop mounds of the batter onto the prepared cookie sheets.
- ❖ Bake for about 11 minutes until they are lightly browned. Enjoy

337)

338)   OLD-FASHIONED RATAFIAS

Preparation Time: 20 minutes

Servings: 8

Ingredients:

- ✓ 2 ounces all-purpose flour
- ✓ 2 ounces almond flour
- ✓ 1 tsp baking powder
- ✓ 2 tbsp applesauce
- ✓ 5 ounces caster sugar
- ✓ 1 ½ ounces vegan butter
- ✓ 4 drops of ratafia essence

Directions:

- ❖ Start by preheating your oven to 330 degrees F. Line a cookie sheet with parchment paper.
- ❖ Thoroughly combine all the ingredients until everything is well incorporated.
- ❖ Use a cookie scoop to drop mounds of the batter onto the prepared cookie sheet.
- ❖ Bake for about 15 minutes until they are lightly browned. Enjoy

339)   JASMINE RICE PUDDING WITH DRIED APRICOTS

Preparation Time: 20 minutes

Servings: 4

Ingredients:

- ✓ 1 cup jasmine rice, rinsed
- ✓ 1 cup water
- ✓ 1 cup almond milk
- ✓ 1/2 cup brown sugar
- ✓ A pinch of salt
- ✓ A pinch of grated nutmeg
- ✓ 1/2 cup dried apricots, chopped
- ✓ 1/4 tsp cinnamon powder
- ✓ 1 tsp vanilla extract

Directions:

- ❖ Add the rice and water to a saucepan. Cover the saucepan and bring the water to a boil.
- ❖ Turn the heat to low; let it simmer for another 10 minutes until all the water is absorbed.
- ❖ Then, add in the remaining ingredients and stir to combine. Let it simmer for 10 minutes more or until the pudding has thickened. Enjoy

340) CHOCOLATE FUDGE WITH NUTS

Preparation Time: 10 minutes + cooling time

Servings: 4

Ingredients:

- ✓ 3 cups chocolate chips
- ✓ ¼ cup thick coconut milk
- ✓ 1 ½ tsp vanilla extract
- ✓ A pinch salt
- ✓ 1 cup chopped mixed nuts

Directions:

- ❖ Line a square pan with baking paper. Melt the chocolate chips, coconut milk, and vanilla in a medium pot over low heat. Mix in the salt and nuts until well distributed and pour the mixture into the square pan. Refrigerate for at least 2 hours. Remove from the fridge, cut into squares, and serve

341) CHOCOLATE AND PEANUT BUTTER COOKIES

Preparation Time: 15 minutes + cooling time

Servings: 4

Ingredients:

- ✓ 1 tbsp flaxseed powder
- ✓ 1 cup pure date sugar + for dusting
- ✓ ½ cup vega butter, softened
- ✓ ½ cup creamy peanut butter
- ✓ 1 tsp vanilla extract
- ✓ 1 ¾ cup whole-wheat flour
- ✓ 1 tsp baking soda
- ✓ ¼ tsp salt
- ✓ ¼ cup unsweetened chocolate chips

Directions:

- ❖ In a small bowl, mix the flaxseed powder with 3 tbsp water and allow thickening for 5 minutes to make the vegan "flax egg." In a medium bowl, whisk the date sugar, plant butter, and peanut butter until light and fluffy. Mix in the flax egg and vanilla until combined. Add in flour, baking soda, salt, and whisk well again. Fold in chocolate chips, cover the bowl with plastic wrap, and refrigerate for 1 hour.
- ❖ Preheat oven to 375 F and line a baking sheet with parchment paper. Use a cookie sheet to scoop mounds of the batter onto the sheet with 1-inch intervals. Bake for 10 minutes. Remove the cookies from the oven, cool for 3 minutes, roll in some date sugar, and serve

342) MIXED BERRY YOGURT ICE POPS

Preparation Time: 5 minutes + chilling time

Servings: 6

Ingredients:

- ✓ 2/3 cup avocado, halved and pitted
- ✓ 2/3 cup frozen berries, thawed
- ✓ 1 cup dairy-free yogurt
- ✓ ½ cup coconut cream
- ✓ 1 tsp vanilla extract

Directions:

- ❖ Pour the avocado pulp, berries, dairy-free yogurt, coconut cream, and vanilla extract. Process until smooth. Pour into ice pop sleeves and freeze for 8 or more hours. Enjoy the ice pops when ready

343) HOLIDAY PECAN TART

Preparation Time: 50 minutes + cooling time

Servings: 4

Ingredients:

- ✓ 4 tbsp flaxseed powder
- ✓ 1/3 cup whole-wheat flour
- ✓ ½ tsp salt
- ✓ ¼ cup cold plant butter, crumbled
- ✓ 3 tbsp pure malt syrup
- ✓ For the filling:
- ✓ 3 tbsp flaxseed powder + 9 tbsp water
- ✓ 2 cups toasted pecans, chopped
- ✓ 1 cup light corn syrup
- ✓ ½ cup pure date sugar
- ✓ 1 tbsp pure pomegranate molasses
- ✓ 4 tbsp plant butter, melted
- ✓ ½ tsp salt
- ✓ 2 tsp vanilla extract

Directions:

- ❖ Preheat oven to 350 F. In a bowl, mix the flaxseed powder with 12 tbsp water and allow thickening for 5 minutes. Do this for the filling's vegan "flax egg" too in a separate bowl. In a bowl, combine flour and salt. Add in plant butter and whisk until crumbly. Pour in the crust's vegan "flax egg" and maple syrup and mix until smooth dough forms. Flatten the dough on a flat surface, cover with plastic wrap, and refrigerate for 1 hour. Dust a working surface with flour, remove the dough onto the surface, and using a rolling pin, flatten the dough into a 1-inch diameter circle. Lay the dough on a greased pie pan and press to fit the shape of the pan. Trim the edges of the pan. Lay a parchment paper on the dough, pour on some baking beans and bake for 20 minutes. Remove, pour out baking beans, and allow cooling.
- ❖ In a bowl, mix the filling's vegan "flax egg," pecans, corn syrup, date sugar, pomegranate molasses, plant butter, salt, and vanilla. Pour and spread the mixture on the piecrust. Bake for 20 minutes or until the filling sets. Remove from the oven, decorate with more pecans, slice, and cool. Slice and serve

344)   COCONUT CHOCOLATE BARKS

Preparation Time: 35 minutes

Servings: 4

Ingredients:

- ✓ 1/3 cup coconut oil, melted
- ✓ ¼ cup almond butter, melted
- ✓ 2 tbsp unsweetened coconut flakes.

- ✓ 1 tsp pure maple syrup
- ✓ A pinch of ground rock salt
- ✓ ¼ cup unsweetened cocoa nibs

Directions:

- ❖ Line a baking tray with baking paper and set aside. In a medium bowl, mix the coconut oil, almond butter, coconut flakes, maple syrup, and fold in the rock salt and cocoa nibs. Pour and spread the mixture on the baking sheet, chill in the refrigerator for 20 minutes or until firm. Remove the dessert, break into shards, and enjoy. Preserve extras in the refrigerator

345)   NUTTY DATE CAKE

Preparation Time: 1 hour 30 minutes

Servings: 4

Ingredients:

- ✓ ½ cup cold plant butter, cut into pieces
- ✓ 1 tbsp flaxseed powder
- ✓ ½ cup whole-wheat flour
- ✓ ¼ cup chopped pecans and walnuts
- ✓ 1 tsp baking powder

- ✓ 1 tsp baking soda
- ✓ 1 tsp cinnamon powder
- ✓ 1 tsp salt
- ✓ 1/3 cup pitted dates, chopped
- ✓ ½ cup pure date sugar
- ✓ 1 tsp vanilla extract
- ✓ ¼ cup pure date syrup for drizzling.

Directions:

- ❖ Preheat oven to 350 F and lightly grease a baking dish with some plant butter. In a small bowl, mix the flaxseed powder with 3 tbsp water and allow thickening for 5 minutes to make the vegan "flax egg."
- ❖ In a food processor, add the flour, nuts, baking powder, baking soda, cinnamon powder, and salt. Blend until well combined. Add 1/3 cup of water, dates, date sugar, and vanilla. Process until smooth with tiny pieces of dates evident.
- ❖ Pour the batter into the baking dish and bake in the oven for 1 hour and 10 minutes or until a toothpick inserted comes out clean. Remove the dish from the oven, invert the cake onto a serving platter to cool, drizzle with the date syrup, slice, and serve

346)   BERRY CUPCAKES WITH CASHEW CHEESE ICING

Preparation Time: 35 minutes + cooling time

Servings: 4

Ingredients:

- ✓ 2 cups whole-wheat flour
- ✓ ¼ cup corn-starch
- ✓ 2 ½ tsp baking powder
- ✓ 1 ½ cups pure date sugar
- ✓ ½ tsp salt
- ✓ ¾ cup plant butter, softened
- ✓ 3 tsp vanilla extract
- ✓ 1 cup strawberries, pureed

- ✓ 1 cup oat milk, room temperature
- ✓ ¾ cup cashew cream
- ✓ 2 tbsp coconut oil, melted
- ✓ 3 tbsp pure maple syrup
- ✓ 1 tsp vanilla extract
- ✓ 1 tsp freshly squeezed lemon juice

Directions:

- ❖ Preheat the oven to 350 F and line a 12-holed muffin tray with cupcake liners. Set aside.
- ❖ In a bowl, mix flour, corn-starch, baking powder, date sugar, and salt. Whisk in plant butter, vanilla extract, strawberries, and oat milk until well combined. Divide the mixture into the muffin cups two-thirds way up and bake for 20-25 minutes. Allow cooling while you make the frosting.
- ❖ In a blender, add cashew cream, coconut oil, maple syrup, vanilla, and lemon juice. Process until smooth. Pour the frosting into a medium bowl and chill for 30 minutes. Transfer the mixture into a piping bag and swirl mounds of the frosting onto the cupcakes. Serve immediately

347)   COCONUT AND CHOCOLATE CAKE

Preparation Time: 40 minutes + cooling time

Servings: 4

Ingredients:

- ✓ 2/3 cup toasted almond flour
- ✓ ¼ cup unsalted plant butter, melted

- ✓ 2 cups chocolate bars, cubed
- ✓ 2 ½ cups coconut cream
- ✓ Fresh berries for topping

Directions:

- ❖ Lightly grease a 9-inch springform pan with some plant butter and set aside.
- ❖ Mix the almond flour and plant butter in a medium bowl and pour the mixture into the springform pan. Use the spoon to spread and press the mixture into the bottom of the pan. Place in the refrigerator to firm for 30 minutes.
- ❖ Meanwhile, pour the chocolate in a safe microwave bowl and melt for 1 minute stirring every 30 seconds. Remove from the microwave and mix in the coconut cream and maple syrup.
- ❖ Remove the cake pan from the oven, pour the chocolate mixture on

top, and shake the pan and even the layer. Chill further for 4 to 6 hours. Take out the pan from the fridge, release the cake and garnish with the raspberries or strawberries. Slice and serve

348)   BERRY MACEDONIA WITH MINT

Preparation Time: 20 minutes   **Servings: 4**

Ingredients:

✓ 2 cups chopped strawberries
✓ 3 cups mixed berries
✓ 8 fresh mint leaves

✓ ¼ cup lemon juice
✓ 4 tsp agave syrup
✓ 2 cups chopped pears

Directions:

❖ Chop half of the mint leaves; reserve.

❖ In a large bowl, combine together pears, strawberries, raspberries, blackberries, and half of the mint leaves. Divide the Macedonia salad between 4 small cups. Top with lemon juice, agave syrup, and mint leaves and serve chilled

349)   CINNAMON PUMPKIN PIE

Preparation Time: 1 hr 10 min + cooling time   **Servings: 4**

Ingredients:

✓ For the piecrust:
✓ 4 tbsp flaxseed powder
✓ 1/3 cup whole-wheat flour
✓ ½ tsp salt
✓ ¼ cup cold plant butter, crumbled
✓ 3 tbsp pure malt syrup

✓ For the filling:
✓ 2 tbsp flaxseed powder + 6 tbsp water
✓ 4 tbsp plant butter
✓ ¼ cup pure maple syrup
✓ ¼ cup pure date sugar
✓ 1 tsp cinnamon powder
✓ ½ tsp ginger powder
✓ 1/8 tsp cloves powder
✓ 1 (15 oz) can pumpkin purée
✓ 1 cup almond milk

Directions:

❖ Preheat oven to 350 F. In a bowl, mix flaxseed powder with 12 tbsp water and allow thickening for 5 minutes. Do this for the filling's vegan "flax egg" too in another bowl. In a bowl, combine flour and salt. Add in plant butter and whisk until crumbly. Pour in crust's vegan "flax egg," maple syrup, vanilla, and mix until smooth dough forms. Flatten, cover with plastic wrap, and refrigerate for 1 hour.

❖ Dust a working surface with flour, remove the dough onto the surface and flatten it into a 1-inch diameter circle. Lay the dough on a greased pie pan and press to fit the shape of the pan. Use a knife to trim the edges of the pan. Lay a parchment paper on the dough, pour on some baking beans and bake for 15-20 minutes. Remove, pour out the baking beans, and allow cooling. In a bowl, whisk filling's flaxseed, butter, maple syrup, date sugar, cinnamon powder, ginger powder, cloves powder, pumpkin puree, and almond milk. Pour the mixture onto the piecrust and bake for 35-40 minutes

350)   PARTY MATCHA AND HAZELNUT CHEESECAKE

Preparation Time: 20 minutes + cooling time   **Servings: 4**

Ingredients:

✓ 2/3 cup toasted rolled oats
✓ ¼ cup plant butter, melted
✓ 3 tbsp pure date sugar
✓ 6 oz cashew cream cheese

✓ ¼ cup almond milk
✓ 1 tbsp matcha powder
✓ ¼ cup just-boiled water
✓ 3 tsp agar agar powder
✓ 2 tbsp toasted hazelnuts, chopped

Directions:

❖ Process the oats, butter, and date sugar in a blender until smooth.

❖ Pour the mixture into a greased 9-inch springform pan and press the mixture onto the bottom of the pan. Refrigerate for 30 minutes until firm while you make the filling.

❖ In a large bowl, using an electric mixer, whisk the cashew cream cheese until smooth. Beat in the almond milk and mix in the matcha powder until smooth.

❖ Mix the boiled water and agar agar until dissolved and whisk this mixture into the creamy mix. Fold in the hazelnuts until well distributed. Remove the cake pan from the fridge and pour in the cream mixture. Shake the pan to ensure a smooth layering on top. Refrigerate further for at least 3 hours. Take out the cake pan, release the cake, slice, and serve

AUTHOR BIBLIOGRAPHY

THE PLANT-BASED COOKBOOK: Cook Your Green Passion: 100+ New Tasty Recipes to Try in All Occasions!

THE PLANT-BASED DIET: Cookbook for Beginners

THE PLANT-BASED DIET FOR WOMEN: Simple, Healthy Recipes to Rise Your Everyday Energy and Balance Hormones

THE PLANT-BASED DIET FOR ATHLETE: Guide and 100+ Tasty Recipes for a Strong Body and a Healthy Life. Lose Weight and Shape the Body, for Beginners and Experts of All Sports.

THE PLANT-BASED RECIPE BOOK: *2 Books in* 1: Easy Beginner's Cookbook with Plant-Based Recipes for Healthy Eating!

THE PLANT-BASED DIET FOR BEGINNERS' WOMEN: *2 Books in* 1: A Special Guide for Beginners with More than 200 Simple, Healthy Recipes to Rise Your Everyday Energy and Balance Hormones!

THE PLANT-BASED DIET COOKBOOK FOR ATHLETE: *2 Books in* 1: All You Need to Know About the Plant-Based Diet + More Than 200 Tasty Recipes for a Strong Body and a Healthy Life. Lose Weight and Shape the Body, for Beginners and Experts of All Sports!

THE MASTER PLANT-BASED DIET: *3 Books in* 1: The Master Guide for Beginners for Vegetarians & Vegans! Try and Taste More than 350 New Recipes and Get to Know About How this Diet Can Help You as Men or Women and Athlete! Special Chapters inside!!!

THE PLANT-BASED DIET QUICK & EASY: *2 Books in* 1: 220+ New Delicious Vegan and Vegetarian Quick & Easy-to-Follow Recipe to Taste!

THE PLANT-BASED DIET FOR MEN: *2 Books in* 1: A Game-Changing Approach to Peak Performance! Guide for Beginners: 240+ Quick & Easy, Affordable Recipes that Novice and Busy People Can Do! Reset and Energize Your Body!

THE PLANT-BASED DIET FOR FITNESS: *2 Books in* 1: The revolutionary diet book with easy and tasty recipes for healthy and smart people! 240 Fantastic Recipes to Get Fit and Lose Weight!

CONCLUSIONS

As an athlete, it may seem that the vegan diet doesn't provide the proper nutrition. Rest assured, you can very well dispel this myth.

Throughout the book, I've given you many tasty and easy-to-make recipes that are sure to provide you with the right amount of carbs and protein. Keep in mind that being a meatless athlete is not easy; this is certainly not a reason to quit!

One of the most significant benefits of switching to vegan is the improved level of health you will undergo, and this will show well beyond your physique. On top of that is the potent combination of healthy plant-based proteins! The vegan diet is famous for its health benefits and especially for weight loss. Many people have done a vegan diet to lose weight and succeeded.

Lose weight, enjoy more energy, and feel good by making a difference in vegetarianism. But before you start a vegan diet, you may be looking for a healthy diet to lose weight, and there are some things you should understand.

Many people make the mistake of giving the word "diet" a negative connotation. This is why most of them cannot stick to a diet when they want to switch to a different lifestyle. You mustn't do. Tell yourself that you are transitioning to a healthier lifestyle that has numerous benefits. Remember that it is okay to indulge in a cheat meal. You can have this meal on days when you have cravings. You should remember not to make it a habit. Once you start leading a vegan lifestyle completely, you will no longer have any cravings for meat.

Those who switch to a vegan diet get immediate benefits on their strength and notice better and faster muscle development. For an athlete, also not to be underestimated is the benefit of boosting the immune system. It allows him to get sick less frequently and, therefore, can better focus on training.

Also, in the vegan diet, there are no pro-inflammatory foods, such as meat and dairy products, which are rich in cholesterol and saturated fats.

However, we must not make the mistake of believing that just being vegan is enough for everything to go well. As with any type of diet, we must incorporate a good variety of nutrient-rich food sources.

It's a good idea to structure an excellent personalized weekly meal plan to make sure you're assimilating everything your body needs. It's also good to feed yourself several times a day and throw out the famous "three meals a day" rule. Top athletes eat up to 8-9 times a day, following their personalized nutrition plan. To be well prepared, the key is to have an unequivocal goal for the occasion, stick to individual plans and preparation procedures, stay on time and limit the effect of interruptions. Remaining positive and hopeful, despite bad luck, and guarding feelings every day are extra tips that can have an essential effect once the rivalry arises. For groups set up for the experience, rivalries give energizing opportunities to exhibit skills and are significant open doors of learning for youthful athletes.

Now that you've learned the benefits of transitioning to a vegan lifestyle and understand that there are ample plant-based or nut-based proteins that can help you provide your body with needed protein and other nutrients, it's time to get started with the recipes.

Audrey Pottery

CPSIA information can be obtained
at www.ICGtesting.com
Printed in the USA
BVHW011657040521
606415BV00007B/2013